WELSH

FOLK-LORE

WELSH FOLK-LORE

A COLLECTION OF THE

FOLK-TALES AND LEGENDS OF

NORTH WALES

BEING THE PRIZE ESSAY OF THE NATIONAL EISTEDDFOD

1887, BY THE

REV. ELIAS OWEN, M.A, F.S.A.

FACSIMILE REPRINT BY
LLANERCH PUBLISHERS
FELINFACH, (1996)

ISBN 1 897853 74 2

PREFACE

To this Essay on the "Folk-lore of North Wales," was awarded the first prize at the Welsh National Eisteddfod, held in London, in 1887. The prize consisted of a silver medal, and £20. The adjudicators were Canon Silvan Evans, Professor Rhys, and Mr Egerton Phillimore, editor of the *Cymmrodor*.

By an arrangement with the Eisteddfod Committee, the work became the property of the publishers, Messrs. Woodall, Minshall, & Co., who, at the request of the author, entrusted it to him for revision, and the present Volume is the result of his labours.

Before undertaking the publishing of the work, it was necessary to obtain a sufficient number of subscribers to secure the publishers from loss. Upwards of two hundred ladies and gentlemen gave their names to the author, and the work of publication was commenced. The names of the subscribers appear at the end of the book, and the writer thanks them one and all for their kind support. It is more than probable that the work would never have been published had it not been for their kind assistance. Although the study of Folk-lore is of growing interest, and its importance to the historian is being acknowledged; still, the publishing of a work on the subject involved a considerable risk of loss to the printers, which, however, has been removed in this case, at least to a certain extent, by those who have subscribed for the work.

The sources of the information contained in this essay are various, but the writer is indebted, chiefly, to the aged

inhabitants of Wales, for his information.   In the discharge
of his official duties, as Diocesan Inspector of Schools, he
visited annually, for seventeen years, every parish in the
Diocese of St. Asaph, and he was thus brought into contact
with young and old.   He spent several years in Carnarvonshire, and he had a brother, the Revd. Elijah Owen, M.A.,
a Vicar in Anglesey, from whom he derived much information.   By his journeys he became acquainted with many
people in North Wales, and he hardly ever failed in obtaining from them much singular and valuable information of
bye-gone days, which there and then he dotted down on
scraps of paper, and afterwards transferred to note books,
which still are in his possession.

It was his custom, after the labour of school inspection
was over, to ask the clergy with whom he was staying to
accompany him to the most aged inhabitants of their parish.
This they willingly did, and often in the dark winter even-
ings, lantern in hand, they sallied forth on their journey,
and in this way a rich deposit of traditions and superstitions
was struck and rescued from oblivion.   Not a few of the
clergy were themselves in full possession of all the quaint
sayings and Folk-lore of their parishes, and they were not
loath to transfer them to the writer's keeping.   In the course
of this work, the writer gives the names of the many aged
friends who supplied him with information, and also the
names of the clergy who so willingly helped him in his
investigations.   But so interesting was the matter obtained
from several of his clerical friends, that he thinks he ought
in justice to acknowledge their services in this preface.
First and foremost comes up to his mind, the Rev. R. Jones,
formerly Rector of Llanycil, Bala, but now of Llysfaen, near
Abergele.   This gentleman's memory is stored with
reminiscences of former days, and often and again his name
occurs in these pages.   The Rev. Canon Owen Jones,
formerly Vicar of Pentrefoelas, but now of Bodelwyddan,
near Rhyl, also supplied much interesting information of

the people's doings in former days, and I may state that
this gentleman is also acquainted with Welsh literature to
an extent seldom to be met with in the person of an
isolated Welsh parson far removed from books and libraries.
To him I am indebted for the perusal of many MSS. To
the Rev. David James, formerly Rector of Garthbeibio, now
of Pennant, and to his predecessor the Rev. W. E. Jones,
Bylchau; the late Rev. Ellis Roberts (Elis Wyn o Wyrfai);
the Rev. M. Hughes, Derwen; the Rev. W. J. Williams,
Llanfihangel-Glyn-Myfyr, and in a great degree to his aged
friend, the Rev. E. Evans, Llanfihangel, near Llanfyllin,
whose conversation in and love of Welsh literature of all
kinds, including old Welsh Almanacks, was almost without
limit, and whose knowledge and thorough sympathy with his
countrymen made his company most enjoyable. To him and
to all these gentlemen above named, and to others, whose
names appear in the body of this work, the writer is greatly
indebted, and he tenders his best thanks to them all.

The many books from which quotations are made are all
mentioned in connection with the information extracted
from their pages.

Welsh Folk-lore is almost inexhaustible, and in these pages
the writer treats of only one branch of popular superstitions.
Ancient customs are herein only incidentally referred to,
but they are very interesting, and worthy of a full
description. Superstitions associated with particular days
and seasons are also omitted. Weather signs are passed over,
Holy wells around which cluster superstitions of bye-gone
days form no part of this essay. But on all these, and other
branches of Folk-lore, the author has collected much information from the aged Welsh peasant, and possibly some
day in the uncertain future he may publish a continuation
of the present volume.

He has already all but finished a volume on the Holy
Wells of North Wales, and this he hopes to publish at no
very distance period.

The author has endeavoured in all instances to give the names of his informants, but often and again, when pencil and paper were produced, he was requested not to mention in print the name of the person who was speaking to him This request was made, not because the information was incorrect, but from false delicacy; still, in every instance, the writer respected this request. He, however, wishes to state emphatically that he has authority for every single bit of Folk-lore recorded. Very often his work was merely that of a translator, for most of his information, derived from the people, was spoken in Welsh, but he has given in every instance a literal rendering of the narrative, just as he heard it, without embellishments or additions of any kind whatsoever.

ELIAS OWEN

Llanyblodwel Vicarage,
       St. Mark's Day, 1896.

INDEX.

ORIGIN OF THE FAIRIES.

(Y TYLWYTH TÊG.)

THE Fairy tales that abound in the Principality have much in common with like legends in other countries. This points to a common origin of all such tales. There is a real and unreal, a mythical and a material aspect to Fairy Folk-Lore. The prevalence, the obscurity, and the different versions of the same Fairy tale show that their origin dates from remote antiquity. The supernatural and the natural are strangely blended together in these legends, and this also points to their great age, and intimates that these wild and imaginative Fairy narratives had some historical foundation. If carefully sifted, these legends will yield a fruitful harvest of ancient thoughts and facts connected with the history of a people, which, as a race, is, perhaps, now extinct, but which has, to a certain extent, been merged into a stronger and more robust race, by whom they were conquered, and dispossessed of much of their land. The conquerors of the Fair Tribe have transmitted to us tales of their timid, unwarlike, but truthful predecessors of the soil, and these tales shew that for a time both races were co-inhabitants of the land, and to a certain extent, by stealth, intermarried.

Fairy tales, much alike in character, are to be heard in many countries, peopled by branches of the Aryan race, and consequently these stories in outline, were most probably in existence before the separation of the families belonging to that race. It is not improbable that the emigrants would carry with them, into all countries whithersoever they went, their ancestral legends, and they would find no difficulty in supplying these interesting stories with a home in their new country. If this supposition be correct, we must look for the origin of Fairy Mythology in the cradle of the Aryan people, and not in any part of the world inhabited by descendants of that great race.

But it is not improbable that incidents in the process of colonization would repeat themselves, or under special circumstances vary, and thus we should have similar and different versions of the same historical event in all countries once inhabited by a diminutive race, which was overcome by a more powerful people.

In Wales Fairy legends have such peculiarities that they seem to be historical fragments of by-gone days. And apparently they refer to a race which immediately preceded the Celt in the occupation of the country, and with which the Celt to a limited degree amalgamated.

NAMES GIVEN TO THE FAIRIES.

The Fairies have, in Wales, at least three common and distinctive names, as well as others that are not nowadays used.

The first and most general name given to the Fairies is " *Y Tylwyth Tég*," or, the Fair Tribe, an expressive and descriptive term. They are spoken of as a people, and not as myths or goblins, and they are said to be a fair or handsome race.

Another common name for the Fairies, is, " *Bendith y Mamau*," or, "The Mothers' Blessing." In Doctor Owen Pughe's Dictionary they are called "Bendith *eu* Mamau," or, " *Their* Mothers' Blessing." The first is the most common expression, at least in North Wales. It is a singularly strange expression, and difficult to explain. Perhaps it hints at a Fairy origin on the mother's side of certain fortunate people.

The third name given to Fairies is "*Ellyll*," an elf, a demon, a goblin. This name conveys these beings to the land of spirits, and makes them resemble the oriental Genii, and Shakespeare's sportive elves. It agrees, likewise, with the modern popular creed respecting goblins and their doings.

Davydd ab Gwilym, in a description of a mountain mist in which he was once enveloped, says:—

> Yr ydoedd ym mhob gobant
> *Ellyllon* mingeimion gant.

> There were in every hollow
> A hundred wrymouthed elves.

The Cambro-Briton, v. I., p. 348.

In Pembrokeshire the Fairies are called *Dynon Buch Tég*, or the *Fair Small People*.

Another name applied to the Fairies is *Plant Annwfn*, or *Plant Annwn*. This, however, is not an appellation in common use. The term is applied to the Fairies in the third paragraph of a Welsh prose poem called *Bardd Cwsg*, thus:—

> Y bwriodd y *Tylwyth T'êg* fi . . . oni bai fy nyfod i mewn pryd i'th achub o gigweiniau *Plant Annwfn*.

> Where the *Tylwyth Têg* threw me . . . if I had not come in time to rescue thee from the clutches of *Plant Annwfn*.

Annwn, or *Annwfn* is defined in Canon Silvan Evans's Dictionary as an abyss, Hades, &c. *Plant Annwn*, therefore, means children of the lower regions. It is a name derived from the supposed place of abode—the bowels of the earth—of the Fairies. *Gwragedd Annwn*, dames of Elfin land, is a term applied to Fairy ladies.

Ellis Wynne, the author of *Bardd Cwsg*, was born in 1671, and the probability is that the words *Plant Annwfn* formed in his days part of the vocabulary of the people. He was born in Merionethshire.

Gwyll, according to Richards, and Dr. Owen Pughe, is a Fairy, a goblin, &c. The plural of *Gwyll* would be *Gwylliaid*, or *Gwyllion*, but this latter word Dr. Pughe defines as ghosts, hobgoblins, &c. Formerly, there was in Merionethshire a red haired family of robbers called *Y Gwylliaid Cochion*, or Red Fairies, of whom I shall speak hereafter.

Coblynau, or Knockers, have been described as a species of Fairies, whose abode was within the rocks, and whose province it was to indicate to the miners by the process of knocking, &c., the presence of rich lodes of lead or other metals in this or that direction of the mine.

That the words *Tylwyth Tég* and *Ellyll* are convertible terms appears from the following stanza, which is taken from the *Cambrian Magazine*, vol. ii., p. 58.

> Pan dramwych ffridd yr Ywen,
> Lle mae *Tylwyth Tég* yn rhodien,
> Dos ymlaen, a phaid a sefyll,
> Gwilia'th droed—rhag dawnsva'r *Ellyll*.

> When the forest of the Yew,
> Where *Fairies* haunt. thou passest through,
> Tarry not, thy footsteps guard
> From the *Goblins'* dancing sward.

Although the poet mentions the *Tylwyth Tég* and *Ellyll* as identical, he might have done so for rhythmical reasons. Undoubtedly, in the first instance a distinction would be drawn between these two words, which originally were intended perhaps to describe two different kinds of beings, but in the course of time the words became interchangeable, and thus their distinctive character was lost. In English the words Fairies and elves are used without any distinction.

It would appear from Brand's *Popular Antiquities*, vol. II., p. 478., that, according to Gervase of Tilbury, there were two kinds of Goblins in England, called *Portuni* and *Grant.* This division suggests a difference between the *Tylwyth Tég* and the *Ellyll.* The *Portuni*, we are told, were very small of stature and old in appearance, " *statura pusilli, dimidium pollicis non habentes*," but then they were " *senili vultu, facie corrugata.*" The wrinkled face and aged countenance of the *Portuni* remind us of nursery Fairy tales in which the wee ancient female Fairy figures. The pranks of the *Portuni* were similar to those of Shakespeare's Puck. The species *Grant* is not described, and consequently it cannot be ascertained how far they resembled any of the many kinds of Welsh Fairies. Gervase, speaking of one of these species, says :—" If anything should be to be carried on in the house, or any kind of laborious work to be done, they join themselves to the work, and expedite it with more than human facility."

In Scotland there were at least two species of elves, the *Brownies* and the *Fairies.* The Brownies were so called from their tawny colour, and the Fairies from their fairness. The *Portuni* of Gervase appear to have corresponded in character to the Brownies, who were said to have employed themselves in the night in the discharge of laborious undertakings acceptable to the family to whose service they had devoted themselves. The Fairies proper of Scotland strongly resembled the Fairies of Wales.

The term *Brownie,* or swarthy elve, suggests a connection between them and the *Gwylliaid Cochion,* or Red Fairies of Wales.

FAIRY LADIES MARRYING MORTALS.

In the mythology of the Greeks, and other nations, gods and goddesses are spoken of as falling in love with human beings, and many an ancient genealogy began with a celestial ancestor. Much the same thing is said of the Fairies. Tradition speaks of them as being enamoured of the inhabitants of this earth, and content, for awhile, to be wedded to mortals. And there are families in Wales who are said to have Fairy blood coursing through their veins, but they are, or were, not so highly esteemed as were the offspring of the gods among the Greeks. The famous physicians of Myddfai, who owed their talent and supposed supernatural knowledge to their Fairy origin, are, however, an exception; for their renown, notwithstanding their parentage, was always great, and increased in greatness, as the rolling years removed them from their traditionary parent, the Fairy lady of the Van Pool.

The *Pellings* are said to have sprung from a Fairy Mother, and the author of *Observations on the Snowdon Mountains* states that the best blood in his veins is fairy blood. There are in some parts of Wales reputed descendants on the female side of the *Gwylliaid Cochion* race; and there are other families among us whom the aged of fifty years ago, with an ominous shake of the head, would say were of Fairy extraction. We are not, therefore, in Wales void of families of doubtful parentage or origin.

All the current tales of men marrying Fairy ladies belong to a class of stories called, technically, Taboo stories. In these tales the lady marries her lover conditionally, and when this condition is broken she deserts husband and children, and hies back to Fairy land.

This kind of tale is current among many people. Max Müller in *Chips from a German Workshop*, vol. ii, pp. 104-6, records one of these ancient stories, which is found in the Brahmana of the Yagur-veda. Omitting a few particulars, the story is as follows :—

" Urvasi, a kind of Fairy, fell in love with Purûravas, the son of Ida, and when she met him she said, 'Embrace me three times a day, but never against my will, and let me never see you without your royal garments, for this is the manner of women.' In this manner she lived with him a long time, and she was with child. Then her former friends, the Gandharvas, said: 'This Urvasi has now dwelt a long time among mortals; let us see that she come back.' Now, there was a ewe, with two lambs, tied to the couch of Urvasi and Purûravas, and the Gandharvas stole one of them. Urvasi said: 'They take away my darling, as if I had lived in a land where there is no hero and no man.' They stole the second, and she upbraided her husband again. Then Purûravas looked and said: 'How can that be a land without heroes and men where I am?' And naked, he sprang up; he thought it too long to put on his dress. Then the Gandharvas sent a flash of lightning, and Urvasi saw her husband naked as by daylight. Then she vanished; 'I come back,' she said, and went.

Purûravas bewailed his love in bitter grief. But whilst walking along the border of a lake full of lotus flowers the Fairies were playing there in the water, in the shape of birds, and Urvasi discovered him and said :—

' That is the man with whom I dwelt so long.' Then her friends said: 'Let us appear to him.' She agreed, and they appeared before him. Then the king recognised her, and said :—

'Lo! my wife, stay, thou cruel in mind! Let us now exchange some words! Our secrets, if they are not told now, will not bring us back on any later day.'

She replied: 'What shall I do with thy speech? I am gone like the first of the dawns. Purûravas, go home again, I am hard to be caught, like the wind.' "

The Fairy wife by and by relents, and her mortal lover became, by a certain sacrifice, one of the Gandharvas.

This ancient Hindu Fairy tale resembles in many particulars similar tales found in Celtic Folk-Lore, and possibly, the original story, in its main features, existed before the Aryan family had separated. The very words, " I am hard to be caught," appear in one of the Welsh legends, which shall be hereafter given :—

> Nid hawdd fy nala,
> I am hard to be caught.

And the scene is similar; in both cases the Fairy ladies are discovered in a lake. The immortal weds the mortal, conditionally, and for awhile the union seems to be a happy one. But, unwittingly, when engaged in an undertaking suggested by, or in agreement with the wife's wishes, the prohibited thing is done, and the lady vanishes away.

Such are the chief features of these mythical marriages. I will now record like tales that have found a home in several parts of Wales.

WELSH LEGENDS OF FAIRY LADIES MARRYING MEN.

1. *The Pentrevoelas Legend.*

I am indebted to the Rev. Owen Jones, Vicar of Pentrevoelas, a mountain parish in West Denbighshire, for the following tale, which was written in Welsh by a native of those parts, and appeared in competition for a prize on the Folk-Lore of that parish.

The son of Hafodgarreg was shepherding his father's flock on the hills, and whilst thus engaged, he, one misty morning, came suddenly upon a lovely girl, seated on the sheltered side of a peat-stack. The maiden appeared to be in great distress, and she was crying bitterly. The young man went up to her, and spoke kindly to her, and his attention and sympathy were not without effect on the comely stranger.

So beautiful was the young woman, that from expressions of sympathy the smitten youth proceeded to words of love, and his advances were not repelled. But whilst the lovers were holding sweet conversation, there appeared on the scene a venerable and aged man, who, addressing the female as her father, bade her follow him. She immediately obeyed, and both departed leaving the young man alone. He lingered about the place until the evening, wishing and hoping that she might return, but she came not. Early the next day, he was at the spot where he first felt what love was. All day long he loitered about the place, vainly hoping that the beautiful girl would pay another visit to the mountain, but he was doomed to disappointment, and night again drove him homewards. Thus daily went he to the place where he had met his beloved, but she was not there, and, love-sick and lonely, he returned to Hafodgarreg. Such devotion deserved its reward. It would seem that the young lady loved the young man quite as much as he loved her. And in the land of allurement and illusion (yn nhir hud a lledrith) she planned a visit to the earth, and met her lover, but she was soon missed by her father, and he, suspecting her love for this young man, again came upon them, and found them conversing lovingly together. Much talk took place between the sire and his daughter, and the shepherd, waxing bold, begged and begged her father to give him his daughter in marriage. The sire, perceiving that the man was in earnest, turned to his daughter, and asked her whether it were her wish to marry a man of the earth? She said it was. Then the father told the shepherd he should have his daughter to wife, and that she should stay with him, until he should strike her with *iron*, and that, as a marriage portion, he would give her a bag filled with bright money. The young couple were duly married, and the promised dowry was received. For many years they lived lovingly and happily together, and children were born to them. One day this man and his wife went together to the hill to catch a couple of ponies, to carry them to the Festival of the Saint of Capel Garmon. The ponies were very wild, and could not be caught. The man, irritated, pursued the nimble creatures. His wife was by his side, and now he thought he had them in his power, but just at the moment he was about to grasp their manes, off they wildly galloped, and the man, in anger, finding that they had again eluded him, threw the bridle after them, and, sad to say, the bit struck the wife, and as this was of *iron* they both knew that their marriage contract was broken. Hardly had they had time to realise the dire accident, ere the aged father of the bride appeared, accompanied by a host of Fairies, and there and then departed with his daughter to the land whence she came, and that, too, without even allowing her to bid farewell to her children. The money, though, and the children were left behind, and these were the only memorials of the lovely wife and the kindest of mothers, that remained to remind the shepherd of the treasure he had lost in the person of his Fairy spouse.

Such is the Pentrevoelas Legend. The writer had evidently not seen the version of this story in the *Cambro-Briton*, nor had he read Williams's tale of a like occurrence, recorded in *Observations on the Snowdon Mountains*. The account, therefore, is all the more valuable, as being an independent production.

A fragmentary variant of the preceding legend was given me by Mr. Lloyd, late schoolmaster of Llanfihangel-Glyn-Myfyr, a native of South Wales, who heard the tale in the parish of Llanfihangel. Although but a fragment, it may not be altogether useless, and I will give it as I received it :—

Shon Rolant, Hafod y Dre, Pentrevoelas, when going

home from Llanrwst market, fortunately caught a Fairy-maid, whom he took home with him. She was a most handsome woman, but rather short and slight in person. She was admired by everybody on account of her great beauty. Shon Rolant fell desperately in love with her, and would have married her, but this she would not allow. He, however, continued pressing her to become his wife, and, by and by, she consented to do so, provided he could find out her name. As Shon was again going home from the market about a month later, he heard some one saying, near the place where he had seized the Fairy-maid, " Where is little Penloi gone? Where is little Penloi gone ?" Shon at once thought that some one was searching for the Fairy he had captured, and when he reached home, he addressed the Fairy by the name he had heard, and Penloi consented to become his wife. She, however, expressed displeasure at marrying a dead man, as the Fairies call us. She informed her lover that she was not to be touched with *iron*, or she would disappear at once. Shon took great care not to touch her with iron. However, one day, when he was on horseback talking to his beloved Penloi, who stood at the horse's head, the horse suddenly threw up its head, and the curb, which was of *iron*, came in contact with Penloi, who immediately vanished out of sight.

The next legend is taken from Williams's *Observations on the Snowdon Mountains.* His work was published in 1802. He, himself, was born in Anglesey, in 1738, and migrated to Carnarvonshire about the year 1760. It was in this latter county that he became a learned antiquary, and a careful recorder of events that came under his notice. His "Observations" throw considerable light upon the life, the customs, and the traditions of the inhabitants of the hill parts and secluded glens of Carnarvonshire. I have thought fit to make these few remarks about the author

I quote from, so as to enable the reader to give to him that credence which he is entitled to. Williams entitles the following story, " A Fairy Tale," but I will for the sake of reference call it " The Ystrad Legend."

2. *The Ystrad Legend.*

" In a meadow belonging to Ystrad, bounded by the river which falls from Cwellyn Lake, they say the Fairies used to assemble, and dance on fair moon-light-nights. One evening a young man, who was the heir and occupier of this farm, hid himself in a thicket close to the spot where they used to gambol; presently they appeared, and when in their merry mood, out he bounced from his covert and seized one of their females; the rest of the company dispersed themselves, and disappeared in an instant. Disregarding her struggles and screams, he hauled her to his home, where he treated her so very kindly that she became content to live with him as his maid servant; but he could not prevail upon her to tell him her name. Some time after, happening again to see the Fairies upon the same spot, he heard one of them saying, ' The last time we met here, our sister *Penelope* was snatched away from us by one of the mortals.' Rejoiced at knowing the name of his *Incognita*, he returned home; and as she was very beautiful, and extremely active, he proposed to marry her, which she would not for a long time consent to; at last, however, she complied, but on this condition, ' That if ever he should strike her with iron, she would leave him, and never return to him again.' They lived happily for many years together, and he had by her a son, and a daughter; and by her industry and prudent management as a house-wife he became one of the richest men in the country. He farmed, besides his own freehold, all the lands on the north side of Nant-y-Bettws to the top of Snowdon, and all Cwmbrwynog in Llanberis; an extent of about five thousand acres or upwards.

Unfortunately, one day Penelope followed her husband into the field to catch a horse; and he, being in a rage at the animal as he ran away from him, threw at him the bridle that was in his hand, which unluckily fell on poor Penelope. She disappeared in an instant, and he never saw her afterwards, but heard her voice in the window of his room one night after, requesting him to take care of the children, in these words :—

> Rhag bod anwyd ar fy mab,
> Yn rhodd rhowch arno gôb ei dâd,
> Rhag bod anwyd ar liw'r cann,
> Rhoddwch arni bais ei mam.

That is—

> Oh! lest my son should suffer cold,
> Him in his father's coat infold,
> Lest cold should seize my darling fair,
> For her, her mother's robe prepare.

These children and their descendants, they say, were called *Pellings;* a word corrupted from their mother's name, Penelope."

Williams proceeds thus with reference to the descendants of this union :—

"The late Thomas Rowlands, Esq., of Caerau, in Anglesey, the father of the late Lady Bulkeley, was a descendant of this lady, if it be true that the name *Pellings* came from her; and there are still living several opulent and respectable people who are known to have sprung from the *Pellings.* The best blood in my own veins is this Fairy's."

This tale was chronicled in the last century, but it is not known whether every particular incident connected therewith was recorded by Williams. *Glasynys*, the Rev. Owen Wynne Jones, a clergyman, relates a tale in the *Brython*, which he regards as the same tale as that given by Williams, and he says that he heard it scores of times when he was a lad. *Glasynys* was born in the parish of Rhostryfan, Carnarvonshire, in 1827, and as his birth place is not far distant from the scene of this legend, he might have heard a different version of Williams's tale, and that too of equal value with Williams's. Possibly, there were not more than from forty to fifty years between the time when the older writer heard the tale and the time when it was heard by the younger man. An octogenarian, or even a younger person, could have conversed with both Williams and *Glasynys*. *Glasynys's* tale appears in Professor Rhys's *Welsh Fairy Tales*, *Cymmrodor*, vol. iv., p. 188. It originally appeared in the *Brython* for 1863, p. 193. It is as follows:—

"One fine sunny morning, as the young heir of Ystrad was busied with his sheep on the side of Moel Eilio, he met a very pretty girl, and when he got home he told the folks there of it. A few days afterwards he met her again, and this happened several times, when he mentioned it to his father, who advised him to seize her when he next met her. The next time he met her he proceeded to do so, but before he could take her away, a little fat old man came to them and begged him to give her back to him, to which the youth would not listen. The little man uttered terrible threats, but he would not yield, so an agreement was made between them that he was to have her to wife until he touched her skin with iron, and great was the joy both of the son and his parents in consequence. They lived together for many years, but once on a time, on the evening of Bettws Fair, the wife's horse got restive, and somehow, as the husband was attending to the horse, the stirrups touched the skin of her bare leg, and that very night she was taken away from him. She had three or four children, and more than one of their descendants, as *Glasynys* maintains, were known to him at the time he wrote in 1863."

3. *The Llanfrothen Legend.*

I am indebted to the Rev. R. Jones, Rector of Llanycil, Bala, for the following legend. I may state that Mr. Jones is a native of Llanfrothen, Merionethshire, a parish in close proximity to the scene of the story. Mr. Jones's informant was his mother, a lady whose mind was well stored with tales of by-gone times, and my friend and informant inherits his mother's retentive memory, as well as her love of ancient lore.

A certain man fell in love with a beautiful Fairy lady, and he wished to marry her. She consented to do so, but warned him that if he ever touched her with iron she would leave him immediately. This stipulation weighed but lightly on the lover. They were married, and for many years they lived most happily together, and several children were born to them. A sad mishap, however, one day overtook them. They were together, crossing Traethmawr, Penrhyndeudraeth, on horseback, when the man's horse became restive, and jerked his head towards the woman, and the bit of the bridle touched the left arm of the Fairy wife. She at once told her husband that they must part for ever. He was greatly distressed, and implored her not to leave him. She said she could not stay. Then the man, appealing to a mother's love for her children, begged that she would for the sake of their offspring continue to dwell with him and them, and, said he, what will become of our children without their mother? Her answer was :—

Gadewch iddynt fod yn bennau cochion a thrwynau hirion.

Let them be redheaded and longnosed.

Having uttered these words, she disappeared and was never seen afterwards.

No Welsh Taboo story can be complete without the pretty tale of the Van Lake Legend, or, as it is called," The Myddfai Legend." Because of its intrinsic beauty and worth, and for the sake of comparison with the preceding stories, I will relate this legend. There are several versions extant. Mr. Wirt Sikes, in his *British Goblins*, has one, the *Cambro-Briton* has one, but the best is that recorded by Professor Rhys, in the *Cymmrodor*, vol. iv., p. 163, in his *Welsh Fairy Tales*. There are other readings of the legend to be met with. I will first of all give an epitome of the Professor's version.

4. *The Myddvai Legend.*

A widow, who had an only son, was obliged, in consequence of the large flocks she possessed, to send, under the care of her son, a portion of her cattle to graze on the Black Mountain near a small lake called Llyn-y-Van-Bach.

One day the son perceived, to his great astonishment, a most beautiful creature with flowing hair sitting on the unruffled surface of the lake combing her tresses, the water serving as a mirror. Suddenly she beheld the young man standing on the brink of the lake with his eyes rivetted on her, and unconsciously offering to herself the provision of barley bread and cheese with which he had been provided when he left his home.

Bewildered by a feeling of love and admiration for the object before him, he continued to hold out his hand towards the lady, who imperceptibly glided near to him, but gently refused the offer of his provisions. He attempted to touch her, but she eluded his grasp, saying

> Cras dy fara ;
> Nid hawdd fy nala.
> Hard baked is thy bread ;
> It is not easy to catch me.

She immediately dived under the water and disappeared, leaving the love-stricken youth to return home a prey to disappointment and regret that he had been unable to make further acquaintance with the lovely maiden with whom he had desperately fallen in love.

On his return home he communicated to his mother the extraordinary vision. She advised him to take some unbaked dough the next time in his pocket, as there must have been some spell connected with the hard baked bread, or " Bara Cras," which prevented his catching the lady.

Next morning, before the sun was up, the young man was at the lake, not for the purpose of looking after the cattle, but that he might again witness the enchanting vision of the previous day. In vain did he glance over the surface of the lake; nothing met his view, save the ripples occasioned by a stiff breeze, and a dark cloud hung heavily on the summit of the Van.

Hours passed on, the wind was hushed, the overhanging clouds had vanished, when the youth was startled by seeing some of his mother's cattle on the precipitous side of the acclivity, nearly on the opposite side of the lake. As he was hastening away to rescue them from their perilous position, the object of his search again appeared to him, and seemed much more beautiful than when he first beheld her. His hand was again held out to her, full of unbaked bread, which he offered to her with an urgent proffer of his heart also, and vows of eternal attachment, all of which were refused by her, saying

> Llaith dy fara !
> Ti ni fynna.'
> Unbaked is thy bread !
> I will not have thee.

But the smiles that played upon her features as the lady vanished beneath the waters forbade him to despair, and

cheered him on his way home. His aged parent was
acquainted with his ill success, and she suggested that his
bread should the next time be but slightly baked, as most
likely to please the mysterious being.

Impelled by love, the youth left his mother's home early
next morning. He was soon near the margin of the lake
impatiently awaiting the reappearance of the lady. The
sheep and goats browsed on the precipitous sides of the
Van, the cattle strayed amongst the rocks, rain and sunshine
came and passed away, unheeded by the youth who was
wrapped up in looking for the appearance of her who had
stolen his heart. The sun was verging towards the west,
and the young man casting a sad look over the waters ere
departing homewards was astonished to see several cows
walking along its surface, and, what was more pleasing to
his sight, the maiden reappeared, even lovelier than ever.
She approached the land and he rushed to meet her in the
water.. A smile encouraged him to seize her hand, and she
accepted the moderately baked bread he offered her, and
after some persuasion she consented to become his wife, on
condition that they should live together until she received
from him three blows without a cause,

Tri ergyd diachos,
Three causeless blows,

when, should he ever happen to strike her three such blows,
she would leave him for ever. These conditions were readily
and joyfully accepted.

Thus the Lady of the Lake became engaged to the young
man, and having loosed her hand for a moment she darted
away and dived into the lake. The grief of the lover at
this disappearance of his affianced was such that he determined to cast himself headlong into its unfathomed depths,
and thus end his life. As he was on the point of commit-

ting this rash act, there emerged out of the lake two most
beautiful ladies, accompanied by a hoary-headed man of
noble mien and extraordinary stature, but having otherwise
all the force and strength of youth. This man addressed
the youth, saying that, as he proposed to marry one of his
daughters, he consented to the union, provided the young
man could distinguish which of the two ladies before him
was the object of his affections. This was no easy task, as
the maidens were perfect counterparts of each other.

Whilst the young man narrowly scanned the two ladies
and failed to perceive the least difference betwixt the two,
one of them thrust her foot a slight degree forward. The
motion, simple as it was, did not escape the observation of
the youth, and he discovered a trifling variation in the mode
in which their sandals were tied. This at once put an
end to the dilemma, for he had on previous occasions noticed
the peculiarity of her shoe-tie, and he boldly took hold of
her hand.

"Thou hast chosen rightly," said the Father, " be to her
a kind and faithful husband, and I will give her, as a dowry,
as many sheep, cattle, goats, and horses, as she can count
of each without heaving or drawing in her breath. But
remember, that if you prove unkind to her at any time and
strike her three times without a cause, she shall return to
me, and shall bring all her stock with her."

Such was the marriage settlement, to which the young
man gladly assented, and the bride was desired to count
the number of sheep she was to have. She immediately
adopted the mode of counting by fives, thus:—One, two,
three, four, five,—one, two, three, four, five ; as many times
as possible in rapid succession, till her breath was exhausted.
The same process of reckoning had to determine the number of goats, cattle, and horses, respectively ; and in an

instant the full number of each came out of the lake, when called upon by the Father.

The young couple were then married, and went to reside at a farm called Esgair Llaethdy, near Myddvai, where they lived in prosperity and happiness for several years, and became the parents of three beautiful sons.

Once upon a time there was a christening in the neighbourhood to which the parents were invited. When the day arrived the wife appeared reluctant to attend the christening, alleging that the distance was too great for her to walk. Her husband told her to fetch one of the horses from the field. "I will," said she, "if you will bring me my gloves which I left in our house." He went for the gloves, and finding she had not gone for the horse, he playfully slapped her shoulder with one of them, saying "dôs, dôs, go go," when she reminded him of the terms on which she consented to marry him, and warned him to be more cautious in the future, as he had now given her one causeless blow.

On another occasion when they were together at a wedding and the assembled guests were greatly enjoying themselves the wife burst into tears and sobbed most piteously. Her husband touched her on the shoulder and inquired the cause of her weeping; she said, "Now people are entering into trouble, and your troubles are likely to commence, as you have the *second* time stricken me without a cause."

Years passed on, and their children had grown up, and were particularly clever young men. Amidst so many worldly blessings the husband almost forgot that only *one* causeless blow would destroy his prosperity. Still he was watchful lest any trivial occurrence should take place which his wife must regard as a breach of their marriage contract. She told him that her affection for him was unabated, and warned him to be careful lest through inadvertence he might give the last and only blow which, by an unalterable destiny, over which she had no control, would separate them for ever.

One day it happened that they went to a funeral together, where, in the midst of mourning and grief at the house of the deceased, she appeared in the gayest of spirits, and indulged in inconsiderate fits of laughter, which so shocked her husband that he touched her, saying—"Hush ! hush ! don't laugh." She said that she laughed because people when they die go out of trouble, and rising up, she went out of the house, saying, " The last blow has been struck, our marriage contract is broken, and at an end. Farewell ! " Then she started off towards Esgair Llaethdy, where she called her cattle and other stock together, each by name, not forgetting, the " little black calf" which had been slaughtered and was suspended on the hook, and away went the calf and all the stock, with the Lady across Myddvai Mountain, and disappeared beneath the waters of the lake whence the Lady had come. The four oxen that were ploughing departed, drawing after them the plough, which made a furrow in the ground, and which remains as a testimony of the truth of this story.

She is said to have appeared to her sons, and accosting Rhiwallon, her firstborn, to have informed him that he was to be a benefactor to mankind, through healing all manner of their diseases, and she furnished him with prescriptions and instructions for the preservation of health. Then, promising to meet him when her counsel was most needed, she vanished. On several other occasions she met her sons, and pointed out to them plants and herbs, and revealed to them their medicinal qualities or virtues.

So ends the Myddvai Legend.

A variant of this tale appears in the form of a letter in the *Cambro-Briton*, vol. ii. pp. 313-315. The editor pre-

faces the legend with the remark that the tale "acquires
an additional interest from its resemblance in one particular
to a similar tradition current in Scotland, wherein certain
beasts, brought from a lake, as in this tale, play much the
same part as is here described." The volume of the *Cambro-
Briton* now referred to was published in 1821 and apparently the writer, who calls himself *Sicncyn ab Tydvil*,
communicates an unwritten tradition afloat in Carmarthenshire, for he does not tell us whence he obtained the story.
As the tale differs in some particulars from that already
given, I will transcribe it.

5. *The Cambro-Briton version of the Myddvai Legend.*

"A man, who lived in the farm-house called Esgair-
llaethdy, in the parish of Myddvai, in Carmarthenshire,
having bought some lambs in a neighbouring fair, led them
to graze near *Llyn y Van Vach*, on the Black Mountains.
Whenever he visited the lambs, three most beautiful female
figures presented themselves to him from the lake, and
often made excursions on the boundaries of it. For some
time he pursued and endeavoured to catch them, but always failed; for the enchanting nymphs ran before him, and,
when they had reached the lake, they tauntingly exclaimed,

> Cras dy fara,
> Anhawdd ein dala,

which, with a little circumlocution, means, ' For thee, who
eatest baked bread, it is difficult to catch us.'

One day some moist bread from the lake came to shore.
The farmer devoured it with great avidity, and on the following day he was successful in his pursuit and caught the
fair damsels. After a little conversation with them, he commanded courage sufficient to make proposals of marriage to
one of them. She consented to accept them on the condition that he would distinguish her from her two sisters

on the following day. This was a new, and a very great
difficulty to the young farmer, for the fair nymphs were so
similar in form and features, that he could scarcely perceive
any difference between them. He observed, however, a
trifling singularity in the strapping of her sandal, by which
he recognized her the following day. Some, indeed, who
relate this legend, say that this Lady of the Lake hinted in
a private conversation with her swain that upon the day of
trial she would place herself between her two sisters, and
that she would turn her right foot a little to the right, and
that by this means he distinguished her from her sisters.
Whatever were the means, the end was secured; he selected
her, and she immediately left the lake and accompanied him
to his farm. Before she quitted, she summoned to attend
her from the lake seven cows, two oxen, and one bull.

This lady engaged to live with him until such time as he
would strike her three times without cause. For some years
they lived together in comfort, and she bore him three sons,
who were the celebrated Meddygon Myddvai.

One day, when preparing for a fair in the neighbourhood,
he desired her to go to the field for his horse. She said she
would; but being rather dilatory, he said to her humor-
ously, ' dôs, dôs, dôs,' i.e., 'go, go, go,' and he slightly touched
her arm *three times* with his glove.

As she now deemed the terms of her marriage broken,
she immediately departed, and summoned with her her
seven cows, her two oxen, and the bull. The oxen were at
that very time ploughing in the field, but they immediately
obeyed her call, and took the plough with them. The
furrow from the field in which they were ploughing, to the
margin of the lake, is to be seen in several parts of that
country to the present day.

After her departure, she once met her two sons in a Cwm,

now called *Cwm Meddygon* (Physicians' Combe), and delivered to each of them a bag containing some articles
which are unknown, but which are supposed to have been
some discoveries in medicine.

The Meddygon Myddvai were Rhiwallon and his sons,
Cadwgan, Gruffydd, and Einion. They were the chief
physicians of their age, and they wrote about A.D. 1230.
A copy of their works is in the Welsh School Library, in
Gray's Inn Lane."

Such are the Welsh Taboo tales. I will now make a few
remarks upon them.

The *age* of these legends is worthy of consideration. The
legend of *Meddygon Myddvai* dates from about the thirteenth century. Rhiwallon and his sons, we are told by
the writer in the *Cambro-Briton*, wrote about 1230 A.D.,
but the editor of that publication speaks of a manuscript
written by these physicians about the year 1300. Modern
experts think that their treatise on medicine in the *Red
Book of Hergest* belongs to the end of the fourteenth century,
about 1380 to 1400.

Dafydd ab Gwilym, who is said to have flourished in the
fourteenth century, says, in one of his poems, as given in
the *Cambro-Briton*, vol. ii., p. 313, alluding to these
physicians :—

> "Meddyg, nis gwnai modd y gwnaeth
> Myddfai, o chai ddyn meddfaeth."
>
> "A Physician he would not make
> As Myddvai made, if he had a mead fostered man."

It would appear, therefore, that these celebrated physicians lived somewhere about the thirteenth century. They
are described as Physicians of Rhys Gryg, a prince of South
Wales, who lived in the early part of the thirteenth century.
Their supposed supernatural origin dates therefore from the
thirteenth, or at the latest, the fourteenth century.

I have mentioned *Y Gwylliaid Cochion*, or, as they are generally styled, *Gwylliaid Cochion Mawddwy*, the Red Fairies of Mawddwy, as being of Fairy origin. The Llanfrothen Legend seems to account for a race of men in Wales differing from their neighbours in certain features. The offspring of the Fairy union were, according to the Fairy mother's prediction in that legend, to have red hair and prominent noses. That a race of men having these characteristics did exist in Wales is undoubted. They were a strong tribe, the men were tall and athletic, and lived by plunder. They had their head quarters at Dinas Mawddwy, Merionethshire, and taxed their neighbours in open day, driving away sheep and cattle to their dens. So unbearable did their depredations become that John Wynn ap Meredydd of Gwydir and Lewis Owen, or as he is called Baron Owen, raised a body of stout men to overcome them, and on Christmas Eve, 1554, succeeded in capturing a large number of the offenders, and, there and then, some hundred or so of the robbers were hung. Tradition says that a mother begged hard for the life of a young son, who was to be destroyed, but Baron Owen would not relent. On perceiving that her request was unheeded, baring her breast she said :—

Y bronau melynion hyn a fagasant y rhai a ddialant waed fy mab, ac a olchant eu dwylaw yn ngwaed calon llofrudd eu brawd.

These yellow breasts have nursed those who will revenge my son's blood, and will wash their hands in the heart's blood of the murderer of their brother.

According to *Pennant* this threat was carried out by the murder of Baron Owen in 1555, when he was passing through the thick woods of Mawddwy on his way to Montgomeryshire Assizes, at a place called to this day *Llidiart y Barwn*, the Baron's Gate, from the deed. Tradition further tells us that the murderers had gone a distance off before they

D

remembered their mother's threat, and returning thrust
their swords into the Baron's breast, and washed their hands
in his heart's blood. This act was followed by vigorous
action, and the banditti were extirpated, the females only
remaining, and the descendants of these women are occasionally still to be met with in Montgomeryshire and Merionethshire.

For the preceding information the writer is indebted to
Yr Hynafion Cymreig, pp. 91-94, *Archæologia Cambrensis*,
for 1854, pp. 119-20, *Pennant*, vol. ii, pp. 225-27, ed. Carnarvon, and the tradition was told him by the Revd. D.
James, Vicar of Garthbeibio, who likewise pointed out to
him the very spot where the Baron was murdered.

But now, who were these *Gwylliaid?* According to the
hint conveyed by their name they were of Fairy parentage,
an idea which a writer in the *Archæologia Cambrensis*,
vol. v., 1854, p. 119, intended, perhaps, to throw out. But
according to *Brut y Tywysogion, Myf. Arch.*, p. 706, A.D.
1114, Denbigh edition, the *Gwylliaid Cochion Mawddwy*
began in the time of Cadwgan ab Bleddyn ab Cynvyn.

From Williams's *Eminent Welshmen*, we gather that
Prince Cadwgan died in 1110, A.D., and, according to the
above-mentioned *Brut*, it was in his days that the Gwylliaid
commenced their career, if not their existence.

Unfortunately for this beginning of the red-headed banditti of Mawddwy, Tacitus states in his Life of Agricola, ch.
xi., that there were in Britain men with red hair who he
surmises were of German extraction. We must. therefore,
look for the commencement of a people of this description
long before the twelfth century, and the Llanfrothen legend
either dates from remote antiquity, or it was a tale that
found in its wanderings a resting place in that locality in
ages long past.

From a legend recorded by *Giraldus Cambrensis*, which shall by and by be given, it would seem that a priest named Elidorus lived among the Fairies in their home in the bowels of the earth, and this would be in the early part of the twelfth century. The question arises, is the priest's tale credible, or did he merely relate a story of himself which had been ascribed to some one else in the traditions of the people? If his tale is true, then, there lived even in that late period a remnant of the aborigines of the country, who had their homes in caves. The Myḍdvai Legend in part corroborates this supposition, for that story apparently belongs to the thirteenth century.

It is difficult to fix the date of the other legends here given, for they are dressed in modern garbs, with, however, trappings of remote times. Probably all these tales have reached, through oral tradition, historic times, but in reality they belong to that far-off distant period, when the prehistoric inhabitants of this island dwelt in Lake-habitations, or in caves. And the marriage of Fairy ladies, with men of a different race, intimates that the more ancient people were not extirpated, but were amalgamated with their conquerors.

Many Fairy tales in Wales are associated with lakes. Fairy ladies emerge from lakes and disappear into lakes. In the oriental legend Purûrvas came upon his absconding wife in a lake. In many Fairy stories lakes seem to be the entrance to the abodes of the Fairies. Evidently, therefore, those people were lake-dwellers. In the lakes of Switzerland and other countries have been discovered vestiges of Lake-villages belonging to the Stone Age, and even to the Bronze Age. Perhaps those that belong to the Stone Age are the most ancient kind of human abodes still traceable in the world. In Ireland and Scotland these kinds of dwellings have been found. I am not in a position to say that they

have been discovered in Wales; but some thirty years ago
Mr. Colliver, a Cornish gentleman, told the writer that
whilst engaged in mining operations near Llyn Llydaw he
had occasion to lower the water level of that lake, when he
discovered embedded in the mud a canoe formed out of the
trunk of a single tree.   He saw another in the lake, but this
he did not disturb, and there it is at the present day.   The
late Professor Peter of Bala believed that he found traces
of Lake-dwellings in Bala Lake, and the people in those
parts have a tradition that a town lies buried beneath its
waters—a tradition, indeed, common to many lakes.   It is
not therefore unlikely that if the lakes of Wales are explored
they will yield evidences of lake-dwellers, and, however un-
romantic it may appear, the Lady of the Van Lake was only
possibly a maiden snatched from her watery home by a
member of a stronger race.

In these legends the lady does not seem to evince much
love for her husband after she has left him.   Possibly he
did nót deserve much, but towards her children she shows
deep affection.   After the husband is deserted, the children
are objects of her solicitation, and they are visited.   The
Lady of the Van Lake promised to meet her son whenever
her counsel or aid was required.   A like trait belongs to
the Homeric goddesses.   Thetis heard from her father's
court far away beneath the ocean the terrible sounds of
grief that burst from her son Achilles on hearing of the
death of his dear friend Patroclus, and quickly ascended to
earth all weeping to learn what ailed her son.   These Fairy
ladies also show a mother's love, immortal though they be.

The children of these marriages depart not with their
mother, they remain with the father, but she takes
with her her dowry.   Thus there are many descendants of
the Lady of the Van Lake still living in South Wales, and as

Professor Rhys remarks—"This brings the legend of the Lady of the Van Lake into connection with a widely spread family;" and, it may be added, shows that the Celts on their advent to Wales found it inhabited by a race with whom they contracted marriages.

The manner in which the lady is seized when dancing in the Ystrad Legend calls to mind the strategy of the tribe of Benjamin to secure wives for themselves of the daughters of Shiloh according to the advice of the elders who commanded them,—"Go and lie in wait in the vineyards; and see, and behold, if the daughters of Shiloh come out to dance in dances, then come ye out of the vineyards, and catch you everyone his wife of the daughters of Shiloh, and go to the land of Benjamin," Judges, ch. xxi. The rape of the Sabine women, who were seized by the followers of Romulus on a day appointed for sacrifice and public games, also serves as a precedent for the action of those young Welshmen who captured Fairy wives whilst enjoying themselves in the dance.

It is a curious fact, that a singular testimony to wife snatching in ancient times is indicated by a custom once general, and still not obsolete in South Wales, of a feigned attempt on the part of the friends of the young woman about to get married to hinder her from carrying out her object. The Rev. Griffith Jones, Vicar of Mostyn, informed the writer that he had witnessed such a struggle. The wedding, he stated, took place at Tregaron, Cardiganshire. The friends of both the young people were on horseback, and according to custom they presented themselves at the house of the young woman, the one to escort her to the church, and the other to hinder her from going there. The friends of the young man were called "*Gwyr shegouts.*" When the young lady was mounted, she was surrounded by the *gwyr shegouts*, and the cavalcade started. All went on peaceably until a lane was reached, down which the lady bolted, and here the struggle commenced, for her friends dashed between her and her husband's friends and endeavoured to force them back, and thus assist her to escape. The parties, Mr. Jones said, rode furiously and madly, and the struggle presented a cavalry charge, and it was not without much apparent danger that the opposition was overcome, and the lady ultimately forced to proceed to the church, where her future husband was anxiously awaiting her arrival. This strange custom of ancient times and obscure origin is suggestive of the way in which the stronger party procured wives in days of old.

Before the marriage of the Fairy lady to the mortal takes place, the father of the lady appears on the scene, sometimes as a supplicant, and at others as a consenting party to the inevitable marriage, but never is he depicted as resorting to force to rescue his daughter. This pusillanimity can only be reasonably accounted for by supposing that the "little man" was physically incapable of encountering and overcoming by brute force the aspirant to the hand of his daughter. From this conduct we must, I think, infer that the Fairy race were a weak people bodily, unaccustomed and disinclined to war. Their safety and existence consisted in living in the inaccessible parts of the mountains, or in lake dwellings far removed from the habitations of the stronger and better equipped race that had invaded their country. In this way they could, and very likely did, occupy parts of Wales contemporaneously with their conquerors, who, through marriage, became connected with the mild race, whom they found in possession of the land.

In the Welsh legends the maid consents to wed her capturer, and remain with him until he strikes her with *iron*.

In every instance where this stipulation is made, it is ultimately broken, and the wife departs never to return. It has been thought that this implies that the people who immediately succeeded the Fair race belonged to the Iron Age, whilst the fair aborigines belonged to the Stone or Bronze age, and that they were overcome by the superior arms of their opponents, quite as much as by their greater bodily strength. Had the tabooed article been in every instance *iron*, the preceding supposition would have carried with it considerable weight, but as this is not the case, all that can be said positively is, that the conquerors of the Fair race were certainly acquainted with iron, and the blow with iron that brought about the catastrophe was undoubtedly inflicted by the mortal who had married the Fairy lady. Why iron should have been tabooed by the Fairy and her father, must remain an open question. But if we could, with reason, suppose, that that metal had brought about their subjugation, then in an age of primitive and imperfect knowledge, and consequent deep superstition, we might not be wrong in supposing that the subjugated race would look upon iron with superstitious dread, and ascribe to it supernatural power inimical to them as a race. They would under such feelings have nothing whatever to do with iron, just as the benighted African, witnessing for the first time the effects of a gun shot, would, with dread, avoid a gun. By this process of reasoning we arrive at the conclusion that the Fairy race belonged to a period anterior to the Iron Age.

With one remark, I will bring my reflections on the preceding legends to an end. Polygamy apparently was unknown in the distant times we are considering. But the marriage bond was not indissoluble, and the initiative in the separation was taken by the woman.

MEN CAPTURED BY FAIRIES.

In the preceding legends, we have accounts of men capturing female Fairies, and marrying them. It would be
strange if the kidnapping were confined to one of the two
races, but Folk-Lore tells us that the Fair Family were not innocent of actions similar to those of mortals, for many a man
was snatched away by them, and carried off to their sub-
terranean abodes, who, in course of time, married the fair
daughters of the *Tylwyth Teg.* Men captured Fairy ladies,
but the Fairies captured handsome men.

The oldest written legend of this class is to be found in
the pages of *Giraldus Cambrensis,* pp. 390-92, Bohn's
edition. The Archdeacon made the tour of Wales in 1188;
the legend therefore which he records can boast of a good
old age, but the tale itself is older than *The Itinerary
through Wales,* for the writer informs us that the priest
Elidorus, who affirmed that he had been in the country of
the Fairies, talked in his old age to David II., bishop of St.
David, of the event. Now David II. was promoted to the
see of St. David in 1147, or, according to others, in 1149,
and died A.D. 1176; therefore the legend had its origin before the last-mentioned date, and, if the priest were a very
old man when he died, his tale would belong to the eleventh
century.

With these prefatory remarks, I will give the legend as
recorded by Giraldus.

1. *Elidorus and the Fairies.*

" A short time before our days, a circumstance worthy of
note occurred in these parts, which Elidorus, a priest, most
strenuously affirmed had befallen to himself.

When a youth of twelve years, and learning his letters,
since, as Solomon says, 'The root of learning is bitter, although the fruit is sweet,' in order to avoid the discipline

and frequent stripes inflicted on him by his preceptor, he ran away and concealed himself under the hollow bank of the river. After fasting in that situation for two days, two little men of pigmy stature appeared to him, saying, 'If you will come with us, we will lead you into a country full of delights and sports.' Assenting and rising up, he followed his guides through a path, at first subterraneous and dark, into a most beautiful country, adorned with rivers and meadows, woods and plains, but obscure, and not illuminated with the full light of the sun. All the days were cloudy, and the nights extremely dark, on account of the absence of the moon and stars. The boy was brought before the King, and introduced to him in the presence of the court; who, having examined him for a long time, delivered him to his son, who was then a boy. These men were of the smallest stature, but very well proportioned in their make; they were all of a fair complexion, with luxuriant hair falling over their shoulders like that of women. They had horses and greyhounds adapted to their size. They neither ate flesh nor fish, but lived on milk diet, made up into messes with saffron. They never took an oath, for they detested nothing so much as lies. As often as they returned from our upper hemisphere, they reprobated our ambition, infidelities, and inconstancies; they had no form of public worship, being strict lovers and reverers, as it seemed, of truth.

The boy frequently returned to our hemisphere, sometimes by the way he had first gone, sometimes by another; at first in company with other persons, and afterwards alone, and made himself known only to his mother, declaring to her the manners, nature, and state of that people. Being desired by her to bring a present of gold, with which that region abounded, he stole, while at play with the king's son, the golden ball with which he used to divert himself, and brought it to his mother in great haste; and when he reached the door of his father's house, but not unpursued, and was entering it in a great hurry, his foot stumbled on the threshold, and falling down into the room where his mother was sitting, the two pigmies seized the ball which had dropped from his hand and departed, showing the boy every mark of contempt and derision. On recovering from his fall, confounded with shame, and execrating the evil counsel of his mother, he returned by the usual track to the subterraneous road, but found no appearance of any passage, though he searched for it on the banks of the river for nearly the space of a year. But since those calamities are often alleviated by time, which reason cannot mitigate, and length of time alone blunts the edge of our afflictions and puts an end to many evils, the youth, having been brought back by his friends and mother, and restored to his right way of thinking, and to his learning, in process of time attained the rank of priesthood.

Whenever David II., Bishop of St. David's, talked to him in his advanced state of life concerning this event, he could never relate the particulars without shedding tears. He had made himself acquainted with the language of that nation, the words of which, in his younger days, he used to recite, which, as the bishop often had informed me, were very conformable to the Greek idiom. When they asked for water, they said 'Ydor ydorum,' which meant 'Bring water,' for Ydor in their language, as well as in the Greek, signifies water, whence vessels for water are called ὕδριαι; and Dŵr, also in the British language signifies water. When they wanted salt they said 'Halgein ydorum,' ' Bring salt.' Salt is called ἁλ in Greek, and Halen in British, for that language, from the length of time which the Britons (then called Trojans and afterwards Britons, from Brito, their leader) remained in Greece after the destruction of Troy, became, in many instances, similar to the Greek."

This legend agrees in a remarkable degree with the popular opinion respecting Fairies. It would almost appear to be the foundation of many subsequent tales that are current in Wales.

The priest's testimony to Fairy temperance and love of truth, and their reprobation of ambition, infidelities, and inconstancies, notwithstanding that they had no form of public worship, and their abhorrence of theft intimate that they possessed virtues worthy of all praise.

Their abode is altogether mysterious, but this ancient description of Fairyland bears out the remarks—perhaps suggested the remarks, of the Rev. Peter Roberts in his book called *The Cambrian Popular Antiquities*. In this work, the author promulgates the theory that the Fairies were a people existing distinct from the known inhabitants of the country and confederated together, and met mysteriously to avoid coming in contact with the stronger race that had taken possession of their land, and he supposes that in these traditionary tales of the Fairies we recognize something of the real history of an ancient people whose customs were those of a regular and consistent policy. Roberts supposes that the smaller race for the purpose of replenishing their ranks stole the children of their conquerors, or slyly exchanged their weak children for their enemies' strong children.

It will be observed that the people among whom Elidorus sojourned had a language cognate with the Irish, Welsh, Greek, and other tongues; in fact, it was similar to that language which at one time extended, with dialectical differences, from Ireland to India; and the *Tylwyth Tég*, in our legends, are described as speaking a language understood by those with whom they conversed. This language they either acquired from their conquerors, or both races must have had a common origin ; the latter, probably, being the more reasonable supposition, and by inference, therefore, the Fairies and other nations by whom they were subdued were descended from a common stock, and ages afterwards, by marriage, the Fairies again commingled with other branches of the family from which they had originally sprung.

Omitting. many embellishments which· the imagination has no difficulty in bestowing, tradition has transmitted one fact, that the *Tylwyth Tég* succeeded in inducing men through the allurements of music and the attractions of their fair daughters to join their ranks. I will now give instances of this belief.

The following tale I received from the mouth of Mr. Richard Jones, Ty'n-y-wern, Bryneglwys, near Corwen. Mr. Jones has stored up in his memory many tales of olden times, and he even thinks that he has himself seen a Fairy. Standing by his farm, he pointed out to me on the opposite side of the valley a Fairy ring still green, where once, he said, the Fairies held their nightly revels. The scene of the tale which Mr. Jones related is wild, and a few years ago it was much more so than at present. At the time that the event is said to have taken place the mountain was unenclosed, and there was not much travelling in those days, and consequently the Fairies could, undisturbed, enjoy their dances. But to proceed with the tale.

2. *A Bryneglwys Man inveigled by the Fairies.*

Two waggoners were sent from Bryneglwys for coals to the works over the hill beyond Minera. On their way they came upon a company of Fairies dancing with all their might. The men stopped to witness their movements, and the Fairies invited them to join in the dance. One of the men stoutly refused to do so, but the other was induced to dance awhile with them. His companion looked on for a short time at the antics of his friend, and then shouted out that he would wait no longer, and desired the man to give up and come away. He, however, turned a deaf ear to the request, and no words could induce him to forego his dance. At last his companion said that he was going, and requested his friend to follow him. Taking the two waggons under his care he proceeded towards the coal pits, expecting every moment to be overtaken by his friend; but he was disappointed, for he never appeared. The waggons and their loads were taken to Bryneglwys, and the man thought that perhaps his companion, having stopped too long in the dance, had turned homewards instead of following him to the coal pit. But on enquiry no one had heard or seen the missing waggoner. One day his companion met a Fairy on the mountain and inquired after his missing friend. The Fairy told him to go to a certain place, which he named, at a certain time, and that he should there see his friend. The man went, and there saw his companion just as he had left him, and the first words that he uttered were "Have the waggons gone far." The poor man never dreamt that months and months had passed away since they had started together for coal.

A variant of the preceding story appears in the *Cambrian Magazine*, vol. ii., pp. 58, 59, where it is styled the Year's Sleep, or "The Forest of the Yewtree," but for the sake of association with like tales I will call it by the following title :—

3. *Story of a man who spent twelve months in Fairyland.*

"In Mathavarn, in the parish of Llanwrin, and the Cantrev of Cyveilioc, there is a wood which is called *Ffridd*

yr Ywen (the Forest of the Yew); it is supposed to be
so called because there is a yew tree growing in the very
middle of it. In many parts of the wood are to be seen
green circles, which are called 'the dancing places of the
goblins,' about which, a considerable time ago, the following
tale was very common in the neighbourhood :—

Two servants of John Pugh, Esq., went out one day to
work in the 'Forest of the Yew.' Pretty early in the
afternoon the whole country was so covered with dark
vapour, that the youths thought night was coming on ; but
when they came to the middle of the 'Forest' it brightened
up around them and the darkness seemed all left behind ;
so, thinking it too early to return home.for the night, they
lay down and slept. One of them, on waking, was much
surprised to find no one there but himself; he wondered a
good deal at the behaviour of his companion, but made up
his mind at last that he had gone on some business of his
own, as he had been talking of it some time before; so the
sleeper went home, and when they inquired after his
companion, he told them he was gone to the cobbler's shop.
The next day they inquired of him again about his fellow-
servant, but he could not give them any account of him ;
but at last confessed how and where they had both gone to
sleep. After searching and searching many days, he went
to a '*gwr cyvarwydd*' (a conjuror), which was a very
common trade in those days, according to the legend; and
the conjuror said to him, 'Go to the same place where you
and the lad slept; go there exactly a year after the boy was
lost; let it be on the same day of the year, and at the same
time of the day, but take care that you do not step inside
the Fairy ring, stand on the border of the green circles you
saw there, and the boy will come out with many of the
goblins to dance, and when you see him so near to you that

you may take hold of him, snatch him out of the ring as
quickly as you can.' He did according to this advice, and
plucked the boy out, and then asked him, ' if he did not feel
hungry,' to which he answered ' No,' for he had still the
remains of his dinner that he had left in his wallet before
going to sleep, and he asked ' if it was not nearly night, and
time to go home,' not knowing that a year had passed by.
His look was like a skeleton, and as soon as he had tasted
food he was a dead man."

A story in its main features similar to that recorded in
the *Cambrian Magazine* was related to me by my friend,
the Rev. R. Jones, Rector of Llanycil. I do not think Mr.
Jones gave me the locality where the occurrence is said to
have taken place ; at least, if he did so, I took no note of it.
The story is as follows :—

4. *A man who spent twelve months and a day with the Fairies.*

A young man, a farm labourer, and his sweetheart were
sauntering along one evening in an unfrequented part of the
mountain, when there appeared suddenly before them two
Fairies, who proceeded to make a circle. This being done,
a large company of Fairies accompanied by musicians
appeared, and commenced dancing over the ring ; their
motions and music were entrancing, and the man, an expert
dancer, by some irresistible power was obliged to throw
himself into the midst of the dancers and join them in their
gambols. The woman looked on enjoying the sight for
several hours, expecting every minute that her lover would
give up the dance and join her, but no, on and on went the
dance, round and round went her lover, until at last daylight
appeared, and then suddenly the music ceased and the
Fairy band vanished, and with them her lover. In great

dismay, the young woman shouted the name of her sweetheart, but all in vain, he came not to her. The sun had
now risen, and, almost broken-hearted, she returned home
and related the events of the previous night. She was
advised to consult a man who was an adept in the black art.
She did so, and the conjuror told her to go to the same
place at the same time of the night one year and one day
from the time that her lover had disappeared and that she
should then and there see him. She was further instructed
how to act. The conjuror warned her from going into the
ring, but told her to seize her lover by the arm as he danced
round, and to jerk him out of the enchanted circle. Twelve
months and a day passed away, and the faithful girl was on
the spot where she lost her lover. At the very moment
that they had in the first instance appeared the Fairies
again came to view, and everything that she had witnessed
previously was repeated. With the Fairy band was her
lover dancing merrily in their midst. The young woman
ran round and round the circle close to the young man,
carefully avoiding the circle, and at last she succeeded in
taking hold of him and desired him to come away with her.
"Oh," said he, "do let me alone a little longer, and then I
will come with you." "You have already been long enough,"
said she. His answer was, "It is so delightful, let me dance
on only a few minutes longer." She saw that he was under
a spell, and grasping the young man's arm with all her
might she followed him round and round the circle, and an
opportunity offering she jerked him out of the circle. He
was greatly annoyed at her conduct, and when told that he
had been with the Fairies a year and a day he would not
believe her, and affirmed that he had been dancing only a
few minutes; however, he went away with the faithful girl,
and when he had reached the farm, his friends had the

greatest difficulty in persuading him that he had been so long from home.

The next Fairy tale that I shall give akin to the preceding stories is to be found in *Y Brython*, vol. iii., pp. 459-60. The writer of the tale was the Rev. Benjamin Williams, whose bardic name was Gwynionydd. I do not know the source whence Mr. Williams derived the story, but most likely he obtained it from some aged person who firmly believed that the tale was a true record of what actually occurred. In the *Brython* the tale is called "Y Tylwyth Têg a Mab Llech y Derwydd," and this title I will retain, merely translating it. The introduction, however, I will not give, as it does not directly bear on the subject now under consideration.

5. *The Son of Llech y Derwydd and the Fairies.*

The son of Llech y Derwydd was the only son of his parents and heir to the farm. He was very dear to his father and mother, yea, he was as the very light of their eyes. The son and the head servant man were bosom friends, they were like two brothers, or rather twins. As they were such close friends the farmer's wife was in the habit of clothing them exactly alike. The two friends fell in love with two young handsome women who were highly respected in the neighbourhood. This event gave the old people great satisfaction, and ere long the two couples were joined in holy wedlock, and great was the merry-making on the occasion. The servant man obtained a convenient place to live in on the grounds of Llech y Derwydd. About six months after the marriage of the son, he and the servant man went out to hunt. The servant penetrated to a ravine filled with brushwood to look for game, and presently returned to his friend, but by the time he came back the son was nowhere to be seen. He continued awhile looking about

F

for his absent friend, shouting and whistling to attract his
attention, but there was no answer to his calls. By and by
he went home to Llech y Derwydd, expecting to find him
there, but no one knew anything about him. Great was the
grief of the family throughout the night, but it was even
greater the next day. They went to inspect the place where
the son had last been seen. His mother and his wife wept
bitterly, but the father had greater control over himself,
still he appeared as half mad. They inspected the place
where the servant man had last seen his friend, and, to their
great surprise and sorrow, observed a Fairy ring close by
the spot, and the servant recollected that he had heard
seductive music somewhere about the time that he parted
with his friend. They came to the conclusion at once that
the man had been so unfortunate as to enter the Fairy ring,
and they conjectured that he had been transported no one
knew where. Weary weeks and months passed away,
and a son was born to the absent man. The little one
grew up the very image of his father, and very precious was
he to his grandfather and grandmother. In fact, he was
everything to them. He grew up to man's estate and married
a pretty girl in the neighbourhood, but her people had not
the reputation of being kind-hearted. The old folks died,
and also their daughter-in-law.

One windy afternoon in the month of October, the family
of Llech y Derwydd saw a tall thin old man with beard and
hair as white as snow, who they thought was a Jew,
approaching slowly, very slowly, towards the house. The
servant girls stared mockingly through the window at him,
and their mistress laughed unfeelingly at the "old Jew,"
and lifted the children up, one after the other, to get a sight
of him as he neared the house. He came to the door, and
entered the house boldly enough, and inquired after his

parents. The mistress answered him in a surly and unusually contemptuous manner, and wished to know " What
the drunken old Jew wanted there," for they thought he
must have been drinking or he would never have spoken in
the way he did. The old man looked at everything in the
house with surprise and bewilderment, but the little children
about the floor took his attention more than anything else.
His looks betrayed sorrow and deep disappointment. He
related his whole history, that yesterday he had gone out to
hunt, and that he had now returned. The mistress told
him that she had heard a story about her husband's father,
which occurred before she was born, that he had been lost
whilst hunting, but that her father had told her that the
story was not true, but that he had been killed. The woman
became uneasy and angry that the old "Jew" did not
depart. The old man was roused and said that the house
was his, and that he would have his rights. He went to
inspect his possessions, and shortly afterwards directed his
steps to the servant's house. To his surprise he saw that
things there were greatly changed. After conversing awhile
with an aged man who sat by the fire, they carefully looked
each other in the face, and the old man by the fire related
the sad history of his lost friend, the son of Llech y Derwydd.
They conversed together deliberately on the events of their
youth, but all seemed like a dream. However, the old man
in the corner came to the conclusion that his visitor was
his dear friend, the son of Llech y Derwydd, returned from
the land of the Fairies after having spent there half a hundred
years. The old man with the white beard believed the story
related by his friend, and long was the talk and many
were the questions which the one gave to the other. The
visitor was informed that the master of Llech y Derwydd
was from home that day, and he was persuaded to eat

some food ; but, to the horror of all, when he had done so, he instantly fell down dead.

Such is the story. The writer adds that the tale relates that the cause of this man's sudden death was that he ate food after having been so long in the land of the Fairies, and he further states that the faithful old servant insisted on his dead friend's being buried with his ancestors, and the rudeness of the mistress of Llech y Derwydd to her father-in-law brought a curse upon the place and family, and her offence was not expiated until the farm had been sold nine times.

The next tale that I shall relate is recorded by Glasynys in *Cymru Fu*, pp. 177-179. Professor Rhys in his *Welsh Fairy Tales, Y Cymmrodor*, vol. v., pp. 81-84, gives a translation of this story. The Professor prefaces the tale with a caution that *Glasynys* had elaborated the story, and that the proper names were undoubtedly his own. The reverend author informs his readers that he heard his mother relate the tale many times, but it certainly appears that he has ornamented the simple narrative after his own fashion, for he was professedly a believer in words ; however, in its general outline, it bears the impress of antiquity, and strongly resembles other Welsh Fairy tales. It belongs to that species of Fairy stories which compose this chapter, and therefore it is here given as translated by Professor Rhys. I will for the sake of reference give the tale a name, and describe it under the following heading.

6. *A young man marries a Fairy Lady in Fairy Land and brings her to live with him among his own people.*

"Once on a time a shepherd boy had gone up the mountain. That day, like many a day before and after, was exceedingly misty. Now, though he was well acquainted with the place, he lost his way, and walked backwards and forwards for many a long hour. At last he got into a low

rushy spot, where he saw before him many circular rings.
He at once recalled the place, and began to fear the worst.
He had heard, many hundreds of times, of the bitter ex-
periences in those rings of many a shepherd who had
happened to chance on the dancing-place or the circles of
the Fair Family. He hastened away as fast as ever he
could, lest he should be ruined like the rest; but though
he exerted himself to the point of perspiring, and losing his
breath, there he was, and there he continued to be, a long
time. At last he was met by a little fat old man with
merry blue eyes, who asked him what he was doing. He
answered that he was trying to find his way homeward.
'Oh,' said he, ' come after me, and do not utter a word
until I bid thee.' This he did, following him on and on
until they came to an oval stone, and the little old fat man
lifted it, after tapping the middle of it three times with his
walking stick. There was there a narrow path with stairs
to be seen here and there, and a sort of whitish light,
inclining to grey and blue, was to be seen radiating from
the stones. ' Follow me fearlessly,' said the fat man, ' no
harm will be done thee.' So on the poor youth went, as
reluctantly as a dog to be hanged ; but presently a fine-
wooded, fertile country spread itself out before them, with
well arranged mansions dotting it over, while every kind of
apparent magnificence met the eye, and seemed to smile in
its landscape ; the bright waters of its rivers meandered in
twisted streams, and its hills were covered with the luxuriant
verdure of their grassy growth, and the mountains with a
glossy fleece of smooth pasture. By the time they had
reached the stout gentleman's mansion, the young man's
senses had been bewildered by the sweet cadence of the
music which the birds poured forth from the groves, then
there was gold there to dazzle his eyes and silver flashing

on his sight. He saw there all kinds of musical instruments and all sorts of things for playing, but he could discern no inhabitant in the whole place; and when he sat down to eat, the dishes on the table came to their places of themselves and disappeared when one had done with them. This puzzled him beyond measure; moreover, he heard people talking together around him, but for the life of him he could see no one but his old friend. At length the fat man said to him, 'Thou canst now talk as much as it may please thee;' 'but when he attempted to move his tongue it would no more stir than if it had been a lump of ice, which greatly frightened him. At this point, a fine old lady, with health and benevolence beaming in her face, came to them and slightly smiled at the shepherd. The mother was followed by her three daughters, who were remarkably beautiful. They gazed with somewhat playful looks at him, and at length began to talk to him, but his tongue would not wag. Then one of the girls came to him, and, playing with his yellow and curly locks, gave him a smart kiss on his ruddy lips. This loosened the string that bound his tongue, and he began to talk freely and eloquently. There he was, under the charm of that kiss, in the bliss of happiness, and there he remained a year and a day without knowing that he had passed more than a day among them, for he had got into a country where there was no reckoning of time. But by and by he began to feel somewhat of a longing to visit his old home, and asked the stout man if he might go. 'Stay a little yet,' said he 'and thou shalt go for a while.' That passed, he stayed on; but Olwen, for that was the name of the damsel that had kissed him, was very unwilling that he should depart. She looked sad every time he talked of going away, nor was he himself without feeling a sort of a cold thrill passing through him

at the thought of leaving her. On condition, however, of
returning, he obtained leave to go, provided with plenty of
gold and silver, of trinkets and gems. When he reached
home, nobody knew who he was; it had been the belief that
he had been killed by another shepherd, who found it
necessary to betake himself hastily far away to America,
lest he should be hanged without delay. But here is
Einion Las at home, and everybody wonders especially to
see that the shepherd had got to look like a wealthy man;
his manners, his dress, his language, and the treasure he
had with him, all conspired to give him the air of a
gentleman. He went back one Thursday night, the first of
the moon that month, as suddenly as he had left the first
time, and nobody knew whither. There was great joy in
the country below when Einion returned thither, and nobody was more rejoiced at it than Olwen, his beloved. The
two were right impatient to get married, but it was necessary
to do that quietly, for the family below hated nothing more
than fuss and noise; so, in a sort of a half-secret fashion,
they were wedded. Einion was very desirous to go once
more among his own people, accompanied, to be sure, by
his wife. After he had been long entreating the old man
for leave, they set out on two white ponies, that were, in
fact, more like snow than anything else in point of colour;
so he arrived with his consort in his old home, and it was
the opinion of all that Einion's wife was the handsomest
person they had anywhere seen. Whilst at home, a son
was born to them, to whom they gave the name of Taliesin.
Einion was now in the enjoyment of high repute, and his
wife received proper respect. Their wealth was immense,
and soon they acquired a large estate; but it was not long
till people began to inquire after the pedigree of Einion's
wife—the country was of opinion that it was not the right

thing to be without a pedigree. Einion was questioned
about it, without his giving any satisfactory answer, and
one came to the conclusion that she was one of the Fair
Family *(Tylwyth Tég)*. 'Certainly,' replied Einion, 'there
can be no doubt that she comes from a very fair family, for
she has two sisters who are as fair as she, and if you saw
them together, you would admit that name to be a capital
one.' This, then, is the reason why the remarkable family
in the land of charm and phantasy *(Hud a Lledrith)* are
called the Fair Family."

7. *A Boy taken to Fairy Land.*

Mrs. Morris, of Cwm Vicarage, near Rhyl, told the writer
the following story. She stated that she had heard it
related in her family that one of their people had in childhood been induced by the Fairies to follow them to their
country. This boy had been sent to discharge some domestic errand, but he did not return. He was sought for in all
directions but could not be found. His parents came to
the conclusion that he had either been murdered or kidnapped, and in time he was forgotten by most people, but
one day he returned with what he had been sent for in
his hand. But so many years had elapsed since he first left
home, that he was now an old grey-headed man, though he
knew it not; he had, he said, followed, for a short time,
delightful music and people; but when convinced, by the
changes around, that years had slipped by since he first left
his home, he was so distressed at the changes he saw that
he said he would return to the Fairies. But alas! he
sought in vain for the place where he had met them, and
therefore he was obliged to remain with his blood relations.

The next tale differs from the preceding, insomuch that
the seductive advances of the Fairies failed in their object.
I am not quite positive whence I obtained the story, but

this much I know, that it belongs to Pentrevoelas, and that a respectable old man was in the habit of repeating it, as an event in his own life.

A Man Refusing the Solicitations of the Fairies.

A Pentrevoelas man was coming home one lovely summer's night, and when within a stone's throw of his house, he heard in the far distance singing of the most enchanting kind. He stopped to listen to the sweet sounds which filled him with a sensation of deep pleasure. He had not listened long ere he perceived that the singers were approaching. By and by they came to the spot where he was, and he saw that they were marching in single file and consisted of a number of small people, robed in close-fitting grey clothes, and they were accompanied by speckled dogs that marched along two deep like soldiers. When the procession came quite opposite the enraptured listener, it stopped, and the small people spoke to him and earnestly begged him to accompany them, but he would not. They tried many ways, and for a long time, to persuade him to join them, but when they saw they could not induce him to do so they departed, dividing themselves into two companies and marching away, the dogs marching two abreast in front of each company. They sang as they went away the most entrancing music that was ever heard. The man, spell-bound, stood where he was, listening to the ravishing music of the Fairies, and he did not enter his house until the last sound had died away in the far-off distance.

Professor Rhys records a tale much like the preceding. (See his *Welsh Fairy Tales*, pp. 34, 35.) It is as follows :—
" One bright moonlight night, as one of the sons of the farmer who lived at Llwyn On in Nant y Bettws was going to pay his addresses to a girl at Clogwyn y Gwin, he beheld the Tylwyth enjoying themselves in full swing on a meadow

G

close to Cwellyn Lake. He approached them and little by
little he was led on by the enchanting sweetness of their
music and the liveliness of their playing until he got within
their circle. Soon some kind of spell passed over him, so
that he lost his knowledge of every place, and found himself
in a country the most beautiful he had ever seen, where
everybody spent his time in mirth and rejoicing. He
had been there seven years, and yet it seemed to him but a
night's dream ; but a faint recollection came to his mind of
the business on which he had left home, and he felt a
longing to see his beloved one : so he went and asked per-
mission to return home, which was granted him, together
with a host of attendants to lead him to his country; and,
suddenly, he found himself, as if waking from a dream, on
the bank where he had seen the Fairy Family amusing
themselves. He turned towards home, but there he found
everything changed : his parents were dead, his brothers
could not recognize him, and his sweetheart was married to
another man. In consequence of such changes, he broke
his heart, and died in less than a week after coming back."

Many variants of the legends already related are still extant in Wales. This much can be said of these tales, that it
was formerly believed that marriages took place between
men and Fairies, and from the tales themselves we can infer
that the men fared better in Fairy land than the Fairy
ladies did in the country of their earthly husbands. This,
perhaps, is what might be expected, if, as we may suppose, the Fair Tribe were supplanted, and overcome, by a
stronger, and bolder people, with whom, to a certain extent,
the weaker and conquered or subdued race commingled by
marriage. Certain striking characteristics of both races
are strongly marked in these legends. The one is a smaller
and more timid people than the other, and far more beauti-

ful in mind and person than their conquerors. The ravishing beauty of the Fairy lady forms a prominent feature in all these legends. The Fairies, too, are spoken of as being without religion. This, perhaps, means nothing more than that they differed from their conquerors in forms, or objects of worship. However this might be, it would appear that their conquerors knew but little of that perfect moral teaching which made the Fairies, according to the testimony of Giraldus, truthful, void of ambition, and honest.

It must, however, be confessed, that there is much that is mythical in these legends, and every part cannot well be made to correspond with ordinary human transactions.

It is somewhat amusing to note how modern ideas, and customs, are mixed up with these ancient stories. They undoubtedly received a gloss from the ages which transmitted the tales.

In the next chapter I shall treat of another phase of Fairy Folk-lore, which will still further connect the Fair Race with their conquerors.

FAIRY CHANGELINGS.

It was firmly believed, at one time, in Wales, that the Fairies exchanged their own weakly or deformed offspring for the strong children of mortals. The child supposed to have been left by the Fairies in the cradle, or elsewhere, was commonly called a changeling. This faith was not confined to Wales; it was as common in Ireland, Scotland, and England, as it was in Wales. Thus, in Spenser's *Faery Queen*, reference is made in the following words to this popular error :—

And her base Elfin brood there for thee left ;
Such, men do chaungelings call, so chaung'd by Faeries theft.

Faery Queen, Bk. I , c. 10.

The same superstition is thus alluded to by Shakespeare :—

> A lovely boy, stol'n from an Indian king,
> She never had so sweet a changeling.
>
> *A Midsummer Night's Dream*, Act II., Sc. 1.

And again, in another of his plays, the Fairy practice
of exchanging children is mentioned :—

> O, that it could be prov'd,
> That some night-tripping Fairy had exchanged
> In cradle-clothes our children, where they lay,
> And call'd mine, Percy, his Plantagenet:
> Then would I have his Harry, and he mine.
>
> *Henry IV.*, Pt. 1., Act I, Sc. 1.

In Scotland and other countries the Fairies were credited
with stealing unbaptized infants, and leaving in their stead
poor, sickly, noisy, thin, babies. But to return to Wales, a
poet in *Y Brython*, vol. iii., p. 103, thus sings :—

> Llawer plentyn teg aeth ganddynt,
> Pan y cym'rynt helynt hir ;
> Oddi ar auwyl dda rieni,
> I drigfanau difri dir.

> Many a lovely child they've taken,
> When long and bitter was the pain ;
> From their parents, loving, dear,
> To the Fairies' dread domain.

John Williams, an old man, who lived in the Penrhyn
quarry district, informed the writer that he could reveal
strange doings of the Fairies in his neighbourhood, for
often had they changed children with even well-to-do families,
he said, but more he would not say, lest he should injure
those prosperous families.

It was believed that the Fairies were particularly busy in
exchanging children on *Nos Wyl Ifan*, or St. John's Eve.

There were, however, effectual means for protecting
children from their machinations. The mother's presence,
the tongs placed cross-ways on the cradle, the early bap-

tism of the child, were all preventives. In the Western Isles of Scotland fire carried round a woman before she was churched, and round the child until he was christened, daily, night and morning, preserved both from the evil designs of the Fairies. (Brand, vol. ii., p. 486.) And it will be shortly shewn that even after an exchange had been accomplished there were means of forcing the Fairies to restore the stolen child.

It can well be believed that mothers who had sickly or idiotic babies would, in uncivilized places, gladly embrace the idea that the child she nursed was a changeling, and then, naturally enough, she would endeavour to recover her own again. The plan adopted for this purpose was extremely dangerous. I will in the following tales show what steps were taken to reclaim the lost child.

Pennant records how a woman who had a peevish child acted to regain from the Fairies her own offspring. His words are:—"Above this is a spreading oak of great antiquity, size, and extent of branches; it has got the name of *Fairy Oak*. In this very century (the eighteenth) a poor cottager, who lived near the spot, had a child who grew uncommonly peevish; the parents attributed this to the *Fairies,* and imagined that it was a changeling. They took the child, put it into a cradle, and left it all night beneath the tree, in hopes that the *Tylwyth Tég*, or *Fairy Family*, or the Fairy folk, would restore their own before the morning. When morning came, they found the child perfectly quiet, so went away with it, quite confirmed in their belief."—*History of Whiteford*, pp. 5, 6.

These people by exposing their infant for a night to the elements ran a risk of losing it altogether; but they acted in agreement with the popular opinion, which was that the Fairies had such affection for their own children that they

would not allow them to be in any danger of losing their
life, and that if the elfin child were thus exposed the
Fairies would rescue it, and restore the exchanged child
to its parents. The following tale exhibits another phase
of this belief.

The story is to be found in the *Cambrian Magazine*,
vol. ii., pp. 86, 87.

1. "*The Egg Shell Pottage.*"

"In the parish of Treveglwys, near Llanidloes, in the
county of Montgomery, there is a little shepherd's cot,
that is commonly called Twt y Cwmrws (the place of strife)
on account of the extraordinary strife that has been there.
The inhabitants of the cottage were a. man and his wife,
and they had born to them twins, whom the woman nursed
with great care and tenderness. Some months afterwards
indispensable business called the wife to the house of one of
her nearest neighbours ; yet, notwithstanding she had not
far to go, she did not like to leave her children by themselves in their cradle, even for a minute, as her house was
solitary, and there were many tales of goblins or the
'*Tylwyth Tég*' (the Fair Family or the Fairies) haunting the
neighbourhood. However, she went, and returned as soon
as she could ; but on coming back she felt herself not a
little terrified on seeing, though it was mid-day, some of 'the
old elves of the blue petticoat,' as they are usually called ;
however, when she got back to her house she was rejoiced
to find everything in the state she had left it.

But after some time had passed by, the good people began
to wonder that the twins did not grow at all, but still continued little dwarfs. The man would have it that they were
not his children ; the woman said that they must be their
children, and about this arose the great strife between them
that gave name to the place. One evening when the woman

was very heavy of heart she determined to go and consult a
Gwr Cyfarwydd (i.e., a wise man, or a conjuror), feeling
assured that everything was known to him, and he gave her
his counsel. Now there was to be a harvest soon of the
rye and oats; so the wise man said to her:—' When you
are preparing dinner for the reapers empty the shell of a
hen's egg, and boil the shell full of pottage and take it out
through the door as if you meant it for a dinner to the
reapers, and then listen what the twins will say; if you hear
the children speaking things above the understanding of
children, return into the house, take them, and throw them
into the waves of Llyn Ebyr, which is very near to you;
but if you don't hear anything remarkable, do them no
injury.' And when the day of the reaping came, the
woman did as her adviser had recommended to her; and as
she went outside the door to listen, she heard one of the
children say to the other:—

> Gwelais vesen cyn gweled derwen,
>   Gwelais wy cyn gweled iâr,
> Erioed ni welais verwi bwyd i vedel
>   Mewn plisgyn wy iâr !

> Acorns before oak I knew,
>   An egg before a hen,
> Never one hen's egg-shell stew
>   Enough for harvest men !

On this the mother returned to her house and took the
two children, and threw them into the Llyn, and suddenly
the goblins in their trousers came to save their dwarfs, and
the woman had her own children back again, and thus the
strife between her and her husband ended."

The writer of the preceding story says that it was translated almost literally from Welsh, as told by the peasantry,
and he remarks that the legend bears a striking resemblance
to one of the Irish tales published by Mr. Croker.

Many variants of the legend are still extant in many parts of Wales. There is one of these recorded in Professor Rhys's *Welsh Fairy Tales, Y Cymmrodor*, vol. iv., pp. 208-209. It is much like that given in the *Cambrian Magazine.*

2. *Corwrion Changeling Legend.*

"Once on a time, in the fourteenth century, the wife of a man at Corwrion had twins, and she complained one day to the witch who lived close by, at Tyddyn y Barcut, that the children were not getting on, but that they were always crying, day and night. 'Are you sure that they are your children?' asked the witch, adding that it did not seem to her that they were like hers. 'I have my doubts also,' said the mother. 'I wonder if somebody has changed children with you,' said the witch. 'I do not know,' said the mother. 'But why do you not seek to know?' asked the other. 'But how am I to go about it?' said the mother. The witch replied, 'Go and do something rather strange before their eyes and watch what they will say to one another.' 'Well I do not know what I should do,' said the mother. 'Oh,' said the other, 'take an egg-shell, and proceed to brew beer in it in a chamber aside, and come here to tell me what the children will say about it.' She went home and did as the witch had directed her, when the two children lifted their heads out of the cradle to see what she was doing, to watch, and to listen. Then one observed to the other :—

'I remember seeing an oak having an acorn,' to which the other replied,

'And I remember seeing a hen having an egg,' and one of the two added,

'But I do not remember before seeing anybody brew beer in the shell of a hen's egg.'

The mother then went to the witch and told her what

the twins had said one to the other, and she directed her to go to a small wooden bridge not far off, with one of the strange children under each arm, and there to drop them from the bridge into the river beneath. The mother went back home again and did as she had been directed. When she reached home this time, to her astonishment, she found that her own children had been brought back."

There is one important difference between these two tales. In the latter, the mother drops the children over the bridge into the waters beneath, and then goes home, without noticing whether the poor children had been rescued by the goblins or not, but on reaching her home she found in the cradle her own two children, presumably conveyed there by the Fairies. In the first tale, we are informed that she saw the goblins save their offspring from a watery grave. Subjecting peevish children to such a terrible ordeal as this must have ended often with a tragedy, but even in such cases superstitious mothers could easily persuade themselves that the destroyed infants were undoubtedly the offspring of elfins, and therefore unworthy of their fostering care. The only safeguard to wholesale infanticide was the test applied as to the super-human precociousness, or ordinary intelligence, of the children.

Another version of this tale was related to me by my young friend, the Rev. D. H. Griffiths, of Clocaenog Rectory, near Ruthin. The tale was told him by Evan Roberts, Ffridd-agored, Llanfwrog. Mr. Roberts is an aged farmer.

3. Llanfwrog Changeling Legend.

A mother took her child to the gleaning field, and left it sleeping under the sheaves of wheat whilst she was busily engaged gleaning. The Fairies came to the field and carried off her pretty baby, leaving in its place one of their own infants. At the time, the mother did not notice any

H

difference between her own child and the one that took its
place, but after awhile she observed with grief that the
baby she was nursing did not thrive, nor did it grow, nor
would it try to walk. She mentioned these facts to her
neighbours, and she was told to do something strange and
then listen to its conversation. She took an egg-shell
and pretended to brew beer in it, and she was then surprised
to hear the child, who had observed her actions intently,
say :—

> Mi welais fesen gan ddcrwen,
> Mi welais ŵy gan iâr,
> Ond ni welais i erioed ddarllaw
> Mewn cibyn ŵy iar.

> I have seen an oak having an acorn,
> I have seen a hen having an egg,
> But I never saw before brewing
> In the shell of a hen's egg.

This conversation proved the origin of the precocious
child who lay in the cradle. The stanza was taken down
from Roberts's lips. But he could not say what was done
to the fairy changeling.

In Ireland a plan for reclaiming the child carried away
by the Fairies was to take the Fairy's changeling and place
it on the top of a dunghill, and then to chant certain invo-
catory lines beseeching the Fairies to restore the stolen
child.

There was, it would seem, in Wales, a certain form of incantation resorted to to reclaim children from the Fairies,
which was as follows :—The mother who had lost her child
was to carry the changeling to a river, but she was to be
accompanied by a conjuror, who was to take a prominent
part in the ceremony. When at the river's brink the conjuror
was to cry out :—

> Crap ar y wrach—
> A grip on the hag ;

and the mother was to respond—

Rhy hwyr gyfraglach —

Too late decrepit one ;

and having uttered these words, she was to throw the child
into the stream, and to depart, and it was believed that on
reaching her home she would there find her own child safe
and sound.

I have already alluded to the horrible nature of such a
proceeding.   I will now relate a tale somewhat resembling
those already given, but in this latter case, the supposed
changeling became the mainstay of his faimily.   I am indebted for the *Gors Goch* legend to an essay, written by Mr.
D. Williams, Llanfachreth, Merionethshire, which took the
prize at the Liverpool Eisteddfod, 1870, and which appears
in a publication called *Y Gordofigion,* pp. 96, 97, published
by Mr. I. Foulkes, Liverpool.

4.   *The Gors Goch Changeling Legend.*

The tale rendered into English is as follows :—" There
was once a happy family living in a place called Gors Goch.
One night, as usual, they went to bed, but they could not
sleep a single wink, because of the noise outside the house.
At last the master of the house got up, and trembling,
enquired ' What was there, and what was wanted.'   A clear
sweet voice answered him thus, ' We want a warm place
where we can tidy the children.'   The door was opened
when there entered half full the house of the *Tylwyth Tég,*
and they began forthwith washing their children.   And when
they had finished, they commenced singing, and the singing
was entrancing.   The dancing and the singing were both
excellent.   On going away they left behind them money
not a little for the use of the house.   And afterwards
they came pretty often to the house, and received a hearty
welcome in consequence of the large presents which they left

behind them on the hob. But at last a sad affair took place
which was no less than an exchange of children. The Gors
Goch baby was a dumpy child, a sweet, pretty, affectionate
little dear, but the child which was left in its stead was
a sickly, thin, shapeless, ugly being, which did nothing but
cry and eat, and although it ate ravenously like a mastiff, it
did not grow. At last the wife of Gors Goch died of a
broken heart, and so also did all her children, but the father
lived a long life and became a rich man, because his new
heir's family brought him abundance of gold and silver."

As I have already given more than one variant of the
same legend, I will supply another version of the Gors Goch
legend which appears in *Cymru Fu*, pp. 177-8, from the pen
of the Revd. Owen Wyn Jones, *Glasynys*, and which in consequence of the additional facts contained in it may be
of some value. I will make use of Professor Rhys's translation. (See *Y Cymmrodor*, vol. v., pp. 79-80.)

5. *Another Version of the Gors Goch Legend.*

" When the people of the Gors Goch one evening had
gone to bed, lo! they heard a great row and disturbance
around the house. One could not at all comprehend what
it might be that made a noise that time of night. Both the
husband and the wife had waked up, quite unable to make
out what there might be there. The children also woke but
no one could utter a word; their tongues had all stuck to
the roofs of their mouths. The husband, however, at last
managed to move, and to ask, 'Who is there'? 'What do
you want'? Then he was answered from without by a small
silvery voice, 'It is room we want to dress our children.'
The door was opened, and a dozen small beings came in, and
began to search for an earthen pitcher with water; there
they remained for some hours, washing and titivating themselves. As the day was breaking they went away, leaving

behind them a fine present for the kindness they had received. Often afterwards did the Gors Goch folks have the company of this family. But once there happened to be a fine roll of a pretty baby in his cradle. The Fair Family came, and, as the baby had not been baptized, they took the liberty of changing him for one of their own. They left behind in his stead an abominable creature that would do nothing but cry and scream every day of the week. The mother was nearly breaking her heart, on account of the misfortune, and greatly afraid of telling anybody about it. But everybody got to see that there was something wrong at Gors Goch, which was proved before long by the mother dying of longing for her child. The other children died broken-hearted after their mother, and the husband was left alone with the little elf without anyone to comfort them. But shortly after, the Fairies began to resort again to the hearth of the Gors Goch to dress children, and the gift which had formerly been silver money became henceforth pure gold. In the course of a few years the elf became the heir of a large farm in North Wales, and that is why the old people used to say, ' Shoe the elf with gold and he will grow.' " (*Fe ddaw gwiddon yn fawr ond ei bedoli âg aur.*)

It will be observed that this latter version differs in one remarkable incident from the preceding tale. In the former there is no allusion to the fact that the changed child had not been baptized; in the latter, this omission is specially mentioned as giving power to the Fairies to exchange their own child for the human baby. This preventive carries these tales into Christian days. Another tale, which I will now relate, also proves that faith in the Fairies and in the efficacy of the Cross existed at one and the same time. The tale is taken from *Y Gordofigion*, p. 96. I will first give it as it originally appeared, and then I will translate the story.

6. Garth Uchaf, Llanuwchllyn, Changeling Legend.

"Yr oedd gwraig Garth Uchaf, yn Llanuwchllyn, un tro wedi myned allan i gweirio gwair, a gadael ei baban yn y cryd; ond fel bu'r anffawd, ni roddodd yr efail yn groes ar wyneb y cryd, ac o ganlyniad, ffeiriwyd ei baban gan y Tylwyth Têg, ac erbyn iddi ddyfod i'r tŷ, nid oedd yn y cryd ond rhyw hen gyfraglach o blentyn fel pe buasai wedi ei haner lewygu o eisiau ymborth, ond magwyd ef er hyny."

The wife of Garth Uchaf, Llanuwchllyn, went out one day to make hay, and left her baby in the cradle. *Unfortunately, she did not place the tongs crossways on the cradle,* and consequently the Fairies changed her baby, and by the time she came home there was nothing in the cradle but some old decrepit changeling, which looked as if it were half famished, but nevertheless, it was nursed.

The reason why the Fairies exchanged babies with human beings, judging from the stories already given, was their desire to obtain healthy well-formed children in the place of their own puny ill-shaped offspring, but this is hardly a satisfactory explanation of such conduct. A mother's love is ever depicted as being so intense that deformity on the part of her child rather increases than diminishes her affection for her unfortunate babe. In Scotland the difficulty is solved in a different way. There it was once thought that the Fairies were obliged every seventh year to pay to the great enemy of mankind an offering of one of their own children, or a human child instead, and as a mother is ever a mother, be she elve's flesh or Eve's flesh, she always endeavoured to substitute some one else's child for her own, and hence the reason for exchanging children.

In Allan Cunningham's *Traditional Tales*, Morley's edition, p. 188, mention is made of this belief. He writes :—

" 'I have heard it said by douce Folk,' 'and sponsible,'
interrupted another, ' that every seven years the elves and
Fairies pay kane, or make an offering of one of their
children, to the grand enemy of salvation, and that they
are permitted to purloin one of the children of men to
present to the fiend,' ' a more acceptable offering, I'll
warrant, than one of their own infernal blood that are
Satan's sib allies, and drink a drop of the deil's blood every
May morning.' "

The Rev. Peter Roberts's theory was that the smaller race
kidnapped the children of the stronger race, who occupied
the country concurrently with themselves, for the purpose
of adding to their own strength as a people.

Gay, in lines, quoted in *Brand's Popular Antiquities*,
vol. ii., p. 485, laughs at the idea of changelings. A Fairy's
tongue ridicules the superstition :—

> Whence sprung the vain conceited lye,
> That we the world with fools supply ?
> What ! Give our sprightly race away
> For the dull helpless sons of clay !
> Besides, by partial fondness shown,
> Like you, we dote upon our own.
> Where ever yet was found a mother
> Who'd give her booby for another ?
> And should we change with human breed,
> Well might we pass for fools, indeed.

With the above fine satire I bring my remarks on Fairy
Changelings to a close.

FAIRY MOTHERS AND HUMAN MIDWIVES.

Fairies are represented in Wales as possessing all the
passions, appetites, and wants of human beings. There are
many tales current of their soliciting help and favours in
their need from men and women. Just as uncivilized
nations acknowledge the superiority of Europeans in medi-

cine, so did the Fairies resort in perplexing cases to
man for aid. There is a class of tales which has reached
our days in which the Fairy lady, who is about to become a
mother, obtains from amongst men a midwife, whom she
rewards with rich presents for her services. Variants of
this story are found in many parts of Wales, and in
many continental countries. I will relate a few of these
legends.

1. *Denbighshire Version of a Fairy Mother and Human
Midwife.*

The following story I received from the lips of David
Roberts, whom I have previously mentioned, a native of
Denbighshire, and he related the tale as one commonly
known. As might be expected, he locates the event in
Denbighshire, but I have no recollection that he gave
names. His narrative was as follows:—

A well-known midwife, whose services were much sought
after in consequence of her great skill, had one night
retired to rest, when she was disturbed by a loud knocking
at her door. She immediately got up and went to the
door, and there saw a beautiful carriage, which she was
urgently requested to enter at once to be conveyed to a
house where her help was required. She did so, and after
a long drive the carriage drew up before the entrance to a
large mansion, which she had never seen before. She successfully performed her work, and stayed on in the place until
her services were no longer required. Then she was conveyed home in the same manner as she had come, but with
her went many valuable presents in grateful recognition of
the services she had rendered.

The midwife somehow or other found out that she had
been attending a Fairy mother. Some time after her return
from Fairy land she went to a fair, and there she saw the

lady whom she had put to bed nimbly going from stall to stall, and making many purchases. For awhile she watched the movements of the lady, and then presuming on her limited acquaintance, addressed her, and asked how she was. The lady seemed surprised and annoyed at the woman's speech, and instead of answering her, said, "And do you see me?" "Yes, I do," said the midwife. "With which eye?" enquired the Fairy. "With this," said the woman, placing her hand on the eye. No sooner had she spoken than the Fairy lady touched that eye, and the midwife could no longer see the Fairy.

Mrs. Lowri Wynn, Clocaenog, near Ruthin, who has reached her eightieth year, and is herself a midwife, gave me a version of the preceding which differed therefrom in one or two particulars. The Fairy gentleman who had driven the woman to and from the Hall was the one that was seen in the fair, said Mrs. Wynn, and he it was that put out the eye or blinded it, she was not sure which, of the inquisitive midwife, and Lowri thought it was the left eye.

2. *Merionethshire Version of the Fairy Mother and Human Midwife.*

A more complete version of this legend is given in the *Gordofigion*, pp. 97, 98. The writer says:—

"Yr oedd bydwraig yn Llanuwchllyn wedi cael ei galw i Goed y Garth, sef Siambra Duon—cartref y Tylwyth Têg— at un o honynt ar enedigaeth baban. Dywedasant wrthi am gymeryd gofal rhag cyffwrdd y dwfr oedd ganddi yn trin y babi yn agos i'w llygaid; ond cyffyrddodd y wraig â'r llygad aswy yn ddigon difeddwl. Yn y Bala, ymhen ychydig, gwelai y fydwraig y gwr, sef tad y babän, a dechreuodd ei holi pa sut yr oeddynt yn Siambra Duon? pa fodd yr oedd y wraig? a sut 'roedd y teulu bach i gyd? Edrychai yntau arni yn graff, a gofynodd, ' A pha lygad yr

I

ydych yn fy ngweled i ?'   'A hwn,' ebe hithau, gan gyfeirio at ei llygad aswy.   Tynodd yntau y llygad hwnw o'i phen, ac yna nis gallai'r wraig ei ganfod."

This in English is :—

There was a midwife who lived at Llanuwchllyn, who was called to Coed y Garth, that is, to Siambra Duon, the home of the Tylwyth Têg, to attend to one of them in child birth. They told her to be careful not to touch her eyes with the water used in washing the baby, but quite unintentionally the woman touched her left eye.   Shortly afterwards the midwife saw the Fairy's husband at Bala, and she began enquiring how they all were at Siambra Duon, how the wife was, and how the little family was?   He looked at her intently, and then asked, "With which eye do you see me?" " With this," she said, pointing to her left eye.   He plucked that eye out of her head, and so the woman could not see him.

With regard to this tale, the woman's eye is said to have been plucked out; in the first tale she was only deprived of her supernatural power of sight ; in other versions the woman becomes blind with one eye.

Professor Rhys in *Y Cymmrodor*, vol. iv., pp. 209, 210, gives a variant of the midwife story which differs in some particulars from that already related.   I will call this the Corwrion version.

3. *The Corwrion Version.*

One of the Fairies came to a midwife who lived at Corwrion and asked her to come with him and attend on his wife.   Off she went with him, and she was astonished to be taken into a splendid palace.   There she continued to go night and morning to dress the baby for some time, until one day the husband asked her to rub her eyes with a certain ointment he offered her.   She did so and found herself sitting on a tuft of rushes, and not in a palace. There was no baby, and all had disappeared. Some time afterwards she happened to go to the town, and whom should she see busily buying various wares but the Fairy on whose wife she had been attending. She addressed him with the question, "How are you, to-day?" Instead of answering her he asked, "How do you see me?" "With my eyes," was the prompt reply. "Which eye?" he asked. "This one," said she, pointing to it; and instantly he disappeared, never more to be seen by her.

There is yet one other variant of this story which I will give, and for the sake of reference I will call it the Nanhwynan version. It appears in the *Brython*, vol. ix., p. 251, and Professor Rhys has rendered it into English in *Y Cymmrodor*, vol. ix., p. 70. I will give the tale as related by the Professor.

4. *The Nanhwynan Version.*

"Once on a time, when a midwife from Nanhwynan had newly got to the Hafodydd Brithion to pursue her calling, a gentleman came to the door on a fine grey steed and bade her come with him at once. Such was the authority with which he spoke, that the poor midwife durst not refuse to go, however much it was her duty to stay where she was. So she mounted behind him, and off they went like the flight of a swallow, through Cwmllan, over the Bwlch, down Nant yr Aran, and over the Gadair to Cwm Hafod Ruffydd, before the poor woman had time to say 'Oh.' When they had got there she saw before her a magnificent mansion, splendidly lit up with such lamps as she had never before seen. They entered the court, and a crowd of servants in expensive liveries came to meet them, and she was at once led through the great hall into a bed-chamber, the like of which she had never seen. There the mistress of the house, to whom she had been fetched, was awaiting her. She got through her duties successfully, and stayed there until the lady had completely recovered; nor had she spent any part of her life so merrily. There was there nought but festivity day and night: dancing, singing, and endless rejoicing reigned there. But merry as it was, she found she must go, and the nobleman gave her a large purse, with the order not to open it until she had got into her own house; then he bade one of his servants escort her the same way she had come. When she reached home she opened the purse, and, to her great joy, it was full of money, and she lived happily on those earnings to the end of her life."

Such are these tales. Perhaps they are one and all fragments of the same story. Each contains a few shreds that are wanting in the others. All, however, agree in one leading idea, that Fairy mothers have, ere now, obtained the aid of human midwives, and this one fact is a connecting link between the people called Fairies and our own remote forefathers.

FAIRY VISITS TO HUMAN ABODES.

Old people often told their children and servant girls, that one condition of the Fairy visits to their houses was cleanliness. They were always instructed to keep the fire place tidy and the floor well swept, the pails filled with water, and to make everything bright and nice before going to bed, and that then, perhaps, the Fairies would come into the house to dance and sing until the morning, and leave on the hearth stone a piece of money as a reward behind them. But should the house be dirty, never would the Fairies enter it to hold their nightly revels, unless, forsooth, they came to punish the slatternly servant. Such was the popular opinion, and it must have acted as an incentive to order and cleanliness. These ideas have found expression in song.

A writer in *Yr Hynafion Cymreig*, p. 153, sings thus of
the place loved by the Fairies :—

> Ysgafn ddrws pren, llawr glân dan nen,
>   A'r aelwyd wen yn wir,
> Tân golau draw, y dwr gerllaw,
>   Yn siriaw'r cylchgrwn clir.

> A light door, and clean white floor,
>   And hearth-stone bright indeed,
> A burning fire, and water near,
>   Supplies our every need.

In a ballad, entitled "The Fairy Queen," in Percy's
Reliques of Ancient English Poetry, Nichols's edition,
vol. iii., p. 172, are stanzas similar to the Welsh verse given
above, which also partially embody the Welsh opinions
of Fairy visits to their houses. Thus chants the " Fairy
Queen ":—

> When mortals are at rest,
> And snoring in their nest,
> Unheard, and un-espy'd,
> Through key-holes we do glide ;
> Over tables, stools, and shelves,
> We trip it with our Fairy elves.

> And, if the house be foul
> With platter, dish, or bowl,
> Upstairs we nimbly creep,
> And find the sluts asleep :
> There we pinch their arms and thighs ;
> None escapes, nor none espies.

> But if the house be swept
> And from uncleanness kept,
> We praise the household maid,
> And duely she is paid :
> For we use before we goe
> To drop a tester in her shoe.

It was not for the sake of mirth only that the Fairies
entered human abodes, but for the performance of more

mundane duties, such as making oatmeal cakes. The Rev. R. Jones, Rector of Llanycil, told me a story, current in his native parish, Llanfrothen, Merionethshire, to the effect that a Fairy woman who had spent the night in baking cakes in a farm house forgot on leaving to take with her the wooden utensil used in turning the cakes on the bake stone; so she returned, and failing to discover the lost article bewailed her loss in these words, "Mi gollais fy mhig," " I have lost my shovel." The people got up and searched for the lost implement, and found it, and gave it to the Fairy, who departed with it in her possession.

Another reason why the Fairies frequented human abodes was to wash and tidy their children. In the Gors Goch legend, already given, is recorded this cause of their visits. Many like stories are extant. It is said that the nightly visitors expected water to be provided for them, and if this were not the case they resented the slight thus shown them and punished those who neglected paying attention to their wants. But tradition says the house-wives were ever careful of the Fairy wants; and, as it was believed that Fairy mothers preferred using the same water in which human children had been washed, the human mother left this water in the bowl for their special use.

In Scotland, also, Fairies were propitiated by attention being paid to their wants. Thus in Allan Cunningham's *Traditional Tales*, p. 11, it is said of Ezra Peden :—" He rebuked a venerable dame, during three successive Sundays for placing a cream bowl and new-baked cake in the paths of the nocturnal elves, who, she imagined, had plotted to steal her grandson from the mother's bosom."

But in the traditions of the Isle of Man we obtain the exact counterpart of Welsh legends respecting the Fairies visiting houses to wash themselves. I will give the following quotation from *Brand*, vol. ii., p. 494, on this point:—

" The Manks confidently assert that the first inhabitants of their island were Fairies, and that these little people have still their residence among them. They call them *the good people*, and say they live in wilds and forests, and on mountains, and shun great cities because of the wickedness acted therein. All the houses are blessed where they visit for they fly vice. A person would be thought impudently profane who should suffer his family to go to bed without having first set a tub, or pail full of clean water for the guests to bathe themselves in, which the natives aver they constantly do, as soon as the eyes of the family are closed, wherever they vouchsafe to come."

Several instances have already been given of the intercourse of Fairies with mortals. In some parts of Wales it is or was thought that they were even so familiar as to borrow from men. I will give one such tale, taken from the *North Wales Chronicle* of March 19th, 1887.

A Fairy Borrowing a Gridiron.

" The following Fairy legend was told to Mr. W. W. Cobb, of Hilton House, Atherstone, by Mrs. Williams, wife of Thomas Williams, pilot, in whose house he lodged when staying in Anglesey :—Mary Roberts, of Newborough, used to receive visits once a week from a little woman who used to bring her a loaf of bread in return for the loan of her gridiron (gradell) for baking bread. The Fairy always told her not to look after her when she left the house, but one day she transgressed, and took a peep as the Fairy went away. The latter went straight to the lake—Lake Rhosddu —near the house at Newborough, and plunged into its waters, and disappeared. This took place about a century ago. The house where Mary Roberts lived is still standing about 100 yards north of the lake."

Compare the preceding with the following lines:—

> If ye will with Mab finde grace,
> Set each platter in its place ;
> Rake the fire up and set
> Water in ere sun be set,
> Wash your pales and cleanse your dairies,
> Sluts are loathsome to the Fairies ;
> Sweep your house ; who doth not so,
> Mab will pinch her by the toe.

Herrick's Hesperides, 1648. (See *Brand*, vol. ii., p. 484.)

Fairy Riches and Gifts.

The riches of the Fairies are often mentioned by the old people, and the source of their wealth is variously given. An old man, who has already been mentioned, John Williams, born about 1770, was of opinion that the Fairies stole the money from bad rich people to give it to good poor folk. This they were enabled to do, he stated, as they could make themselves invisible. In a conversation which we once had on this subject, my old friend posed me with this question, "Who do you think robbed . . . . . . of his money without his knowledge?" "Who do you think took . . . . . money only twenty years ago?" "Why, the Fairies," added he, "for no one ever found out the thief."

Shakespeare, in *Midsummer Night's Dream*, A. iii., S. 1, gives a very different source to the Fairy riches:—

> I will give thee Fairies to attend on thee,
> And they *shall fetch thee jewels from the deep.*

Without inquiring too curiously into the source of these riches, it shall now be shown how, and for what services, they were bestowed on mortals. Gratitude is a noble trait in the Fairy character, and favours received they ever repaid. But the following stories illustrate alike their commiseration, their caprice, and their grateful bounty.

The Fairies Placing Money on the Ground for a Poor Man.

The following tale was told me by Thomas Jones, a small mountain farmer, who occupies land near Pont Petrual, a place between Ruthin and Llanfihangel Glyn Myfyr. Jones informed me that he was acquainted with all the parties mentioned in the tale. His story was as follows :—

A shoemaker, whose health would not permit him to pursue his own trade, obtained work in a tanyard at Penybont, near Corwen. The shoemaker lived in a house called Ty'n-y-graig, belonging to Clegir isa farm. He walked daily to his employment, a distance of several miles, because he could not afford to pay for lodgings. One day, he noticed a round bit of green ground, close to one of the gates on Tan-y-Coed farm, and going up to it discovered a piece of silver lying on the sward. Day after day, from the same spot, he picked up a silver coin. By this means, as well as by the wage he received, he became a well-to-do man. His wife noticed the many new coins he brought home, and ques-tioned him about them, but he kept the secret of their origin to himself. At last, however, in consequence of repeated inquiries, he told her all about the silver pieces, which daily he had picked up from the green plot. The next day he passed the place, but there was no silver, as in days gone by, and he never discovered another shilling, although he looked for it every day. The poor man did not live long after he had informed his wife whence he had obtained the bright silver coins.

The Fairies and their Chest of Gold.

The following tale I obtained from the Rev. Owen Jones, Vicar of Pentrevoelas. The scene lies amongst the wildest mountains of Merionethshire.

David, the weaver, lived in a house called Ifurig, near

J

Cerniogau Mawr, between Pentrevoelas and Cerrig-y-Drudion. One day David was going over the hill to Bala. On the top of the Garn two Fairies met him, and desired him to follow them, promising, if he would do so, that they would show him a chest filled with gold, and furthermore, they told him that the gold should be his. David was in want of money, and he was therefore quite willing to follow these good natured Fairies. He walked many miles with them across the bleak, bare mountain, and at last, descending from the summit, they reached a deep secluded glen, lying at the foot of the mountain, and there the Fairies exposed to his view a chest, which had never before been seen by mortal eye, and they informed him that it was his. David was delighted when he heard the good news, and mentally bade farewell to weaving. He knew, though, from tradition, that he must in some way or other, there and then, take possession of his treasure, or it would disappear. He could not carry the chest away, as it was too heavy, but to show his ownership thereto he thrust his walking stick into the middle of the gold, and there it stood erect. Then he started homewards, and often and again, as he left the glen, he turned round to see whether the Fairies had taken his stick away, and with it the chest; but no, there it remained. At last the ridge hid all from view, and, instead of going on to Bala, he hastened home to tell his good wife of his riches. Quickly did he travel to his cottage, and when there it was not long before his wife knew all about the chest of gold, and where it was, and how that David had taken possession of his riches by thrusting his walking stick into the middle of the gold. It was too late for them to set out to carry the chest home, but they arranged to start before the sun was up the next day. David, well acquainted with Fairy doings, cautioned his wife not to tell anyone of their good fortune, "For, if you do," said he, "we shall vex the Fairies, and the chest, after all, will not be ours." She promised to obey, but alas, what woman possesses a silent tongue! No sooner had the husband revealed the secret to his wife than she was impatient to step to her next door neighbour's house, just to let them know what a great woman she had all at once become. Now, this neighbour was a shrewd miller, called Samuel. David went out to attend to some little business, leaving his wife alone, and she, spying her opportunity, rushed to the miller's house, and told him and his wife every whit, and how that she and David had arranged to go for the chest next morning before the sun was up. Then she hurried home, but never told David where she had been, nor what she had done. The good couple sat up late that night, talking over their good fortune and planning their future. It was consequently far after sunrise when they got up next day, and when they reached the secluded valley, where the chest had been, it had disappeared, and with it David's stick. They returned home sad and weary, but this time there was no visit made to the miller's house. Ere long it was quite clearly seen that Samuel the miller had come into a fortune, and David's wife knew that she had done all the mischief by foolishly boasting of the Fairy gift, designed for her husband, to her early rising and crafty neighbour, who had forestalled David and his wife, and had himself taken possession of the precious chest.

The Fairy Shilling.

The Rev. Owen Jones, Pentrevoelas, whom I have already mentioned as having supplied me with the Folk-lore of his parish, kindly gave me the following tale :—

There was a clean, tidy, hardworking woman, who was most particular about keeping her house in order. She had

a place for everything, and kept everything in its place.
Every night, before retiring to rest, she was in the habit of
brushing up the ashes around the fire place, and putting a
few fresh peat on the fire to keep it in all night, and she
was careful to sweep the floor before going to bed. It was
a sight worth seeing to see her clean cottage. One night
the Fairies, in their rambles, came that way and entered
her house. It was just such a place as they liked. They
were delighted with the warm fire, the clean floor and
hearth, and they stayed there all night and enjoyed themselves greatly. In the morning, on leaving, they left a
bright new shilling on the hearthstone for the woman.
Night after night, they spent in this woman's cottage,
and every morning she picked up a new shilling. This
went on for so long a time that the woman's worldly
condition was much improved. This her neighbours
with envy and surprise perceived, and great was their talk
about her. At last it was noticed that she always paid for
the things she bought with new shilling pieces, and the
neighbours could not make out where she got all these
bright shillings from. They were determined, if possible,
to ascertain, and one of their number was deputed to take
upon her the work of obtaining from the woman the history
of these new shillings. She found no difficulty whatever in
doing so, for the woman, in her simplicity, informed her gossip
that every morning the coin was found on the hearthstone.
Next morning the woman, as usual, expected to find a
shilling, but never afterwards did she discover one, and the
Fairies came no more to her house, for they were offended
with her for divulging the secret.

This tale is exactly like many others that may be heard
related by old people, in many a secluded abode, to their
grandchildren.

A lesson constantly inculcated by Fairy tales is this—
Embrace opportunities as they occur, or they will be lost
for ever. The following stories have reterence to this belief.

The Hidden Golden Chair.

It is a good many years since Mrs. Mary Jones, Corlanau,
Llandinorwig, Carnarvonshire, told me the following tale.
The scene of the story is the unenclosed mountain between
Corlanau, a small farm, and the hamlet, Rhiwlas. There is
still current in those parts a tale of a hidden golden chair,
and Mrs. Jones said that it had once been seen by a young
girl, who might have taken possession of it, but unfortunately
she did not do so, and from that day to this it has not been
discovered. The tale is this :—

There was once a beautiful girl, the daughter of poor
hardworking parents, who held a farm on the side of the
hill, and their handsome industrious daughter took care of
the sheep. At certain times of the year she visited the
sheep-walk daily, but she never went to the mountain
without her knitting needles, and when looking after the
sheep she was always knitting stockings, and she was so
clever with her needles that she could knit as she walked
along. The Fairies who lived in those mountains noticed
this young woman's good qualities. One day, when she
was far from home, watching her father's sheep, she saw
before her a most beautiful golden chair. She went up to
it and found that it was so massive that she could not move
it. She knew the Fairy-lore of her neighbourhood, and she
understood that the Fairies had, by revealing the chair,
intended it for her, but there she was on the wild mountain,
far away from home, without anyone near to assist her in
carrying it away. And often had she heard that such
treasures were to be taken possession of at once, or they
would disappear for ever. She did not know what to do,

but all at once she thought, if she could by attaching the
yarn in her hand to the chair connect it thus with her
home, the chair would be hers for ever. Acting upon this
suggestion she forthwith tied the yarn to the foot of
the chair, and commenced unrolling the ball, walking the
while homewards. But long before she could reach her
home the yarn in the ball was exhausted; she, however,
tied it to the yarn in the stocking which she had been
knitting, and again started towards her home, hoping to reach
it before the yarn in the stocking would be finished, but
she was doomed to disappointment, for that gave out before
she could arrive at her father's house. She had nothing
else with her to attach to the yarn. She, however, could
now see her home, and she began to shout, hoping to gain
the ear of her parents, but no one appeared. In her distress
she fastened the end of the yarn to a large stone, and ran
home as fast as she could. She told her parents what
she had done, and all three proceeded immediately towards
the stone to which the yarn had been tied, but they failed
to discover it. The yarn, too, had disappeared. They continued a futile search for the golden chair until driven away
by the approaching night. The next day they renewed
their search, but all in vain, for the girl was unable to find
the spot where she had first seen the golden chair. It was
believed by everybody that the Fairies had not only removed
the golden chair, but also the yarn, and stone to which the
yarn had been attached, but people thought that if the yarn
had been long enough to reach from the chair to the girl's
home then the golden chair would have been hers for ever.

Such is the tale. People believe the golden chair is still
hidden away in the mountain, and that some day or other
it will be given to those for whom it is intended. But it is,
they say, no use anyone looking for it, as it is not to be got

by searching, but it will be revealed, as if by accident, to those fated to possess it.

Fairy Treasures seen by a Man near Ogwen Lake.

Another tale, similar to the preceding one, is told by my friend, Mr. Hugh Derfel Hughes, in his *Hynafiaethau Llandegai a Llanllechid*, pp. 35, 36. The following is a translation of Mr. Hughes's story :—

It is said that a servant man penetrated into the recesses of the mountains in the neighbourhood of Ogwen Lake, and that he there discovered a cave within which there was a large quantity of brazen vessels of every shape and description. In the joy of his heart at his good fortune, he seized one of the vessels, with the intention of carrying it away with him, as an earnest that the rest likewise were his. But, alas, it was too heavy for any man to move. Therefore, with the intention of returning the following morning to the cave with a friend to assist him in carrying the vessels away, he closed its mouth with stones, and thus he securely hid from view the entrance to the cave. When he had done this it flashed upon his mind that he had heard of people who had accidentally come across caves, just as he had, but that they, poor things, had afterwards lost all traces of them. And lest a similar misfortune should befall him, he determined to place a mark on the mouth of the cave, which would enable him to come upon it again, and also he bethought himself that it would be necessary, for further security, to indicate by some marks the way from his house to the cave. He had however nothing at hand to enable him to carry out this latter design, but his walking stick. This he began to chip with his knife, and he placed the chips at certain distances all along the way homewards. In this way he cut up his staff, and he was satisfied with what he had done, for he hoped to find the cave by means of

the chips.   Early the next morning he and a friend started
for the mountain in the fond hope of securing the treasures,
but when they arrived at the spot where the chip-marked
pathway ought to begin, they failed to discover a single chip,
because, as it was reported—"They had been gathered up
by the Fairies."   And thus this vision was in vain.

The author adds to the tale these words :—" But, reader,
things are not always to be so.   There is a tradition in the
Nant, that a Gwyddel is to have these treasures and this is
how it will come to pass.   A Gwyddel Shepherd will come
to live in the neighbourhood, and on one of his journeys to
the mountain to shepherd his sheep, when fate shall see fit
to bring it about, there will run before-him into the cave a
black sheep with a speckled head, and the Gwyddel shepherd will follow it into the cave to catch it, and on entering,
to his great astonishment, he will discover the treasures and
take possession of them.   And in this way it will come to
pass, in some future age, that the property of the Gwyddelod
will return to them."

The Fairies giving Money to a Man for joining them in their Dance.

The following story came to me through the Rev. Owen
Jones, Vicar of Pentrevoelas.   The occurrence is said to
have taken place near Pentrevoelas.   The following are the
particulars :—

Tomas Moris, Ty'n-y-Pant, returning home one delightful summer night from Llanrwst fair, came suddenly upon a
company of Fairies dancing in a ring.   In the centre of the
circle were a number of speckled dogs, small in size, and
they too were dancing with all their might.   After the
dance came to an end, the Fairies persuaded Tomas to accompany them to Hafod Bryn Mullt, and there the dance

was resumed, and did not terminate until the break of day.
Ere the Fairies departed they requested their visitor to join
them the following night at the same place, and they
promised, if he would do so, to enrich him with gifts of
money, but they made him promise that he would not reveal
to any one the place where they held their revels. This
Tomas did, and night after night was spent pleasantly by
him in the company of his merry newly-made friends. True
to their word, he nightly parted company with them, laden
with money, and thus he had no need to spend his days as
heretofore, in manual labour. This went on as long as
Tomas Moris kept his word, but alas, one day, he divulged
to a neighbour the secret of his riches. That night, as
usual, he went to Hafod Bryn Mullt, but his generous
friends were not there, and he noticed that in the place
where they were wont to dance there was nothing but
cockle shells.

In certain parts of Wales it was believed that Fairy
money, on close inspection, would be found to be cockle
shells. Mrs. Hugh Jones, Corlanau, who has already been
mentioned, told the writer that a man found a crock filled,
as he thought when he first saw it, with gold, but on taking
it home he discovered that he had carried home from the
mountain nothing but cockle shells. This Mrs. Jones told
me was Fairy money.

The Fairies rewarding a Woman for taking care of their Dog.

Mention has already been made of Fairy Dogs. It would
appear that now and again these dogs, just like any other
dogs, strayed from home; but the Fairies were fond of their
pets, and when lost, sought for them, and rewarded those
mortals who had shown kindness to the animals. For the
following tale I am indebted to the Rev. Owen Jones.

One day when going home from Pentrevoelas Church, the wife of Hafod y Gareg found on the ground in an exhausted state a Fairy dog. She took it up tenderly, and carried it home in her apron. She showed this kindness to the poor little thing from fear, for she remembered what had happened to the wife of Bryn Heilyn, who had found one of the Fairy dogs, but had behaved cruelly towards it, and consequently had fallen down dead. The wife of Hafod y Gareg therefore, made a nice soft bed for the Fairy dog in the pantry, and placed over it a brass pot. In the night succeeding the day that she had found the dog, a company of Fairies came to Hafod y Gareg to make inquiries after it. The woman told them that it was safe and sound, and that they were welcome to take it away with them. She willingly gave it up to its masters. Her conduct pleased the Fairies greatly, and so, before departing with the dog, they asked her which she would prefer, a clean or a dirty cow? Her answer was, " A dirty one," And so it came to pass that from that time forward to the end of her life, her cows gave more milk than the very best cows, in the very best farms in her neighbourhood. In this way was she rewarded for her kindness to the dog, by the Fairies.

FAIRY MONEY TURNED TO DROSS.

Fairies' treasure was of uncertain value, and depended for its very existence on Fairy intentions. Often and again, when they had lavishly bestowed money on this or that person, it was discovered to be only leaves or some equally worthless substance ; but people said that the recipients of the money richly deserved the deception that had been played upon them by the Fairies.

In this chapter a few tales shall be given of this trait of Fairy mythology.

1. *A Cruel Man and a Fairy Dog.*

The person from whom the following tale was derived was David Roberts, Tycerrig, Clocaenog, near Ruthin.

A Fairy dog lost its master and wandered about here and there seeking him. A farmer saw the dog, and took it home with him, but he behaved very unkindly towards the wee thing, and gave it little to eat, and shouted at it, and altogether he showed a hard heart. One evening a little old man called at this farmer's house, and inquired if any stray dog was there. He gave a few particulars respecting the dog, and mentioned the day that it had been lost. The farmer answered in the affirmative, and the stranger said that the dog was his, and asked the farmer to give it up to him. This the farmer willingly did, for he placed no value on the dog. The little man was very glad to get possession of his lost dog, and on departing he placed a well filled purse in the farmer's hand. Some time afterwards the farmer looked into the purse, intending to take a coin out of it, when to his surprise and annoyance he found therein nothing but leaves.

Roberts told the writer that the farmer got what he deserved, for he had been very cruel to the wee dog.

Another tale much like the preceding one, I have heard, but I have forgotten the source of the information. A person discovered a lost Fairy dog wandering about, and took it home, but he did not nurse the half-starved animal, nor did he nourish it. After a while some of the Fairy folk called on this person to inquire after their lost dog, and he gave it to them. They rewarded this man for his kindness with a pot filled with money and then departed. On further inspection, the money was found to be cockle shells.

Such lessons as these taught by the Fairies were not without their effect on people who lived in days gone by.

2. *Dick the Fiddler and the Fairy Crown-Piece.*

For the following story I am indebted to my friend, Mr Hamer, who records it in his " Parochial account of Llanidloes," published in the *Montgomeryshire Collections*, vol. x., pp. 252-3-4. Mr Hamer states that the tale was related to him by Mr. Nicholas Bennett, Glanrafon, Trefeglwys.

" Dick the Fiddler was in the habit of going about the country to play at merry-makings, fairs, &c. This worthy, after a week's *fuddle* at Darowen, wending his way homeward, had to walk down ' Fairy Green Lane,' just above the farmstead of Cefn Cloddiau, and to banish fear, which he felt was gradually obtaining the mastery over him, instead of whistling, drew out from the skirt pocket of his longtailed great coat his favourite instrument. After tuning it, he commenced elbowing his way through his favourite air, *Aden Ddu'r Fran* (the Crow's Black Wing). When he passed over the green sward where the *Tylwyth Têg*, or Fairies, held their merry meetings, he heard something rattle in his fiddle, and this something continued rattling and tinkling until he reached Llwybr Scriw Riw, his home, almost out of his senses at the fright caused by that everlasting ' tink, rink, jink,' which was ever sounding in his ears. Having entered the cottage he soon heard music of a different kind, in the harsh angry voice of his better half, who justly incensed at his absence, began lecturing him in a style, which, unfortunately, Dick, from habit, could not wholly appreciate. He was called a worthless fool, a regular drunkard and idler. ' How is it possible for me to beg enough for myself and half a house-full of children nearly naked, while you go about the country and bring me nothing home.' ' Hush, hush, my good woman,' said Dick, ' see what's in the blessed old fiddle.' She obeyed, shook it, and out tumbled, to their great surprise, a five-shilling piece. The wife looked

up into the husband's face, saw that it was 'as pale as a
sheet' with fright: and also noting that he had such an
unusually large sum in his possession, she came to the conclusion that he could not live long, and accordingly changed
her style saying, 'Good man go to Llanidloes to-morrow, it
is market-day and buy some shirting for yourself, for it may
never be your good fortune to have such a sum of money
again.' The following day, according to his wife's wishes,
Dick wended his way to Llanidloes, musing, as he went
along, upon his extraordinary luck, and unable to account
for it. Arrived in the town, he entered Richard Evans's
shop, and called for shirting linen to the value of five shillings,
for which he gave the shopkeeper the crown piece taken out
of the fiddle. Mr. Evans placed it in the till, and our
worthy Dick betook himself to Betty Brunt's public-house
(now known as the Unicorn) in high glee with the capital piece
of linen in the skirt pocket of his long-tailed top coat. He
had not, however, been long seated before Mr. Evans came
in, and made sharp enquiries as to how and where he obtained possession of the crown piece with which he had
paid for the linen. Dick assumed a solemn look, and then
briefly related where and how he had received the coin.
'Say you so,' said Evans, 'I thought as much, for when I
looked into the till, shortly after you left the shop, to my
great surprise it was changed into a heap of musty horse
dung.' "

FAIRIES WORKING FOR MEN.

It was once thought that kind Fairies took compassion
on good folk, who were unable to accomplish in due time
their undertakings, and finished in the night these works
for them; and it was always observed that the Fairy work-
man excelled as a tradesman the mortal whom he assisted.
Many an industrious shoemaker, it is said, has ere this

found in the morning that the Fairies had finished in the
night the pair of shoes which he had only commenced the
evening before. Farmers too, who had in part ploughed a
field, have in the morning been surprised to find it finished.
These kind offices, it was firmly believed, were accomplished
by Fairy friends.

Milton in *L'Allegro* alludes to this belief in the following
lines:—

> Tells how the drudging Goblin swet,
> To earn his cream-bowl duly set,
> When in one night, ere glimpse of morn,
> His shadowy flail hath thresh'd the corn,
> That ten day-labourers could not end.
>
> MILTON, *L'Allegro*, lines 105-9.

In Scotland the sprite, or Fairy, called Browny, haunted
family abodes, and did all manner of work in the night for
those who treated him kindly. In England, Robin Good-
fellow was supposed to perform like functions. Thus sings
Robin:—

> Yet now and then, the maids to please,
> At midnight I card up their wooll;
> And while they sleepe, and take their ease,
> With wheel to threads their flax I pull.
> I grind at mill
> Their malt up still;
> I dress their hemp, I spin their tow.
> If any 'wake
> And would me take,
> I wend me, laughing, ho, ho, ho!
>
> *Percy's Reliques*, vol. iii., p. 169.

Welsh Fairies are not described as ordinarily inclined to
lessen men's labours by themselves undertaking them; but
there are a few tales current of their having assisted worthy
persons in their manual works. Professor Rhys records one
of these stories in *Y Cymmrodor*, vol. iv. 210. He writes
thus:—

" One day Guto, the Farmer of Corwrion, complained to his wife that he was in need of men to mow his hay, and she answered, ' Why fret about it ? look yonder ! there you have a field full of them at it, and stripped to their shirt sleeves.' When he went to the spot the sham workmen of the Fairy family had disappeared. This same Guto, or somebody else, happened another time to be ploughing, when he heard some person he could not see calling out to him, ' I have got the *bins* (that is the *vice*) of my plough broken.' ' Bring it to me,' said the driver of Guto's team, ' that I may mend it.' When they brought the furrow to an end, there they found the broken vice, and a barrel of beer placed near it. One of the men sat down and mended it. Then they made another furrow, and when they returned to the spot they found there a two-eared dish, filled to the brim with *bara a chwrw*, or bread and beer."

FAIRY DANCES.

The one occupation of the Fairy folk celebrated in song and prose was dancing. Their green rings, circular or ovoidal in form, abounded in all parts of the country, and it was in these circles they were said to dance through the livelong night. In " *Cân y Tylwyth Tég*," or the Fairies' Song, thus they chant :—

> O'r glaswellt glân a'r rhedyn mân,
> Gyfeillion dyddan, dewch,
> E ddarfu'r nawn—mae'r lloer yn llawn,
> Y nos yn gyflawn gewch ;
> O'r chwarau sydd ar dwyn y dydd,
> I'r Dolydd awn ar daith,
> Nyni sydd lon, ni chaiff gerbron,
> Farwoliou ran o'n gwaith.

Yr Hynafion Cymraeg, p. 153.

> From grasses bright, and bracken light,
> Come, sweet companions, come,

> The full moon shines, the sun declines,
>   We'll spend the night in fun ;
> With playful mirth, we'll trip the earth,
>   To meadows green let's go,
> We're full of joy, without alloy,
>   Which mortals may not know.

The spots where the Fairies held their nightly revels
were preserved from intrusion by traditional superstitions.
The farmer dared not plough the land where Fairy circles
were, lest misfortune should overtake him. Thus were
these mythical beings left in undisturbed possession of
many fertile plots of ground, and here they were believed to
dance merrily through many a summer night.

> Canu, canu, drwy y nos,
> Dawnsio, dawnsio, ar waen y rhos,
> Yn ngoleuni'r lleuad dlos ;
>   Hapus ydym ni !
> Pawb o honom sydd yn llon,
> Heb un gofid dan ei fron :
> Canu, dawnsio, ar y ton —
>   Dedwydd ydym ni !

> Singing, singing, through the night,
> Dancing, dancing, with our might,
> Where the moon the moor doth light :
>   Happy ever we !
> One and all of merry mien,
> Without sorrow are we seen,
> Singing, dancing on the green :
>   Gladsome ever we !

Professor Rhys's Fairy Tales.

These words correctly describe the popular opinion of
Fairy dance and song, an opinion which reached the early
part of the present century.

Since so much has reached our days of Fairy song and
dance, it is not surprising that we are told that the beautiful
Welsh melody, *Toriad y Dydd,* or the Dawn of Day, is the

work of a Fairy minstrel, and that this song was chanted
by the Fairy company just as the pale light in the east
announced the approach of returning day.

Chaucer (1340 c. to 1400 c.), alluding to the Fairies and
their dances, in his 'Wife of Bath's Tale,' writes :—

> In olde dayes of King Artour,
> Of which the Bretons speken gret honour,
> All was this lond ful-filled of Faerie ;
> The elf-quene with hire joly compagnie
> Danced ful oft in many a grene mede.
> This was the old opinion as I rede ;
> I speke of many hundred yeres ago ;
> But now can no man see non elves mo.
>
> Tyrwhitt's Chaucer i., p. 255.

In the days of the Father of English poets, the elves
had disappeared, and he speaks of "many hundred yeres
ago," when he says that the Fairy Queen and her jolly company danced full often in many a green meadow.

Number 419 of the *Spectator*, published July 1st, 1712,
states that formerly "every large common had a circle of
Fairies belonging to it." Here again the past is spoken of,
but in Wales it would seem that up to quite modern days
some one, or other, was said to have seen the Fairies at their
dance, or had heard of some one who had witnessed their
gambols. Robert Roberts, Tycerrig, Clocaenog, enumerated
several places, such as Nantddu, Clocaenog, Craig-fron-Bannog,
on Mynydd Hiraethog, and Fron-y-Go, Llanfwrog, where the
Fairies used to hold their revels, and other places, such as
Moel Fammau, have been mentioned as being Fairy dancing
ground. Many an aged person in Wales will give the name
of spots dedicated to Fairy sports. Information of this kind
is interesting, for it shows how long lived traditions are, and,
in a manner, places associated with the Fair Tribe bring
these mysterious beings right to our doors.

L

I will now relate a few tales of mortals witnessing or joining in Fairy dances.

The first was related to me by David Roberts. The scene of the dance was the hill side by Pont Petrual between Ruthin and Cerrig-y-Drudion.

1. *A Man who found himself on a Heap of Ferns after joining in a Fairy Dance.*

A man who went to witness a Fairy dance was invited to join them. He did so, and all night long he greatly enjoyed himself. At the break of day the company broke up, and the Fairies took their companion with them. The man found himself in a beautiful hall with everything he could desire at his command, and here he pleasantly passed the time ere he retired to rest. In the morning when he awoke, instead of finding himself on a couch in Fairy Hall, he found himself lying on a heap of fern on the wild mountain side.

Although somewhat unfortunate, this man fared better than most men who joined the Fairy dances.

2. *The Fairies threw dust into a Man's Eyes who Saw them Dance.*

This tale is taken from *Cymru Fu*, p. 176, and is from the pen of *Glasynys*. I give it in English.

William Ellis, of Cilwern, was once fishing in Llyn Cwm Silin, on a dark cloudy day, when he observed close by, in the rushes, a great number of men, or beings in the form of men, about a foot high, jumping and singing.

He watched them for hours, and he never heard in all his life such singing. But William went too near them, and they threw some kind of dust into his eyes, and whilst he was rubbing his eyes, the little family disappeared and fled somewhere out of sight and never afterwards was Ellis able to get a sight of them.

The next tale *Glasynys* shall relate in his own words. It appears in *Cymru Fu* immediately after the one just related.

3. *A Man Dancing with the Fairies for Three Days.*

" Y mae chwedl go debyg am le o'r enw Llyn-y-Ffynonau. Yr oedd yno rasio a dawnsio, a thelynio a ffidlo enbydus, a gwas o Gelli Ffrydau a'i ddau gi yn eu canol yn neidio ac yn prancio mor sionc â neb. Buont wrthi hi felly am dridiau a theirnos, yn ddi-dor-derfyn; ac oni bai bod ryw wr cyfarwydd yn byw heb fod yn neppell, ac i hwnw gael gwybod pa sut yr oedd pethau yn myned yn mlaen, y mae'n ddiddadl y buasai i'r creadur gwirion ddawnsio 'i hun i farwolaeth. Ond gwaredwyd ef y tro hwn." This in English is as follows :—

" There is a tale somewhat like the preceding one told in connection with a place called Llyn-y-Ffynonau. There was there racing and dancing, and harping and furious fiddling, and the servant man of Gelli Ffrydau with his two dogs in their midst jumping and dancing like mad. There they were for three days and three nights without a break dancing as if for very life, and were it not that there lived near by a conjuror, who knew how things were going on, without a doubt the poor creature would have danced himself to death. But he was spared this time."

The next tale I received from Mr. David Lloyd, schoolmaster, Llanfihangel-Glyn-Myfyr, and he heard it in that parish.

4. *A Harper and the Fairies.*

There once lived in a remote part of Denbighshire, called Hafod Elwy, an old harper, named Shon Robert, who used to be invited to parties to play for the dancers, or to accompany the singers. One evening he went to Llechwedd Llyfn, in the neighbourhood of Cefn Brith, to hold a merry meeting, and it was late before the lads and lasses separated. At last the harper wended his way homeward. His path was over the bare mountain. As he came near a lake called Llyn-dau-ychain, he saw on its verge a grand palace, vividly illuminated. He was greatly surprised at the sight, for he had never seen such a building there before. He, however, proceeded on his way, and when he came in front of this beautiful palace he was hailed by a footman, and invited to enter. He accepted the invitation, and was ushered into a magnificent room, where a grand ball was being held. The guests surrounded the harper and became very friendly, and, to his wonder, addressed him by name. This hall was magnificently furnished. The furniture was of the most costly materials, many things were made of solid gold. A waiter handed him a golden cup filled with sparkling wine, which the harper gladly quaffed. He was then asked to play for the company, and this he did to the manifest satisfaction of the guests. By and by one of the company took Shon Robert's hat round and collected money for the harper's benefit, and brought it back to him filled with silver and gold. The feast was carried on with great pomp and merriment until near the dawn of day, when, one by one, the guests disappeared, and at last Shon was left alone. Perceiving a magnificent couch near, he laid himself thereon, and was soon fast asleep. He did not awake until mid-day, and then, to his surprise, he found himself lying on a heap of heather, the grand palace had vanished away, and the gold and silver, which he had transferred from his hat the night before into his bag, was changed to withered leaves.

The following tale told me by the Rev. R. Jones shows that those who witness a Fairy dance know not how time passes.

5. *A Three Hours Fairy Dance seeming as a Few Minutes.*

The Rev. R. Jones's mother, when a young unmarried woman, started one evening from a house called Tyddyn Heilyn, Penrhyndeudraeth, to her home, Penrhyn isaf, accompanied by their servant man, David Williams, called on account of his great strength and stature, Dafydd Fawr, Big David. David was carrying home on his back a flitch of bacon. The night was dark, but calm. Williams walked somewhat in the rear of his young mistress, and she, thinking he was following, went straight home. But three hours passed before David appeared with the pork on his back.

He was interrogated as to the cause of his delay, and in answer said he had only been about three minutes after his young mistress. He was told that she had arrived three hours before him, but this David would not believe. At length, however, he was convinced that he was wrong in his time, and then he proceeded to account for his lagging behind as follows:—

He observed, he said, a brilliant meteor passing through the air, which was followed by a ring or hoop of fire, and within this hoop stood a man and woman of small size, handsomely dressed. With one arm they embraced each other, and with the other they took hold of the hoop, and their feet rested on the concave surface of the ring. When the hoop reached the earth these two beings jumped out of it, and immediately proceeded to make a circle on the ground. As soon as this was done, a large number of men and women instantly appeared, and to the sweetest music that ear ever heard commenced dancing round and round the circle. The sight was so entrancing that the man stayed, as he thought, a few minutes to witness the scene. The ground all around was lit up by a kind of subdued light, and he observed every movement of these beings. By and by the meteor which had at first attracted his attention appeared again, and then the fiery hoop came to view, and when it reached the spot where the dancing was, the lady and gentleman who had arrived in it jumped into the hoop, and disappeared in the same manner in which they had reached the place. Immediately after their departure the Fairies vanished from sight, and the man found himself alone and in darkness, and then he proceeded homewards. In this way he accounted for his delay on the way.

In Mr. Sikes's *British Goblins*, pp. 79-81, is a graphic account of a mad dance which Tudur ap Einion Gloff had with the Fairies, or Goblins, at a place called Nant-yr-Ellyllon, a hollow half way up the hill to Castell Dinas Bran, in the neighbourhood of Llangollen. All night, and into the next day, Tudur danced frantically in the Nant, but he was rescued by his master, who understood how to break the spell, and release his servant from the hold the Goblins had over him! This he did by pronouncing certain pious words, and Tudur returned home with his master.

Mr. Evan Davies, carpenter, Brynllan, Efenechtyd, who is between seventy and eighty years old, informed the writer that his friend John Morris told him that he had seen a company of Fairies dancing, and that they were the handsomest men and women that he had ever seen. It was night and dark, but the place on which the dance took place was strangely illuminated, so that every movement of the singular beings could be observed, but when the Fairies disappeared it became suddenly quite dark.

Although from the tales already given it would appear that the Fairies held revelry irrespective of set times of meeting, still it was thought that they had special days for their great banquets, and the eve of the first of May, old

style, was one of these days, and another was *Nos Wyl
Ifan*, St. John's Eve, or the evening of June 23rd.

Thus sings *Glasynys*, in *Y Brython*, vol. iii. p. 270 :—

Nos Wyl Ifan.

T'ylwyth Têg yn lluoedd llawen,
O dan nodded tawel Dwynwen,
Welir yn y cêl encilion,
Yn perori mwyn alawon,
Ac yn taenu hyd y twyni,
Ac ar leiniau'r deiliog lwyni,
Hud a Lledrith ar y glesni,
Ac yn sibrwd'dwyfol desni !

I am indebted to my friend Mr Richard Williams,
F.R.H.S., Newtown, Montgomeryshire, for the following
translation of the preceding Welsh lines :—

The Fairy Tribe in merry crowds,
Under Dwynwen's calm protection,
Are seen in shady retreats
Chanting sweet melodies,
And spreading over the bushes
And the leafy groves
Illusion and phantasy on all that is green,
And whispering their mystic lore.

May-day dances and revelling have reached our days, and
probably they have, like the Midsummer Eve's festivities,
their origin in the far off times when the Fairy Tribe inhabited Britain and other countries, and to us have they
bequeathed these Festivals, as well as that which ushers in
winter, and is called in Wales, *Nos glan gaua*, or All Hallow Eve. If so, they have left us a legacy for which we
thank them, and they have also given us a proof of their
intelligence and love of nature.

But I will now briefly refer to Fairy doings on *Nos Wyl
Ifan* as recorded by England's greatest poet, and, further
on, I shall have more to say of this night.

Shakespeare introduces into his *Midsummer Night's Dream* the prevailing opinions respecting Fairies in England, but they are almost identical with those entertained by the people of Wales; so much so are they British in character, that it is no great stretch of the imagination to suppose that he must have derived much of his information from an inhabitant of Wales. However, in one particular, the poet's description of the Fairies differs from the more early opinion of them in Wales. Shakespeare's Fairies are, to a degree, diminutive; they are not so small in Wales. But as to their habits in both countries they had much in common. I will briefly allude to similarities between English and Welsh Fairies, confining my remarks to Fairy music and dancing.

To begin, both danced in rings. A Fairy says to Puck :—

> And I serve the Fairy Queen
> To dew her orbs upon the green.
> *Midsummer Night's Dream*, Act II., S. I.

And allusion is made in the same play to these circles in these words :—

> If you will patiently dance in our round
> And see our moonlight revels, go with us.
> Act II., S. I.

Then again Welsh and English Fairies frequented like spots to hold their revels on. I quote from the same play :—

> And now they never meet in grove or green,
> By fountain clear, or spangled starlight sheen.
> Act II., S. I.

And again :—

> And never since the middle summer's spring
> Met we on hill, in dale, forest, or mead
> By paved fountain or by rushy brook
> Or by the beached margent of the sea,
> To dance our ringlets to the whistling wind.
> Act II., S. I

And further the Fairies in both countries meet at night, and hold their Balls throughout the hours of darkness, and separate in early morn. Thus Puck addressing Oberon :—

> Fairy King, attend and hark ;
> I do hear the morning lark.

Act IV., S. I.

> Now until the break of day
> Through this house each Fairy stray
>
> .   .   .   .
>
> .   .   .   .
>
> Trip away, make no stay,
> Meet we all at break of day.

Act V., S. I.

In the Welsh tales given of Fairy dances the music is always spoken of as most entrancing, and Shakespeare in felicitous terms gives utterance to the same thought—

> Music, lo ! music, such as charmeth sleep.

I am indebted to the courtesy of the Rev. R. O. Williams, M.A., Vicar of Holywell, for the following singular testimony to Fairy dancing. The writer was the Rev. Dr. Edward Williams, at one time of Oswestry, and afterwards Principal of the Independent Academy at Rotherham in Yorkshire, who was born at Glan Clwyd, Bodfari, Nov. 14th, 1750, and died March 9, 1813. The extract is to be seen in the autobiography of Dr. Williams, which has been published, but the quotation now given is copied from the doctor's own handwriting, which now lies before me.

It may be stated that Mr. Wirt Sikes, in his *British Goblins*, refers to the Dwarfs of Cae Caled, Bodfari, as Knockers, but he was not justified, as will be seen from the extract, in thus describing them. For the sake of reference the incident shall be called—The Elf Dancers of Cae Caled.

The Elf Dancers of Cae Caled.

Dr. Edward Williams, under the year 1757, writes as follows:—

"I am now going to relate a circumstance in this young period of my life which probably will excite an alternate smile and thoughtful reflection, as it has often done in myself, however singular the fact and strong the evidence of its authenticity, and, though I have often in mature age called to my mind the principles of religion and philosophy to account for it, I am forced to class it among my *unknowables*. And yet I may say that not only the fact itself, but also the consideration of its being to my own mind inexplicable, has afforded some useful reflections, with which this relation need not be accompanied.

"On a fine summer day (about midsummer) between the hours of 12 at noon and one, my eldest sister and myself, our next neighbour's children Barbara and Ann Evans, both older than myself, were in a field called Cae Caled near their house, all innocently engaged at play by a hedge under a tree, and not far from the stile next to that house, when one of us observed on the middle of the field a company of—what shall I call them?—*Beings*, neither men, women, nor children, dancing with great briskness. They were full in view less than a hundred yards from us, consisting of about seven or eight couples: we could not well reckon them, owing to the briskness of their motions and the consternation with which we were struck at a sight so unusual. They were all clothed in red, a dress not unlike a military uniform, without hats, but their heads tied with handkerchiefs of a reddish colour, sprigged or spotted with yellow, all uniform in this as in habit, all tied behind with the corners hanging down their backs, and white handkerchiefs in their hands held loose by the corners. They appeared of a size somewhat less than our own, but more like dwarfs than children. On the first discovery we began, with no small dread, to question one another as to what they could be, as there were no soldiers in the country, nor was it the time for May dancers, and as they differed much from all the human beings we had ever seen. Thus alarmed we dropped our play, left our station, and made for the stile. Still keeping our eyes upon them we observed one of their company starting from the rest and making towards us with a running pace. I being the youngest was the last at the stile, and, though struck with an inexpressi-ble panic, saw the *grim elf* just at my heels, having a full and clear, though terrific view of him, with his ancient, swarthy, and grim complexion. I screamed out exceedingly; my sister also and our companions set up a roar, and the former dragged me with violence over the stile on which, at the instant I was disengaged from it, this warlike Liliputian leaned and stretched himself after me, but came not over. With palpitating hearts and loud cries we ran towards the house, alarmed the family, and told them our trouble. The men instantly left their dinner, with whom still trembling we went to the place, and made the most solici-tous and diligent enquiry in all the neighbourhood, both at that time and after, but never found the least vestige of any circumstance that could contribute to a solution of this re-markable phenomenon. Were any disposed to question the sufficiency of this quadruple evidence, the fact having been uniformly and often attested by each of the parties and various and separate examinations, and call it a childish deception, it would do them no harm to admit that, com-paring themselves with the scale of universal existence, beings with which they certainly and others with whom it is possible they may be surrounded every moment, they are

but children of a larger size. I know but few less credulous
than the relator, but he is no Sadducee. 'He who hath
delivered will yet deliver.'"

My friend, Mr. R. Prys Jones, B.A., kindly informs me
that he has several intelligent boys in his school, the Boys'
Board School, Denbigh, from Bodfari, and to them he read
the preceding story, but not one of them had ever heard of
it. It is singular that the story should have died so soon
in the neighbourhood that gave it birth.

FAIRY TRICKS WITH MORTALS.

It was formerly believed in Wales that the Fairies, for a
little fun, sportively carried men in mid air from place to
place, and, having conveyed them to a strange neighbourhood, left them to return to their homes as best they could.
Benighted travellers were ever fearful of encountering a
throng of Fairies lest they should by them be seized, and
carried to a strange part of the country.

Allusion is made to this freak of the Fairies in the
Cambro-Briton, vol. i., p. 348 :—

"And it seems that there was some reason to be appre-
hensive of encountering these 'Fair people' in a mist;
for, although allowed not to be maliciously disposed, they
had a very inconvenient practice of seizing an unwary pil-
grim, and hurrying him through the air, first giving him
the choice, however, of travelling above wind, mid-wind, or
below wind. If he chose the former, he was borne to an
altitude somewhat equal to that of a balloon ; if the latter,
he had the full benefit of all the brakes and briars in his
way, his contact with which seldom failed to terminate in
his discomfiture. Experienced travellers, therefore, always
kept in mind the advice of Apollo to Phaeton (In medio
tutissimus ibis) and selected the middle course, which en-

sured them a pleasant voyage at a moderate elevation, equally removed from the branches and the clouds."

This description of an aerial voyage of a hapless traveller through Fairy agency corresponds with the popular faith in every particular, and it would not have been difficult some sixty, or so, years back, to have collected many tales in various parts of Wales of persons who had been subjected to this kind of conveyance.

The first mention that I have been able to find of this Fairy prank is in a small book of prose poetry called *Gweledigaeth Cwrs y Byd*, or *Y Bardd Cwsg*, which was written by the Revd. Ellis Wynne (born 1670-1, died 1734), rector of Llanfair, near Harlech. The "Visions of the Sleeping Bard" were published in 1703, and in the work appear many superstitions of the people, some of which shall by and by be mentioned.

In the very commencement of this work, the poet gives a description of a journey which he had made through the air with the Fairies. Addressing these beings, he says:—
"Atolwg, lan gynnulleidfa, yr wyf yn deall mai rhai o bell ydych, a gymmerwch chwi Fardd i'ch plith sy'n chwennych trafaelio?" which in English is—"May it please you, comely assembly, as I understand that you come from afar, to take into your company a Bard who wishes to travel?"

The poet's request is granted, and then he describes his aerial passage in these words:—

"Codasant fi ar eu hysgwyddau, fel codi Marchog Sir; ac yna ymaith â ni fel y gwynt, tros dai a thiroedd, dinasoedd a theyrnasoedd, a moroedd a mynyddoedd, heb allu dal sylw ar ddim, gan gyflymed yr oeddynt yn hedeg." This translated is:—

"They raised me on their shoulders, as they do a Knight of

the Shire, and away we went like the wind, over houses and fields, over cities and kingdoms, over seas and mountains, but I was unable to notice particularly anything, because of the rapidity with which they flew."

What the poet writes of his own flight with the Fairies depicts the then prevailing notions respecting aerial journeys by Fairy agencies, and they bear a striking resemblance to like stories in oriental fiction. That the belief in this form of transit survived the days of *Bardd Cwsg* will be seen from the following tale related by my friend Mr. E. Hamer in his Parochial Account of Llanidloes :—

A Man Carried Through the Air by the Fairies.

"One Edward Jones, or 'Ned the Jockey,' as he was familiarly called, resided, within the memory of the writer, in one of the roadside cottages a short distance from Llanidloes, on the Newtown road. While returning home late one evening, it was his fate to fall in with a troop of Fairies, who were not pleased to have their gambols disturbed by a mortal. Requesting him to depart, they politely offered him the choice of three means of locomotion, viz., being carried off by a 'high wind, middle wind, or low wind.' The jockey soon made up his mind, and elected to make his trip through the air by the assistance of a high wind. No sooner had he given his decision, than he found himself whisked high up into the air and his senses completely bewildered by the rapidity of his flight; he did not recover himself till he came in contact with the earth, being suddenly dropped in the middle of a garden near Ty Gough, on the Bryndu road, many miles distant from the spot whence he started on his aerial journey. Ned, when relating this story, would vouch for its genuineness in the most solemn manner, and the person who narrated it to the writer brought forward as a proof of its truth, 'that there was not the slightest trace of any person going into the garden while Ned was found in the middle of it.' "

Montgomeryshire Collections, vol. x., p. 247.

Mr. Hamer records another tale much like the foregoing, but the one I have given is a type of all such stories.

Fairy illusion and phantasy were formerly firmly believed in by the inhabitants of Wales. Fairies were credited with being able to deceive the eyesight, if not also the other senses of man. One illustrative tale of this kind I will now record. Like stories are heard in many parts. The following story is taken from *Y Gordofigion*, p. 99, a book which has more than once been laid under contribution.

Fairy Illusions.

" Ryw dro͏̄yr oedd brodor o Nefyn yn dyfod adref o ffair Pwllheli, ac wrth yr Efail Newydd gwelai *Inn* fawreddog, a chan ei fod yn gwybod nad oedd yr un gwesty i fod yno, gofynodd i un o'r gweision os oedd ganddynt ystabl iddo roddi ei farch. Atebwyd yn gadarnhaol. Rhoddwyd y march yn yr ystabl, ac aeth yntau i mewn i'r ty, gofynodd am *beint* o gwrw, ac ni chafodd erioed well cwrw na'r cwrw hwnw. Yn mhen ychydig, gofynodd am fyned i orphwys, a chafodd hyny hefyd. Aeth i'w orweddle, yr hwn ydoedd o ran gwychder yn deilwng i'r brenhin; ond wchw fawr ! erbyn iddo ddeffro, cafodd ei hun yn gorwedd ar ei hyd mewn tomen ludw, a'r ceffyl wedi ei rwymo wrth bolyn clawdd gwrysg."

This in English is as follows :—" Once upon a time a native of Nefyn was returning from Pwllheli fair, and when near Efail Newydd he saw a magnificent Inn, and, as he knew that no such public-house was really there, he went up to it and asked one of the servants whether they had a stable where he could put up his horse. He was answered in the affirmative. The horse was placed in the stable, and the man entered the house and asked for a pint of beer, which he thought was the best he had ever drunk. After awhile he inquired whether he could go to rest. This also was granted him, and he retired to his room, which in splendour was worthy of the king. But alas! when he awoke he found himself sleeping on his back on a heap of ashes, and the horse tied to a pole in the hedge."

FAIRY MEN CAPTURED.

There are many tales current of wee Fairy men having been captured. These tales are, however, evidently variants of the same story. The dwarfs are generally spoken of as having been caught by a trapper in his net, or bag, and the hunter, quite unconscious of the fact that a Fairy is in his bag, proceeds homewards, supposing that he has captured a badger, or some other kind of vermin, but, all at once, he hears the being in the bag speak, and throwing the bag down he runs away in a terrible fright. Such in short is the tale. I will proceed to give several versions of this story.

1. *Gwyddelwern Version.*

The following tale was told by Mr. Evan Roberts, Ffridd Agored, a farmer in the parish of Llanfwrog. Roberts heard the story when he was a youth in the parish of Gwyddelwern. It is as follows :—

A man went from his house for peat to the stack on the hill. As he intended to carry away only a small quantity for immediate use, he took with him a bag to carry it home. When he got to the hill he saw something running before him, and he gave chase and caught it and bundled it into the bag. He had not proceeded far on his way before he heard a small voice shout somewhere near him, "Neddy, Neddy." And then he heard another small voice in the bag saying, "There is daddy calling me." No sooner did the man hear these words than in a terrible fright he threw the bag down, and ran home as fast as he could.

2. *The Llandrillo Version.*

I am indebted for the following tale to Mr. E. S. Roberts, schoolmaster, Llantysilio, near Llangollen :—

Two men whilst otter-hunting in Cwm Pennant, Llandrillo, saw something reddish scampering away across the ground just before them. They thought it was an otter, and watching it saw that it entered a hole by the side of the river. When they reached the place they found, underneath the roots of a tree, two burrows. They immediately set to work to catch their prey. Whilst one of the men pushed a long pole into one of the burrows, the other held the mouth of a sack to the other, and very shortly into the sack rushed their prey and it was secured. The men now went homewards, but they had not gone far, ere they heard a voice in the bag say, " My mother is calling me." The frightened men instantly threw the sack to the ground, and they saw a small man, clothed in red, emerge therefrom, and the wee creature ran away with all his might to the brushwood that grew along the banks of the river.

3. *The Snowdon Version.*

The following tale is taken from *Y Gordofigion*, p. 98 :—

" Aeth trigolion ardaloedd cylchynol y Wyddfa un tro i hela pryf llwyd. Methasant a chael golwg ar yr un y diwrnod cyntaf ; ond cynllwynasant am un erbyn trannoeth, trwy osod sach a'i cheg yn agored ar dwll yr arferai y pryf fyned iddo, ond ni byddai byth yn dyfod allan drwyddo am ei fod yn rhy serth a llithrig. A'r modd a gosodasant y sach oedd rhoddi cortyn trwy dyllau yn ei cheg, yn y fath fodd ag y crychai, ac y ceuai ei cheg pan elai rhywbeth iddi. Felly fu ; aeth pawb i'w fan, ac i'w wely y noson hono. Gyda'r wawr bore dranoeth, awd i edrych y sach, ac erbyn

M

dyfod ati yr oedd ei cheg wedi crychu, yn arwydd fod rhyw-beth oddifewn. Codwyd hi, a thaflodd un hi ar ei ysgwydd i'w dwyn adref. Ond pan yn agos i Bryn y Fedw wele dor-pyn o ddynan bychan yn sefyll ar delpyn o graig gerllaw ac yn gwaeddi, 'Meirig, wyt ti yna, dwad?' 'Ydwyf,' attebai llais dieithr (ond dychrynedig) o'r sach. Ar hyn, wele'r helwyr yn dechreu rhedeg ymaith, a da oedd ganddynt wneyd hyny, er gadael y sach i'r pryf, gan dybied eu bod wedi dal yn y sach un o ysbrydion y pwll diwaelod, ond deallasant ar ol hyny mai un o'r Tylwyth Teg oedd yn y sach."

The tale in English reads thus :—"Once the people who lived in the neighbourhood of Snowdon went badger-hunting. They failed the first day to get sight of one. But they laid a trap for one by the next day. This they did by placing a sack's open mouth with a noose through it at the entrance to the badger's den. The vermin was in the habit of entering his abode by one passage and leaving it by another. The one by which he entered was too pre-cipitous and slippery to be used as an exit, and the trappers placed the sack in this hole, well knowing that the running noose in the mouth of the sack would close if anything entered. The next morning the hunters returned to the snare, and at once observed that the mouth of the sack was tightly drawn up, a sign that there was something in it. The bag was taken up and thrown on the shoulders of one of the men to be carried home. But when they were near Bryn y Fedw they saw a lump of a little fellow, standing on the top of a rock close by and shouting, 'Meirig, are you there, say?' 'I am,' was the answer in a strange but nervous voice. Upon this, the hunters, throwing down the bag, began to run away, and they were glad to do so, although they had to leave their sack behind them, believing, as they did, that they had captured one of the spirits of the bottomless pit. But afterwards they understood that it was one of the Fairy Tribe that was in the sack."

There was at one time a tale much like this current in the parish of Gyffylliog, near Ruthin, but in this latter case the voice in the bag said, " My father is calling me," though no one was heard to do so. The bag, however, was cast away, and the trapper reported that he had captured a Fairy !

4. *The Llanfair Dyffryn Clwyd Version.*

Mr. Evan Davies, carpenter, Bryn Llan, Efenechtyd, told the writer that Robert Jones, innkeeper, in the same parish, told him the following tale, mentioning at the same time the man who figures in the narrative, whose name, however, I have forgotten. The story runs thus :—

A man, wishing to catch a fox, laid a bag with its mouth open, but well secured, at the entrance to a fox's den in Coed Cochion, Llanfair Dyffryn Clwyd parish, and hid himself to await the result. He had seen the fox enter its lair, and he calculated that it would ere long emerge therefrom. By and by, he observed that something had entered the bag, and going up to it, he immediately secured its mouth, and, throwing the bag over his shoulder, proceeded homewards, but he had not gone far on his way before he heard someone say, "Where is my son John ? " The man, however, though it was dark, was not frightened, for he thought that possibly some one was in search of a lad who had wandered from home. He was rather troubled to find that the question was repeated time after time by some one who apparently was following him. But what was his terror when, ere long, he heard a small voice issue from the bag he was carrying, saying

"There is dear father calling me." The man in a terrible fright threw the bag down, and ran away as fast as his feet could carry him, and never stopped until he reached his home, and when he came to himself he related the story of his adventure in the wood to his wife.

FAIRIES IN MARKETS AND FAIRS.

It was once firmly believed by the Welsh that the Fairy Tribe visited markets and fairs, and that their presence made business brisk. If there was a buzz in the market place, it was thought that the sound was made by the Fairies, and on such occasions the farmers' wives disposed quickly of their commodities; if, however, on the other hand, there was no buzz, the Fairies were absent, and there was then no business transacted.

Mr. Richard Jones, Ty'n-y-Wern, Bryneglwys, who, when a youth, lived in Llanbedr parish, near Ruthin, informed the writer that his mother, after attending a market at Ruthin, would return home occasionally with the sad news that "They were not there," meaning that the Fairies were not present in the market, and this implied a bad market and no sweets for Richard. On the other hand, should the market have been a good one, she would tell them that "They filled the whole place," and the children always had the benefit of their presence.

This belief that the Fairies sharpened the market was, I think, general. I find in *Y Gordofigion*, p. 97, the following words :—

"Byddai y Tylwyth Têg yn arfer myned i farchnadoedd y Bala, ac yn gwneud twrw mawr heb i neb eu gweled, ac yr oedd hyny yn arwydd fod y farchnad ar godi," which is:—

The Fairies were in the habit of frequenting Bala markets, and they made a great noise, without any one seeing them, and this was a sign that the market was sharpening.

NAMES OF THINGS ATTRIBUTED TO THE FAIRIES.

Many small stone utensils found in the ground, the use, or the origin, of which was unknown to the finders, were formerly attributed to the Fairies. Thus, flint arrow-heads were called elf shots, from the belief that they once belonged to Elves or Fairies. And celts, and other stone implements, were, by the peasants of Wales and other places, ascribed to the same small folk. Very small clay pipes were also attributed to the same people. All this is curious evidence of a pre-existing race, which the Celts supplanted, and from whom, in many respects, they differed. Although we cannot derive much positive knowledge from an enumeration of the articles popularly associated with the Fairies, still, such a list, though an imperfect one, will not be void of interest. I will, therefore, describe certain pre-historic remains, which have been attributed to the aboriginal people of Britain.

Fairy Pipes.

Cetyn y Tylwyth Tég, or Fairy Pipes, are small clay pipes, with bowls that will barely admit the tip of the little finger. They are found in many places, generally with the stem broken off, though usually the bowl is perfect.

A short time ago I stayed awhile to talk with some workmen who were engaged in carting away the remains of a small farm house, once called *Y Bwlch*, in the parish of Efenechtyd, Denbighshire, and they told me that they had just found a Fairy Pipe, or, as they called it, *Cetyn y Tylwyth Tég*, which they gave me. A similar pipe was also picked up by Lewis Jones, Brynffynon, on Coed Marchan, in the same parish, when he was enclosing a part of the mountain allotted to his farm. In March, 1887, the workmen employed in taking down what were at one time buildings belonging to a bettermost kind of residence, opposite Llanfwrog Church, near Ruthin, also discovered one of these wee pipes. Pipes, identical in shape and size, have been found in all parts of Wales, and they are always known by the name of *Cetyn y Tylwyth Tég*, or Fairy Pipes.

In Shropshire they have also been discovered in the Fens, and the late Rev. Canon Lee, Hanmer, had one in his possession, which had been found in those parts, and, it was called a Fairy Pipe.

Fairy Whetstone.

The small spindle whorls which belong to the stone age, and which have been discovered in the circular huts, called *Cyttiau'r Gwyddelod*, which are the earliest remains of human abodes in Wales, are by the people called Fairy Whetstones, but, undoubtedly, this name was given them from their resemblance to the large circular whetstone at present in common use, the finders being ignorant of the original use of these whorls.

Fairy Hammer and Fairy or Elf Stones.

Stone hammers of small size have been ascribed to the Fairies, and an intelligent Welsh miner once told the writer that he had himself seen, in a very ancient diminutive mine level, stone hammers which, he said, had once belonged to the Fairies.

Other pre-historic implements, as celts, have been denominated Fairy remains. Under this head will come flint, or stone arrow-heads. These in Scotland are known by the name Elf Shots or Fairy Stones.

Pennant's *Tour in Scotland*, 1769, p. 115, has the following reference to these arrow-heads:—

"*Elf Shots*, i.e., the stone arrow-heads of the old inhabitants of this island, are supposed to be weapons shot by Fairies at cattle, to which are attributed any disorders they have."

Jamieson states in his Dictionary, under the heading Elf Shot :—" The *Elf Shot* or *Elfin Arrow* is still used in the Highlands as an amulet."

Tradition, in thus connecting stone implements with the Fairies, throws a dim light on the elfin community. But evidence is not wanting that the Celts themselves used stone utensils.

The things which shall now be mentioned, as being connected with the Fairies, owe their names to no foundation in fact, but are the offspring of a fanciful imagination, and are attributed to the Fairies in agreement with the more modern and grotesque notions concerning those beings and their doings. This will be seen when it is stated that the Fox Glove becomes a Fairy Glove, and the Mushroom, Fairy Food.

Ymenyn y Tylwyth Tég, or Fairy Butter.

I cannot do better than quote Pennant on this matter. His words are :—

" Petroleum, rock oil, or what the Welsh call it, *Ymenin tylwyth tég*, or Fairies' butter, has been found in the lime stone strata in our mineral country. It is a greasy substance, of an agreeable smell, and, I suppose, ascribed to the benign part of those imaginary beings. It is esteemed serviceable in rheumatic cases, rubbed on the parts affected. It retains a place in our dispensary."

Pennant's Whiteford, p. 131.

Bwyd Ellyllon, or Goblins' Food.

This was a kind of fungus or mushroom. The word is given in Dr. Owen Pughe's dictionary under the head *Ellyll*.

Menyg y Tylwyth Tég, or Fairy Gloves.

The Fox Glove is so called, but in Dr. Owen Pughe's dictionary, under the head *Ellyll*, the Fox Glove is called *Menyg Ellyllon*.

Yr Ellyll Dân, or Goblin Fire.

The Rev. T. H. Evans, in his *History of the Parish of Llanwddyn*, states that in that parish "Will of the Wisp" is called "*Yr Ellyll Dân.*" This is indeed the common name for the *Ignis fatuus* in most, if not in all parts of Wales, but in some places where English is spoken it is better known by the English term, "Jack o' Lantern," or "Jack y Lantern."

Rhaffau'r Tylwyth Tég, or the Ropes of the Fairies.

Professor Rhys, in his Welsh Fairy Tales—*Y Cymmrodor* vol. v., p. 75—says, that gossamer, which is generally called in North Wales *edafedd gwawn*, or *gwawn* yarn, used to be called, according to an informant, *Rhaffau'r·Tylwyth Tég*, that is to say, the Ropes of the Fair Family, thus associating the Fairies with marshy, or rushy, places, or with ferns and heather as their dwelling places. It was supposed that if a man lay down to sleep in such places the Fairies would come and bind him with their ropes, and cover him with a gossamer sheet, which would make him invisible, and incapable of moving.

FAIRY KNOCKERS, OR COBLYNAU.

The *Coblynau* or *Knockers* were supposed to be a species of Fairies who had their abode in the rocks, and whose province it was to indicate by knocks, and other sounds, the presence of ore in mines.

It would seem that many people had dim traditions of a small race who had their dwellings in the rocks. This wide-spread belief in the existence of cave men has, in our days, been shown to have had a foundation in fact, and many vestiges of this people have been revealed by intelligent cave hunters. But the age in which the cave men lived cannot even approximately be ascertained. In various parts of Wales, in the lime rock, their abodes have been brought to light. It is not improbable that the people who occupied the caves of ancient days were, in reality, the original Fairy Knockers. These people were invested, in after ages, by the wonder-loving mind of man, with supernatural powers.

Æschylus, the Greek tragic poet, who died in the 69th year of his age, B.C. 456, in *Prometheus Vinctus*, refers to cave dwellers in a way that indicates that even then they belonged to a dateless antiquity.

In Prometheus's speech to the chorus—κοῦτε πλινθυφεῖς .. ἐν μυχοῖς ἀηλίοις—lines 458-461, is a reference to this ancient tradition. His words, put into English, are these:—"And neither knew the warm brick-built houses exposed to the sun, nor working in wood, *but they dwelt underground*, like as little ants, *in the sunless recesses of caves.*"

The above quotation proves that the Greeks had a tradition that men in a low, or the lowest state of civilization, had their abodes in caves, and possibly the reference to ants would convey the idea that the cave dwellers were small people. Be this as it may, it is very remarkable that the word applied to a *dwarf* in the dialects of the northern countries of Europe signifies also a *Fairy*, and the dwarfs, or Fairies, are there said to inhabit the rocks. The following quotation from Jamieson's *Scottish Dictionary* under the word *Droich*, a dwarf, a pigmy, shows this to have been the case :—

" In the northern dialects, *dwerg* does not merely signify a dwarf, but also a *Fairy !* The ancient Northern nations, it is said, prostrated themselves before rocks, believing that they were inhabited by these pigmies, and that they thence gave forth oracles. Hence they called the echo *dwergamal*, as believing it to be their voice or speech. . . .

N

They were accounted excellent artificers, especially as
smiths, from which circumstance some suppose that they
have received their name. . . Other Isl. writers assert
that their ancestors did not worship the pigmies as they did
the *genii* or spirits, also supposed to reside in the rocks."

Bishop Percy, in a letter to the Rev. Evan Evans *(Ieuan
Prydydd Hir)*, writes :—

"Nay, I make no doubt but Fairies are derived from the
Duergar, or Dwarfs, whose existence was so generally believed among all the northern nations."

The Cambro-Briton, vol. i., p. 331.

And again in Percy's *Reliques of Ancient Poetry*, vol. iii.,
p. 171, are these remarks :—

"It is well known that our Saxon ancestors, long before
they left their German forests, believed in the existence of a
kind of diminutive demons, or middle species between men
and spirits, whom they called *Duergar*, or Dwarfs, and to
whom they attributed wonderful performances, far exceeding
human art."

Pennant, in his *Tour in Scotland*, 1772, pp. 55-56, when
describing the collieries of Newcastle, describes the Knockers
thus :—

"The immense caverns that lay between the pillars exhibited a most gloomy appearance. I could not help
enquiring here after the imaginary inhabitant, the creation
of the labourer's fancy,

The swart Fairy of the mine ;

and was seriously answered by a black fellow at my elbow
that he really had never met with any, but that his grandfather had found the little implements and tools belonging
to this diminutive race of subterraneous spirits. The
Germans believed in two species ; one fierce and malevolent,
the other a gentle race, appearing like little old men, dressed

like the miners, and not much above two feet high ; these wander about the drifts and chambers of the works, seem perpetually employed, yet do nothing. Some seem to cut the ore, or fling what is cut into vessels, or turn the windlass, but never do any harm to the miners, except provoked ; as the sensible Agricola, in this point credulous, relates in his book, *de Animantibus Subterraneis.*"

Jamieson, under the word *Farefolkis*, writes :—" Besides the Fairies, which are more commonly the subject of popular tradition, it appears that our forefathers believed in the existence of a class of spirits under this name that wrought in the mines;" and again, quoting from a work dated 1658, the author of which says :—

" In northerne kingdomes there are great armies of devils that have their services which they perform with the inhabitants of these countries, but they are most frequent in rocks and *mines*, where they break, cleave, and make them hollow ; which also thrust in pitchers and buckets, and carefully fit wheels and screws, whereby they are drawn upwards; and they show themselves to the labourers, when they list, like phantoms and ghosts."

The preceding quotations from Pennant and Jamieson correspond with the Welsh miners' ideas of the *Coblynau,* or Knockers. There is a difficulty in tracing to their origin these opinions, but, on the whole, I am strongly inclined to say that they have come down to modern times from that remote period when cave-men existed as a distinct people.

But now let us hear what our Welsh miners have to say about the *Coblynau.* I have spoken to several miners on this subject, and, although they confessed that they had not themselves heard these good little people at work, still they believed in their existence, and could name mines in which they had been heard. I was told that they are generally heard at work in new mines, and that they lead the men to the ore by knocking in its direction, and when the lode is reached the knocking ceases.

But the following extracts from two letters written by Lewis Morris, a well-known and learned Welshman, fully express the current opinion of miners in Wales respecting Knockers. The first letter was written Oct. 14, 1754, and the latter is dated Dec. 4, 1754. They appear in Bingley's *North Wales*, vol. ii., pp. 269—272. Lewis Morris writes :—

"People who know very little of arts or sciences, or the powers of nature (which, in other words, are the powers of the author of nature), will laugh at us Cardiganshire miners, who maintain the existence of *Knockers* in mines, a kind of good natured impalpable people not to be seen, but heard, and who seem to us to work in the mines; that is to say, they are the types or forerunners of working in mines, as dreams are of some accidents, which happen to us. The barometer falls before rain, or storms. If we do not know the construction of it, we should call it a kind of dream that foretells rain ; but we know it is natural, and produced by natural means, comprehended by us. Now, how are we sure, or anybody sure, but that our dreams are produced by the same natural means ? There is some faint resemblance of this in the sense of hearing ; the bird is killed before we hear the report of the gun. However this is, I must speak well of the *Knockers*, for they have actually stood my good friends, whether they are aerial beings called spirits, or whether they are a people made of matter, not to be felt by our gross bodies, as air and fire and the like.

"Before the discovery of the *Esgair y Mwyn* mine, these little people, as we call them here, worked hard there day and night ; and there are abundance of honest, sober people, who have heard them, and some persons who have no

notion of them or of mines either; but after the discovery
of the great ore they were heard no more.

" When I began to work at Llwyn Llwyd, they worked so
fresh there for a considerable time that they frightened some
young workmen out of the work. This was when we were
driving levels, and before we had got any ore; but when
we came to the ore, they then gave over, and I heard
no more talk of them.

" Our old miners are no more concerned at hearing
them *blasting*, boring holes, landing *deads*, &c., than if
they were some of their own people; and a single miner
will stay in the work, in the dead of the night, without
any man near him, and never think of any fear or of any
harm they will do him. The miners have a notion that
the *Knockers* are of their own tribe and profession, and are
a harmless people who mean well. Three or four miners
together shall hear them sometimes, but if the miners stop
to take notice of them, the *Knockers* will also stop; but,
let the miners go on at their work, suppose it is *boring*, the
Knockers will at the same time go on as brisk as can be in
landing, *blasting*, or beating down the *loose*, and they are
always heard a little distance from them before they come
to the ore.

" These are odd assertions, but they are certainly facts,
though we cannot, and do not pretend to account for them.
We have now very good ore at *Llwyn Llwyd*, where the
Knockers were heard to work, but have now yielded up the
place, and are no more heard. Let who will laugh, we
have the greatest reason to rejoice, and thank the *Knockers*,
or rather God, who sends us these notices."

The second letter is as follows :—

"I have no time to answer your objection against
Knockers; I have a large treatise collected on that head, and

what Mr. Derham says is nothing to the purpose. If sounds
of voices, whispers, blasts, working, or pumping, can be
carried on a mile underground, they should always be heard
in the same place, and under the same advantages, and
not once in a month, a year, or two years. Just before the
discovery of ore last week, three men together in our work
at *Llwyn Llwyd* were ear-witnesses of *Knockers* pumping,
driving a wheelbarrow, &c.; but there is no pump in the
work, nor any mine within less than a mile of it, in which
there are pumps constantly going. If they were these
pumps that they had heard, why were they never heard
but that once in the space of a year? And why are they
not now heard? But the pumps make so little noise that
they cannot be heard in the other end of *Esgair y Mwyn*
mine when they are at work.

"We have a dumb and deaf tailor in this neighbourhood
who has a particular language of his own by signs, and by
practice I can understand him, and make him understand
me pretty well, and I am sure I could make him learn to
write, and be understood by letters very soon, for he can
distinguish men already by the letters of their names. Now
letters are marks to convey ideas, just after the same
manner as the motion of fingers, hands, eyes, &c. If this
man had really seen ore in the bottom of a sink of water in
a mine, and wanted to tell me how to come at it, he would
take two sticks like a pump, and would make the motions
of a pumper at the very sink where he knew the ore was, and
would make the motions of driving a wheelbarrow. And
what I should infer from thence would be that I ought to
take out the water and sink or drive in the place, and wheel
the stuff out. By parity of reasoning, the language of
Knockers, by imitating the sound of pumping, wheeling, &c.,
signifies that we should take out the water and drive there.

This is the opinion of all old miners, who pretend to understand the language of the *Knockers*. Our agent and manager, upon the strength of this notice, goes on and expects great things. You, and everybody that is not convinced of the being of *Knockers*, will laugh at these things, for they sound like dreams; so does every dark science. Can you make any illiterate man believe that it is possible to know the distance of two places by looking at them? Human knowledge is but of small extent, its bounds are within our view, we see nothing beyond these; the great universal creation contains powers, &c., that we cannot so much as guess at. May there not exist beings, and vast powers infinitely smaller than the particles of air, to whom air is as hard a body as the diamond is to us? Why not? There is neither great nor small, but by comparison. Our *Knockers* are some of these powers, the guardians of mines.

" You remember the story in Selden's Table-Talk of Sir Robert Cotton and others disputing about Moses's shoe. Lady Cotton came in and asked, 'Gentlemen, are you sure it *is* a shoe?' So the first thing is to convince mankind that there is a set of creatures, a degree or so finer than we are, to whom we have given the name of *Knockers* from the sounds we hear in our mines. This is to be done by a collection of their actions well attested, and that is what I have begun to do, and then let everyone judge for himself."

The preceding remarks, made by an intelligent and reliable person, conversant with mines, and apparently uninfluenced by superstition, are at least worthy of consideration. The writer of these interesting letters states positively that sounds were heard; whether his attempt to solve the cause of these noises is satisfactory, and conclusive, is open to doubt. We must believe the facts asserted, although dis-

agreeing with the solution of the difficulty connected with
the sounds. Miners in all parts of England, Scotland,
Wales, Germany, and other parts, believe in the existence
of *Knockers*, whatever these may be, and here, as far as I
am concerned, I leave the subject, with one remark only,
which is, that I have never heard it said that anyone in
Wales ever *saw* one of these *Knockers*. In this they differ
from Fairies, who, according to popular notions, have, time
and again, been seen by mortal eyes; but this must have
been when time was young.

The writer is aware that Mr. Sikes, in his *British Goblins*,
p. 28, gives an account of *Coblynau* or *Knockers* which he
affirms had been seen by some children who were playing in
a field in the parish of Bodfari, near Denbigh, and that they
were dancing like mad, and terribly frightened the children.
But in the autobiography of Dr. Edward Williams, already
referred to, p. 98, whence Mr. Sikes derived his information
of the Dwarfs of Cae Caled, they are called "*Beings*," and
not *Coblynau*.

Before concluding my remarks on Fairy Knockers I will
give one more quotation from Bingley, who sums up the
matter in the following words :—

"I am acquainted with the subject only from report, but
I can assure my readers that I found few people in Wales
that did not give full credence to it. The elucidation of
these extraordinary facts must be left to those persons who
have better opportunities of inquiring into them than I
have. I may be permitted to express a hope that the subject will not be neglected, and that those who reside in any
neighbourhood where the noises are heard will carefully
investigate their cause, and, if possible, give to the world a
more accurate account of them than the present. In the
year 1799 they were heard in some mines in the parish of

Llanvihangel Ysgeiviog, in Anglesea, where they continued, at intervals, for some weeks."

Bingley's North Wales, vol. ii., p. 275.

In conclusion, I may remark that in living miners' days, as already stated, Knockers have not been heard. Possibly Davy's Safety Lamp and good ventilation have been their destruction. Their existence was believed in when mining operations, such as now prevail, were unknown, and their origin is to be sought for among the dim traditions that many countries have of the existence of small cave men.

The Pwka, or Pwca.

Another imaginary being, closely allied to the Fairy family, was the *Pwka*. He seems to have possessed many of the mischievous qualities of Shakespeare's Puck, whom, also, he resembled in name, and it is said that the *Pwka*, in common with the *Brownie*, was a willing worker.

The Rev. Edmund Jones in his *Book of Apparitions* gives an account of one of these goblins, which visited the house of Job John Harry, who lived at a place called the Trwyn, and hence the visitor is called Pwka'r Trwyn, and many strange tales are related of this spirit. The writer of the *Apparitions* states that the spirit stayed in Job's house from some time before Christmas until Easter Wednesday. He writes :—" At first it came knocking at the door, chiefly by night, which it continued to do for a length of time, by which they were often deceived, by opening it. At last it spoke to one who opened the door, upon which they were much terrified, which being known, brought many of the neighbours to watch with the family. T. E. foolishly brought a gun with him to shoot the spirit, as he said, and sat in the corner. As Job was coming home that night the spirit met him, and told him that there was a man come to the house to shoot him, ' but,' said he, 'thou shalt see how I will beat him.' As soon as Job was come to the house stones were thrown at the man that brought the gun, from which he received severe blows. The company tried to defend him from the blows of the stones, which did strike him and no other person; but it was in vain, so that he was obliged to go home that night, though it was very late; he had a great way to go. When the spirit spoke, which was not very often, it was mostly out of the oven by the hearth's side. He would sometimes in the night make music with Harry Job's fiddle. One time he struck the cupboard with stones, the marks of which were to be seen, if they are not there still. Another time he gave Job a gentle stroke upon his toe, when he was going to bed, upon which Job said, 'Thou art curious in smiting,' to which the spirit answered, 'I can smite thee where I please.' They were at length grown fearless and bold to speak to it, and its speeches and actions were a recreation to them, seeing it was a familiar kind of spirit which did not hurt them, and informed them of some things which they did not know. One old man, more bold than wise, on hearing the spirit just by him, threatened to stick him with his knife, to which he answered, 'Thou fool, how can thou stick what thou cannot see with thine eyes.' The spirit told them that he came from Pwll-y-Gaseg, i.e., Mare's Pit, a place so called in the adjacent mountain, and that he knew them all before he came there. . . . On Easter Wednesday he left the house and took his farewell in these words:—'Dos yn iach, Job,' i.e., 'Farewell, Job,' to which Job said, 'Where goest thou?' He was answered, 'Where God pleases.' "

The Pwka was credited with maliciously leading benighted men astray. He would appear with a lantern or candle in hand, some little distance in front of the traveller, and without any exertion keep ahead of him, and leading him through rocky and dangerous places, would suddenly, with an ironical laugh blow out the candle, and disappear, and leave the man to his fate.

The following tale, taken from Croker's *Fairy Legends of Ireland*, vol. ii., pp. 231-3, well illustrates this mischievous trait in the character of the Pwka. The writer has seen the tale elsewhere, but as it differs only slightly from that recorded by Croker, he gives it in the words of this author. His words are as follows :—

"Cwm Pwcca, or the Pwcca's Valley, forms part of the deep and romantic glen of the Clydach, which, before the establishment of the iron works of Messrs. Frere and Powell, was one of the most secluded spots in Wales, and therefore well calculated for the haunt of goblins and fairies ; but the bustle of a manufactory has now in a great measure scared these beings away, and of late it is very rarely that any of its former inhabitants, the Pwccas, are seen. Such, however, is their attachment to their ancient haunt, that they have not entirely deserted it, as there was lately living near this valley a man who used to assert that he had seen one, and had a narrow escape of losing his life, through the maliciousness of the goblin. As he was one night returning home over the mountain from his work, he perceived at some distance before him a light, which seemed to proceed from a candle in a lantern, and upon looking more attentively, he saw what he took to be a human figure carrying it, which he concluded to be one of his neighbours likewise returning from his work. As he perceived that the figure was going the same way with himself, he quickened his pace in order that he might overtake him, and have the benefit of his light to descend the steep and rocky path which led into the valley ; but he rather wondered that such a short person as appeared to carry the lantern should be able to walk so fast. However, he re-doubled his exertions, determined to come up with him, and although he had some misgivings that he was not going along the usual track, yet he thought that the man with the lantern must know better than himself, and he followed the direction taken by him without further hesitation. Having, by dint of hard walking, overtaken him, he suddenly found himself on the brink of one of the tremendous precipices of Cwm Pwcca, down which another step would have carried him headlong into the roaring torrent beneath. And, to complete his consternation, at the very instant he stopped, the little fellow with the lantern made a spring right across the glen to the opposite side, and there, holding up the light above his head, turned round and uttered with all his might a loud and most malicious laugh, upon which he blew out his candle, and disappeared up the opposite hill."

This spirit is also said to have assisted men in their labours, and servant girls and servant men often had their arduous burdens lightened by his willing hands. But he punished those who offended him in a vindictive manner. The Pwka could hide himself in a jug of barm or in a ball of yarn, and when he left a place, it was for ever.

In the next chapter I will treat of another phase of legendary lore, which, although highly imaginative, seems to intimate that the people who transmitted these tales had some knowledge, though an exaggerated one, of a people and system which they supplanted.

FAIRY, OR MYTHIC ANIMALS.

From the Myddvai Legend it would appear that the Fairies possessed sheep, cattle, goats, and horses, and from other tales we see that they had dogs, &c. Their stock, therefore, was much like that of ordinary farmers in our days. But Fairy animals, like their owners, have, in the course of ages, been endowed with supernatural powers. In this chapter shall be given a short history of these mythical animals.

Cwn Annwn, or Dogs of the Abyss.

The words *Cwn Annwn* are variously translated as Dogs of Hell, Dogs of Elfinland. In some parts of Wales they are called *Cwn Wybir*, Dogs of the Sky, and in other places *Cwn Bendith y Mamau.* We have seen that "*Bendith y Mamau*" is a name given to the Fairies, and in this way these dogs become Fairy Dogs.

A description of these Fairy dogs is given in *Y Brython*, vol. iii., p. 22. Briefly stated it is as follows :—*Cwn Bendith y Mamau* were a pack of small hounds, headed by a large dog. Their howl was something terrible to listen to, and it foretold death. At their approach all other dogs ceased barking, and fled before them in terror, taking refuge in their kennels. The birds of the air stopped singing in the groves when they heard their cry, and even the owl was silent when they were near. The laugh of the young, and the talk at the fireside were hushed when the dreadful howl of these Hell hounds was heard, and pale and trembling with fear the inmates crowded together for mutual protection. And what was worse than all, these dogs often foretold a death in some particular family in the neighbourhood where they appeared, and should a member of this family be in a public-house, or other place of amusement, his fright would be so great that he could not move, believing that already had death seized upon some one in his house.

The Fairy dogs howled more at Cross-roads, and such like public places, than elsewhere. And woe betide any one who stood in their way, for they bit them, and were likely even to drag a man away with them, and their bite was often fatal. They collected together in huge numbers in the churchyard where the person whose death they announced was to be buried, and, howling around the place that was to be his grave, disappeared on that very spot, sinking there into the earth, and afterwards they were not to be seen.

A somewhat different description of *Cwn Annwn* is given in the *Cambro-Briton*, vol. i., p. 350. Here we are told that " these terrific animals are supposed to be devils under the semblance of hunting dogs . . . . and they are usually accompanied by fire in some form or other. Their appearance is supposed to indicate the death of some friend or relative of the person to whom they shew themselves. They have never been known to commit any mischief on the persons of either man or woman, goat, sheep, or cow, &c."

In Motley's *Tales of the Cymry*, p. 58, that author says: —" I have met with but a few old people who still cherished a belief in these infernal hounds which were supposed after death to hunt the souls of the wretched to their allotted place of torment."

It was, however, once firmly and generally believed, that these awful creatures could be heard of a wild stormy night in full cry pursuing the souls of the unbaptized and unshriven. Mr. Chapman, Dolfor, near Newtown, Montgomeryshire, writes to me thus :—" These mysterious animals are never seen, only heard. A whole pack were recently heard on the borders of Radnorshire and Montgomeryshire. They went from the Kerry hills towards the Llanbadarn road, and a funeral quickly followed the same route. The sound was similar to that made by a pack of hounds in full cry, but softer in tone."

The Rev. Edmund Jones, in his work entitled " An Account of Apparitions of Spirits in the county of Monmouth," says that, " The nearer these dogs are to a man, the less their voice is, and the farther the louder, and sometimes,

like the voice of a great hound, or like that of a blood hound,
a deep hollow voice." It is needless to say that this gentleman believed implicitly in the existence of *Cwn Annwn*,
and adduces instances of their appearance.

The following is one of his tales :—

" As Thomas Andrews was coming towards home one
night with some persons with him, he heard, as he thought,
the sound of hunting. He was afraid it was some person
hunting the sheep, so he hastened on to meet, and hinder
them ; he heard them coming towards him, though he saw
them not. When they came near him, their voices were
but small, but increasing as they went from him ; they went
down the steep towards the river *Ebwy*, dividing between
this parish and *Mynyddislwyn*, whereby he knew they
were what are called *Cwn wybir* (Sky dogs), but in the in-
ward part of Wales *Cwn Annwn* (Dogs of Hell). I have
heard say that these spiritual hunting-dogs have been heard
to pass by the eaves of several houses before the death of
someone in the family. Thomas Andrews was an honest,
religious man, and would not have told an untruth either
for fear or for favour."

The colour of these dogs is variously given, as white, with
red ears, and an old man informed Mr. Motley that their
colour was blood-red, and that they always were dripping
with gore, and that their eyes and teeth were of fire. This
person confessed that he had never seen these dogs, but
that he described them from what he had heard.—*Tales of the
Cymry*, p. 60. There is in *The Cambro-Briton*, vol. ii., p.
271, another and more natural description of *Cwn Annwn*.
It is there stated that Pwyll, prince of Dyved, went out to hunt,
and :—

" He sounded his horn and began to enter upon the chase,
following his dogs and separating from his companions.

And, as he was listening to the cry of his pack, he could
distinctly hear the cry of another pack, different from that
of his own, and which was coming in an opposite direction.
He could also discern an opening in the wood towards a level
plain; and as his pack was entering the skirt of the opening,
he perceived a stag before the other pack, and about the
middle of the glade the pack in the rear coming up and
throwing the stag on the ground; upon this he fixed his
attention on the colour of the pack without recollecting to
look at the stag; and, of all the hounds in the world he had
ever seen, he never saw any like them in colour. Their
colour was a shining clear white, with red ears; and the
whiteness of the dogs, and the redness of their ears, were
equally conspicuous."

We are informed that these dogs belonged to Arawn, or
the silver-tongued King of Annwn, of the lower or southern
regions. In this way these dogs are identified with the
creàtures treated of in this chapter. But their work was less
weird than soul-hunting.

A superstition akin to that attached to *Cwn Annwn*
prevails in many countries, as in Normandy and Bretagne.
In Devonshire, the Wish, or Wisked Hounds, were once
believed in, and certain places on Dartmoor were thought
to be their peculiar resort, and it was supposed that they
hunted on certain nights, one of which was always St.
John's Eve. These terrible creations of a cruel mind indicate a phase of faith antagonistic to, and therefore more
ancient than, Christianity.

With another quotation from *Tales of the Cymry* (p.
61-62), I will conclude my remarks:—

"In the north of Devon the spectral pack are called
Yesh hounds and Yell hounds. There is another legend,
evidently of Christian origin, which represents them in

incessant pursuit of a lost spirit. In the northern quarter
of the moor the Wish hounds, in pursuit of the spirit of a
man who had been well known in the country, entered a
cottage, the door of which had been incautiously left open,
and ran round the kitchen, but quietly, without their usual
cry. The Sunday after the same man appeared in church,
and the person whose house the dogs had entered, made
bold by the consecrated place in which they were, ventured
to ask why he had been with the Wish hounds. 'Why
should not my spirit wander,' he replied, 'as well as another
man's?' Another version represents the hounds as following the spirit of a beautiful woman, changed into the form
of a hare; and the reader will find a similar legend, with
some remarkable additions, in the Disquisitiones Magicæ
of the Jesuit Delrio, lib. vi., c. 2."

The preceding paragraph is from the pen of " R. J. K.," and
appears in the *Athenæum*, March 27, 1847, Art. Folk-lore.

The Fairy Cow.

There are many traditions afloat about a wonderful cow,
that supplied whole neighbourhoods with milk, which ceased
when wantonly wasted. In some parts of England this is
called the Dun Cow; in Shropshire she becomes also the
White Cow; in Wales she is, *Y Fuwch Frech*, or *Y Fuwch
Gyfeiliorn*. This mystic cow has found a home in many
places. One of these is the wild mountain land between
Llanfihangel Glyn Myfyr and a hamlet called Clawdd
Newydd about four miles from Ruthin. About midway
between these two places is a bridge called Pontpetrual, and
about half a mile from the bridge to the north is a small
mountain farm called *Cefn Bannog*, and near this farm, but
on the unenclosed mountain, are traces of primitive abodes,
and it was here that, tradition says, the *Fuwch Frech* had her
home. But I will now give the history of this strange cow as I
heard it from the mouth of Thomas Jones, Cefn Bannog.

P

Y Fuwch Frech.   The Freckled Cow.

In ages long gone by, my informant knew not how long
ago, a wonderful cow had her pasture land on the hill close
to the farm, called Cefn Bannog, after the mountain ridge
so named.   It would seem that the cow was carefully looked
after, as indicated by the names of places bearing her name.
The site of the cow house is still pointed out, and retains its
name, *Preseb y Fuwch Frech*—the Crib of the Freckled
Cow.   Close to this place are traces of a small enclosure
called *Gwal Erw y Fuwch Frech*, or the Freckled Cow's
Meadow.   There is what was once a track way leading from
the ruins of the cow house to a spring called *Ffynon y
Fuwch Frech,* or the Freckled Cow's Well, and it was, tradition
says, at this well that the cow quenched her thirst.
The well is about 150 yards from the cow house.   Then
there is the feeding ground of the cow called, *Waen Banawg,*
which is about half a mile from the cow house.   There are
traces of walls several feet thick in these places.   The spot
is a lonely one, but ferns and heather flourish luxuriantly
all about this ancient homestead.   It is also said that this
cow was the mother of the *Ychain Banawg,* or large-horned
oxen.   But now to proceed to the tradition that makes the
memory of this cow dear to the inhabitants of the Denbighshire moorland.

Old people have transmitted from generation to generation the following strange tale of the Freckled Cow.   Whenever any one was in want of milk they went to this cow,
taking with them a vessel into which they milked the cow,
and, however big this vessel was, they always departed with
the pail filled with rich milk, and it made no difference,
however often she was milked, she could never be milked dry.
This continued for a long time, and glad indeed the people
were to avail themselves of the inexhaustible supply of

new milk, freely given to them all.   At last a wicked hag,
filled with envy at the people's prosperity, determined to
milk the cow dry, and for this purpose she took a riddle
with her, and milked and milked the cow, until at last
she could get no more milk from her.   But, sad to say, the
cow immediately, upon this treatment, left the country, and
was never more seen.   Such is the local history of the
Freckled Cow.

Tradition further states that she went straight to a lake
four miles off, bellowing as she went, and that she was followed
by her two children the *Dau Eidion Banawg*, the two long-
horned oxen, to *Llyn dau ychain*, the Lake of the Two Oxen,
in the parish of Cerrig-y-drudion, and that she entered the
lake and the two long-horned oxen, bellowing horribly,
went, one on either side the lake, and with their mother
disappeared within its waters, and none were ever afterwards seen.

Notwithstanding that tradition buries these celebrated
cattle in this lake, I find in a book published by Dr. John
Williams, the father of the Rev. John Williams, M.A., Vicar
of Llanwddyn, in the year 1830, on the "Natural History
of Llanrwst," the following statement.   The author in page
17, when speaking of *Gwydir*, says :—

" In the middle court (which was once surrounded by the
house), there is a large bone, which appears to be the rib of
some species of whale, but according to the vulgar opinion,
it is the rib of the Dun Cow (*y Fuwch Frech*), killed by the
Earl of Warwick."

It may be stated that Llanrwst is not many miles distant
from Cerrig-y-drudion, and yet we have in these places
conflicting traditions, which I will not endeavour to reconcile.

The Shropshire tale of the Fairy Cow is much the same
as the preceding.   There she is known as *The White Cow of*

Mitchell's Fold. This place is situated on the Corndon Hill, a bare moorland in the extreme west of Shropshire. To this day there is to be seen there a stone circle known as Mitchell's Fold.

The story of the Shropshire Cow is this. There was a dire famine in those parts, and the people depended for support on a beautiful white cow, a Fairy cow, that gave milk to everybody, and it mattered not how many came, there was always enough for all, and it was to be so, so long as every one who came only took one pailful. The cow came night and morning to be milked, and it made no difference what size the vessel was that was brought by each person, for she always gave enough milk to fill it, and all the other pails. At last, there came an old witch to Mitchell's Fold, and in spite and malice she brought a riddle and milked the cow into it; she milked and milked, and at last she milked her dry, and after that the cow was never seen. Folk say she was turned into a stone.

I am indebted to Miss Burne's *Shropshire Folk-Lore* for the particulars above given.

A like tale is to be heard in Warwickshire, and also in Lancashire, near Preston, where the Dun cow gave freely her milk to all in time of drought, and disappeared on being subjected to the treatment of the Welsh and Shropshire cow.

Mr. Lloyd, Llanfihangel Glyn Myfyr, gave me a different tale of the *Dau ychain Banawg* to that already related. His story is as follows :—

The Legend of Llyn y ddau ychain.

The speckled cow had two calves, which, when they grew up, became strong oxen. In those days there was a wicked spirit that troubled Cerrig-y-drudion Church, and the people greatly feared this spirit, and everybody was afraid, even in the day-time, to pass the church, for there, day after day, they saw the evil one looking out of the church windows and grinning at them. They did not know what to do to get rid of this spirit, but at last they consulted a famous conjuror, who told them that no one could dislodge their enemy but the *Dau ychain Banawg*. They knew of the two long-horned cattle which fed on Waen Banawg. There, therefore, they went, and brought the powerful yoke to the church. After considerable difficulty they succeeded in dislodging the spirit, and in securing it to a sledge to which these oxen were yoked, and now struggling to get free, he was dragged along by the powerful oxen towards a lake on Hiraethog Mountain, but so ponderous was their load and so fearful was the spirit's contentions that the sledge ploughed the land between the church and the lake as they went along, leaving in the course that they took deep furrows, and when they came to the hill so terrible were the struggles of the oxen to get along that the marks of their hoofs were left in the rocks where they may still be seen. When at last they reached the lake the spirit would not yield, and therefore oxen, sledge, and spirit were driven into the lake, and thus was the country rid of the evil one, and hence the name of the lake—the Lake of the Two Oxen—for the oxen likewise perished in the lake.

The foregoing legend is evidently founded on the older and more obscure story of Hu Gardarn, or Hu the Mighty, who with his *Dau ychain Banawg* drew to land the *avanc* out of *Llyn Llion*, so that the lake burst out no more to deluge the earth. For, be it known, it was this *avanc* that had occasioned the flood. However, there is a rival claimant for the honour of having destroyed the *avanc*, whatever that might have been, for, in Hindu Mythology, Vishnu is credited with having slain the monster that had occasioned the Deluge.

This last bit of Folk-lore about Hu Gadarn, which is found in the *Triads*, shows how widespread, and how very ancient, Welsh tales are. Hu Gadarn is by some writers identified with Noah. He was endowed, it would seem, with all the qualities of the gods of the Greeks, Egyptians, and Orientals, and his name is applied by the Welsh poets of the middle ages to the Supreme Being.

Y *Fuwch Gyfeiliorn. The Stray Cow.*

The history of the Fairy Stray Cow appears in *Y Brython*, vol. iii., pp. 183-4. The writer of the story states that he obtained his materials from a Paper by the late Dr. Pugh, Penhelyg, Aberdovey. The article alluded to by Gwilym Droedddu, the writer of the account in the *Brython*, appeared in the *Archæologia Cambrensis* for 1853, pp. 201-5. The tale, as given by Dr. Pugh, is reproduced by Professor Rhys in his Welsh Fairy Tales, and it is much less embellished in English than in Welsh. I will quote as much of the Doctor's account as refers to the Stray Cow.

" A shrewd old hill farmer (Thomas Abergroes by name), well skilled in the folk-lore of the district, informed me that, in years gone by, though when, exactly, he was too young to remember, those dames (*Gwragedd Annwn*) were wont to make their appearance, arrayed in green, in the neighbourhood of Llyn Barfog, chiefly at eventide, accompanied by their kine and hounds, and that, on quiet summer nights in particular, these ban-hounds were often to be heard in full cry, pursuing their prey—the souls of doomed men dying without baptism and penance—along the upland township of Cefnrhosucha. Many a farmer had a sight of their comely, milk-white kine; many a swain had his soul turned to romance and poesy by a sudden vision of themselves in the guise of damsels arrayed in green, and radiant in beauty and grace; and many a sportsman had his path crossed by their white hounds of supernatural fleetness and comeliness, the *Cwn Annwn*; but never had any one been favoured with more than a passing view of either, till an old farmer residing at Dyssyrnant, in the adjoining valley of Dyffryn Gwyn, became at last the lucky captor of one of their milk-white kine. The acquaintance which the *Gwartheg y Llyn*, the kine of the lake, had formed with the farmer's cattle, like the loves of the angels for the daughters of men, became the means of capture; and the farmer was thereby enabled to add the mystic cow to his own herd, an event in all cases believed to be most conducive to the worldly prosperity of him who should make so fortunate an acquisition. Never was there such a cow, never were there such calves, never such milk and butter, or cheese; and the fame of the *Fuwch Gyfeiliorn*, the stray cow, was soon spread abroad through that central part of Wales known as the district of Rhwng y ddwy Afon, from the banks of the Mawddach to those of the Dofwy (Dovey)—from Aberdiswnwy to Abercorris. The farmer, from a small beginning, rapidly became, like Job, a man of substance, possessed of thriving herds of cattle—a very patriarch among the mountains. But, alas! wanting Job's restraining grace, his wealth made him proud, his pride made him forget his obligation to the elfin cow, and fearing she might soon become too old to be profitable, he fattened her for the butcher, and then even she did not fail to distinguish herself, for a more monstrously fat beast was never seen. At last the day of slaughter came—an eventful day in the annals of a mountain farm—the killing of a fat cow, and such a monster of obesity. No wonder all the neighbours were gathered together to see the sight. The old farmer looked upon the preparations in self-pleased importance; the butcher felt he was about no common feat of his craft,

and, baring his arm, he struck the blow—not now fatal, for
before even a hair had been injured, his arm was paralysed,
the knife dropped from his hand, and the whole company
was electrified by a piercing cry that awakened an echo in a
dozen hills, and made the welkin ring again; and lo and
behold! the whole assemblage saw a female figure, clad in
green, with uplifted arms, standing on one of the rocks
overhanging Llyn Barfog, and heard her calling with a voice
loud as thunder:—

'Dere di velen Einion,
Cyrn cyveiliorn—braith y Llyn,
A'r voel Dodin,
Codwch, dewch adre.

Come thou Einion's yellow one,
Stray horns—speckled one of the Lake,
And the hornless Dodin,
Arise, come home.

And no sooner were these words of power uttered, than
the original lake cow, and all her progeny to the third and
fourth generations, were in full flight towards the heights of
Llyn Barfog, as if pursued by the evil one. Self-interest
quickly roused the farmer, who followed in pursuit, till,
breathless and panting, he gained an eminence overlooking
the lake, but with no better success than to behold the
green-attired dame leisurely descending mid-lake, accompanied by the fugitive cows, and her calves formed in a
circle around her; they tossed their tails, she waved her
hands in scorn, as much as to say, 'You may catch us, my
friend, if you can,' as they disappeared beneath the dark
waters of the lake, leaving only the yellow water-lily to
mark the spot where they vanished, and to perpetuate the
memory of this strange event. Meanwhile, the farmer
looked with rueful countenance upon the spot where the
elfin herd disappeared, and had ample leisure to deplore

the effects of his greediness, as with them also departed the
prosperity which had hitherto attended him, and he became
impoverished to a degree below his original circumstances,
and in his altered circumstances few felt pity for one who, in
the noontide flow of prosperity, had shown himself so far
forgetful of favours received, as to purpose slaying his
benefactor." Thus ends Dr. Pugh's account of the Stray
Cow.

A tale very much like the preceding is recorded of a
Scotch farmer. It is to be found in vol. ii., pp. 45-6, of
Croker's *Fairy Legends of Ireland*, and is as follows :—

"A farmer who lived near a river had a cow which
regularly every year, on a certain day in May, left the
meadow and went slowly along the banks of the river till
she came opposite to a small island overgrown with bushes ;
she went into the water and waded or swam towards the
island, where she passed some time, and then returned to
her pasture. This continued for several years ; and every
year, at the usual season, she produced a calf which perfectly
resembled the elf bull. One afternoon, about Martinmas,
the farmer, when all the corn was got in and measured, was
sitting at his fireside, and the subject of the conversation
was, which of the cattle should be killed for Christmas.
He said : 'We'll have the cow; she is well fed, and has
rendered good services in ploughing, and filled the stalls
with fine oxen, now we will pick her old bones.' Scarcely
had he uttered these words when the cow with her young
ones rushed through the walls as if they had been made of
paper, went round the dunghill, bellowed at each of her
calves, and then drove them all before her, according to
their age, towards the river, where they got into the water,
reached the island, and vanished among the bushes. They
were never more heard of."

Q

⁓·ffyl y Dwfr.   The Water Horse.

The super...tion respecting the water-horse, in one form
or other, is common to the Celtic race.   He was supposed to
intimate by preternatural lights and noises the death of
those about to perish by water, and it was vulgarly believed
that he even assisted in drowning his victims.   The water-
horse was thought to be an evil spirit, who, assuming the
shape of a horse, tried to allure the unwary to mount him,
and then soaring into the clouds, or rushing over mountain,
and water, would suddenly vanish into air or mist, and pre-
cipitate his rider to destruction.

The Welsh water-horse resembles the Kelpie of the Scotch.
Jamieson, under the word *Kelpie,* in his *Scottish Dictionary,*
quoting from various authors, as is his custom, says :—

"This is described as an aquatic demon, who drowns not
only men but ships.   The ancient Northern nations believed
that he had the form of a horse ; and the same opinion is
still held by the vulgar in Iceland.

" Loccenius informs us that in Sweden the vulgar are still
afraid of his power, and that swimmers are on their guard
against his attacks ; being persuaded that he suffocates and
carries off those whom he catches under water." "Therefore,"
adds this writer, " it would seem that ferry-men warn those
who are crossing dangerous places in some rivers not so
much as to mention his name ; lest, as they say, they should
meet with a storm and be in danger of losing their lives.
Hence, doubtless, has this superstition originated ; that, in
these places formerly, during the time of paganism, those
who worshipped their sea-deity *Nekr,* did so, as it were
with a sacred silence, for the reason already given."

The Scotch Kelpie closely resembled the Irish Phoocah,
or Poocah, a mischievous being, who was particularly
dreaded on the night of All Hallow E'en, when it was

thought he had especial power; he delighted to assume the form of a black horse, and should any luckless wight bestride the fiendish steed, he was carried through brake and mire, over water and land at a bewildering pace. Woe-betide the timid rider, for the Poocah made short work of such an one, and soon made him kiss the ground. But to the bold fearless rider the Poocah submitted willingly, and became his obedient beast of burden.

The following quotation from the *Tales of the Cymry*, p. 151, which is itself an extract from Mrs. S. C. Hall's Ireland, graphically describes the Irish water fiend :—

"The great object of the Poocah seems to be to obtain a rider, and then he is in all his most malignant glory Headlong he dashes through briar and brake, through flood and fall, over mountain, valley, moor, and river indiscriminately; up and down precipice is alike to him, provided he gratifies the malevolence that seems to inspire him. He bounds and flies over and beyond them, gratified by the distress, and utterly reckless and ruthless of the cries, and danger, and suffering of the luckless wight who bestrides him."

Sometimes the Poocah assumed the form of a goat, an eagle, or of some other animal, and leaped upon the shoulders of the unwary traveller, and clung to him, however frantic were the exertions to get rid of the monster.

Allied to the water-horse were the horses upon which magicians in various lands were supposed to perform their aerial journeys.

It was believed in Wales that the clergy could, without danger, ride the water-horse, and the writer has heard a tale of a clergyman, who, when bestride one of these horses, had compassion on his parish clerk, who was trudging by his side, and permitted him to mount behind him, on condition that he should keep silence when upon the horse's back. For awhile the loquacious parish clerk said no word, but ere long the wondrous pace of the horse caused him to utter a pious ejaculation, and no sooner were the words uttered than he was thrown to the ground; his master kept his seat, and, on parting with the fallen parish official, shouted out, "Serve you right, why did you not keep your noisy tongue quiet?"

The weird legends and gloomy creations of the Celt assume a mild and frolicsome feature when interpreted by the Saxon mind. The malevolent Poocah becomes in England the fun-loving Puck, who delights in playing his pranks on village maidens, and who says:—

> I am that merry wanderer of the night;
> Jest to Oberon, and make him smile,
> When I a fat and bean-fed horse beguile,
> Neighing in likeness of a filly foal;
> And sometimes lurk I in a gossip's bowl,
> In very likeness of a roasted crab;
> And when she drinks against her lips I bob,
> And on her withered dew-lap pour the ale.
>
> *Midsummer Night's Dream*, Act I, Sc. I.

The *Ceffyl-y-Dwfr* was very different to Chaucer's wonderful brass horse, which could be ridden, without harm, by a sleeping rider:—

> This steed of brasse, and easilie and well
> Can in the space of a day naturél,
> This is to say, in foure and twenty houres,
> Where so ye liste, in drought or ellés showers,
> Baren youre bodie into everie place,
> In which your hearté willeth for to pace,
> Withouten wemme of you through foul or fair,
> Or if you liste to flee as high in th' aire
> As doth an eagle when him liste to soare,
> This same steed shall bear you evermore,
> Withouten harm, till ye be there you leste,

Though that ye sleepen on his back or reste ;
And turn againe with writhing of a pinne,
He that it wroughte he couldé many a gin,
He waited many a constellation,
Ere he had done this operation.

Chaucer's Squire's Tale, 137-152.

The rider of the magic horse was made acquainted with
the charm that secured its obedience, for otherwise he took
an aerial ride at his peril. This kind of invention is oriental,
but it is sufficiently like the Celtic in outline to indicate that
all figments of the kind had undoubtedly a common origin.

I have seen it somewhere stated, but where I cannot recall to mind, that the Water Horses did, in olden times,
sport, on the Welsh mountains, with the puny native ponies,
before they became a mixed breed.

It was believed that the initiated could conjure up the
River Horse by shaking a magic bridle over the pool wherein
it dwelt.

There is much curious information respecting this mythic
animal in the *Tales of the Cymry* and from this work I have
culled many thoughts.

The Torrent Spectre.

This spectre was supposed to be an old man, or malignant
spirit, who directed, and ruled over, the mountain torrents.
He delighted in devastating the lands. His appearance was
horrible to behold, and it was believed that in the midst of
the rushing stream his terrible form could be discerned apparently moving with the torrent, but in reality remaining
stationary. Now he would raise himself half out of the
water, and ascend like a mist half as high as the near mountain, and then he would dwindle down to the size of a man.
His laugh accorded with his savage visage, and his long hair
stood on end, and a mist always surrounded him.

Davies, in his *Mythology of the Druids*, says that believers
in this strange superstition are yet to be met with in

Glamorganshire. Davies was born in the parish of Llan-
vareth, Radnorshire, in 1756, and died January 1st, 1831.

Gwrach y Rhibyn, or Hag of the Mist.

Another supernatural being associated with water was the
Gwrach y Rhibyn. She was supposed to reside in the
dripping fog, but was seldom, if ever seen. It was believed
that her shriek foretold misfortune, if not death, to the
hearer, and some even thought that, in a shrill tenor, and
lengthened voice, she called the person shortly to die by name.

Yr Hen Chrwchwd, or The Old Humpbacked, a fiend in
the shape of an old woman, is thought to be identical with
this Gwrach y Rhibyn.

In Carmarthenshire the spirit of the mist is represented,
not as a shrivelled up old woman, but as a hoary headed old
man, who seats himself on the hill sides, just where the
clouds appear to touch them, and he is called *Y Brenhin
Llwyd,* or The Grey King. I know not what functions this
venerable personage, or king of the mist, performed, unless it
were, that he directed the mist's journey through the air.

Mermaids and Mermen.

It is said that these fabulous beings frequented the sea-
coasts of Wales to the great danger of the inhabitants. The
description of the Welsh mermaid was just as it is all over
the world; she is depicted as being above the waist a most
lovely young woman, whilst below she is like a fish with
fins and spreading tail. Both mermen and mermaids were
fond, it is said, of combing their long hair, and the siren-like
song of the latter was thought to be so seductive as to entice
men to destruction. It was believed that beautiful mermaids fell in love with comely young men and even induced
them to enter their abodes in the depth of the sea.

I heard the following tale, I believe in Carnarvonshire,
but I have no notes of it, and write from memory.

A man captured a mermaid, and took her home to his house, but she did nothing but beg and beg to be allowed to return to the sea, but notwithstanding her entreaties her captor kept her safe enough in a room, and fastened the door so that she could not escape.   She lingered several days, pitifully beseeching the man to release her, and then she died.   But ever after that event a curse seemed to rest upon the man, for he went from bad to worse, and died miserably poor.

It was always considered most unlucky to do anything unkind to these beings. Fear acted as a powerful incentive, in days of old, to generous conduct.   For it was formerly believed that vengeance ever overtook the cruel.

An Isle of Man legend, related by Waldron, in his account of the Isle of Man, and reproduced by Croker, vol. i., p. 56, states, that some persons captured a mermaid, and carried her to a house and treated her tenderly, but she refused meat and drink, neither would she speak, when addressed, though they knew these creatures could speak.   Seeing that she began to look ill, and fearing some great calamity would befall the island if she died, they opened the door, after three days, and she glided swiftly to the sea side.   Her keeper followed at a distance and saw her plunge into the sea, where she was met by a great number of her own species, one of whom asked her what she had seen among those on land, to which she answered, "Nothing, but that they are so ignorant as to throw away the very water they boil their eggs in."

STORIES OF SATAN, GHOSTS, &c.

Although Max Müller, in *Chips from a German Workshop*, vol. ii., p. 238, states that "The Aryan nations had no Devil," this certainly cannot at present be affirmed of that branch of the Celtic race which inhabits Wales. In the Principality the Devil occupies a prominent position in the foreground of Welsh Folk-Lore. He is, however, generally depicted as inferior in cunning and intellect to a bright, witted Welshman, and when worsted in a contest he acknowledges his inferiority by disappearing in a ball or wheel of fire. Men, it was supposed, could sell themselves to the Evil One for a term of years, but they easily managed to elude the fulfilment of the contract, for there was usually a loop-hole by which they escaped from the clutches of the stupid Devil. For instance, a man disposes of his soul for riches, pleasures, and supernatural knowledge and power, which he is to enjoy for a long number of years, and in the contract it is stipulated that the agreement holds good if the man is buried either *in* or *outside* the church. To all appearance the victim is irretrievably lost, but no, after enjoying all the fruits of his contract, he cheats the Devil of his due, by being buried *in* or *under* the church walls.

In many tales Satan is made to act a part detrimental to his own interests; thus Sabbath breakers, card players, and those who practised divination, have been frightened almost to death by the appearance of the Devil, and there and then, being terrified by the horrible aspect of the enemy, they commenced a new life. This thought comes out strongly in *Y Bardd Cwsg*. The poet introduces one of the fallen angels as appearing to act the part given to the Devil, in the play of Faust, when it was being performed at Shrewsbury, and this appearance drove the frequenters of the theatre from their pleasures to their prayers. His words are:—

" Dyma walch, ail i hwnw yn y Mwythig, y dydd arall, ar ganol interlud Doctor Ffaustus; a rhai . . . . pan oeddynt brysuraf, ymddangosodd y diawl ei hun i chwareu ei bart ac wrth hynny gyrodd bawb o'i bleser i'w weddiau."

In English this is :—" Here's a fine fellow, second to that at Shrewsbury, who the other day, when the interlude of Doctor Faustus was being acted, in the middle of the play, all being busily engaged, the devil himself appeared to take his own part, and by so doing, drove everyone from pleasure to prayer."

The absurd conduct of the Evil Spirit on this occasion is held up to ridicule by the poet, but the idea, which is an old one, that demons were, by a superior power, obliged to frustrate their own designs, does not seem to have been taken into consideration by him. He depicts the Devil as a strange mixture of stupidity and remorseless animosity. But this, undoubtedly, was the then general opinion. The bard revels in harrowing descriptions of the tortures of the damned in Gehenna—the abode of the Arch-fiend and his angels. This portion of his work was in part the offspring of his own fervid imagination; but in part it might have been suggested to him by what had been written already on the subject; and from the people amongst whom he lived he could have, and did derive, materials for these descriptions. In any case he did not outrage, by any of his horrible depictions of Pandemonium, the sentiments of his fellow countrymen, and his delineation of Satan was in full accord with the popular opinion of his days. The bard did not create but gave utterance to the fleeting thoughts which then prevailed respecting the Devil. Indeed there does not seem to be in Wales any distinct attributes ascribed to Satan, which are not also believed to be his specialities in other countries. His personal appearance is the same in most places. He is described as being black, with horns, and hoofs and tail, he breathes fire and brimstone, and he is accompanied with the clank of chains. Such was the uncouth form which Satan was supposed to

R

assume, and such was the picture drawn of him formerly
in Wales.

There is a strong family likeness in this description
between Satan and *Pan*, who belongs to Greek and Egyptian
mythology. Pan had two small horns on his head, his nose
was flat, and his legs, thighs, tail, and feet were those of a
goat. His face is described as ruddy, and he is said to
have possessed many qualities which are also ascribed to
Satan. His votaries were not encumbered with an exalted
code of morality.

The *Fauni*, certain deities of Italy, are also represented
as having the legs, feet, and ears of goats, and the rest of
the body human, and the *Satyri* of the Greeks are also
described as having the feet and legs of goats, with short
horns on the head, and the whole body covered with thick
hair. These demigods revelled in riot and lasciviousness.
The satyrs attended upon Bacchus, and made themselves
conspicuous in his orgies. The Romans called their satyrs
Fauni, Panes, and Sylvani.

It is difficult to ascertain whether the Celt of Britain
obtained through the Romans their gross notions of the
material body of Satan, or whether it was in later times
that they became possessed of this idea. It may well have
been that the Fauni, and other disreputable deities of the
conquerors of the world, on the introduction of Christianity
were looked upon as demons, and their forms consequently
became fit representations of the Spirit of Evil, from whom
they differed little, if any, in general attributes. In this way
god after god would be removed from their pedestals in
the world's pantheon, and would be relegated to the regions
occupied by the great enemy of all that is pure, noble, and
good in mankind. Thus the god of one age would become
the devil of the succeeding age, retaining, nevertheless,

by a cruel irony, the same form and qualities in his changed position that he had in his exalted state.

It is by some such reasoning as the preceding that we can account for the striking personal resemblance between the Satan of mediæval and later times and the mythical deities already mentioned.

Reference has been made to the rustic belief that from his mouth Satan emits fire and brimstone, and here again we observe traces of classic lore. The fabulous monsters, Typhæus, or Typhon, and Chimæra, are probably in this matter his prototypes. It is said that real flames of devouring fire darted from the mouth and eyes of Typhon, and that he uttered horrible yells, like the shrieks of different animals, and Chimæra is described as continually vomiting flames.

Just as the gods of old could assume different shapes, so could Satan. The tales which follow show that he could change himself at will into the form of a lovely woman, a mouse, a pig, a black dog, a cock, a fish, a headless horse, and into other animals or monstrous beings. But the form which, it is said, he usually assumed to enable him to escape when discovered in his intrigues was a ball or hoop of fire.

The first series of tales which I shall relate depict Satan as taking a part in the pastimes of the people.

Satan Playing Cards.

A good many years ago I travelled from Pentrevoelas to Yspytty in company with Mr. Lloyd, the then vicar of the latter parish, who, when crossing over a bridge that spanned a foaming mountain torrent, called my attention to the spot, and related to me the following tale connected with the place :—

A man was returning home late one night from a

friend's house, where he had spent the evening in card
playing, and as he was walking along he was joined by a
gentleman, whose conversation was very interesting. At
last they commenced talking about card playing, and the
stranger invited the countryman to try his skill with him,
but as it was late, and the man wanted to go home, he
declined, but when they were on the bridge his companion
again pressed him to have a game on the parapet, and proceeded to take out of his pocket a pack of cards, and at
once commenced dealing them out ; consequently, the man
could not now refuse to comply with the request. With
varying success game after game was played, but ultimately
the stranger proved himself the more skilful player. Just
at this juncture a card fell into the water, and in their
excitement both players looked over the bridge after it, and
the countryman saw to his horror that his opponent's head,
reflected in the water, had on it *two horns*. He immediately
turned round to have a careful look at his companion ; he,
however, did not see him, but in his place was a *ball of fire*,
which flashed away from his sight.

I must say that when I looked over the bridge I came to
the conclusion that nothing could have been reflected in
the water, for it was a rushing foaming torrent, with no
single placid spot upon its surface.

Another version of the preceding tale I obtained from the
Rev. Owen Jones. In this instance *the cloven foot* and not
the *horned head* was detected. The scene of this tale is
laid in the parish of Rhuddlan near Rhyl.

Satan Playing Cards at a Merry Meeting.

It was formerly a general custom in Wales for young
lads and lasses to meet and spend a pleasant evening
together in various farmhouses. Many kinds of amusements,
such as dancing, singing, and card playing, were resorted to,

to while away the time. The Rev. Owen Jones informed
me that once upon a time a merry party met at Hênafon
near Rhuddlan, and when the fun was at its height a
gentleman came to the farm, and joined heartily in all the
merriment. By and by, card playing was introduced, and
the stranger played better than any present. At last a card
fell to the ground, and the party who picked it up discovered that the clever player had a cloven foot. In his
fright the man screamed out, and immediately the Evil One
—for he it was that had joined the party—transformed
himself into a wheel of fire, and disappeared up the chimney.

For the next tale I am also indebted to my friend the
Rev. Owen Jones. The story appears in a Welsh MS. in
his possession, which he kindly lent me. I will, first of all,
give the tale in the vernacular, and then I will, for the
benefit of my English readers, supply an English translation.

Satan Playing Cards on Rhyd-y-Cae Bridge, Pentrevoelas.

"Gwas yn y Gilar a phen campwr ei oes am chwareu
cardiau oedd Robert Llwyd Hari. Ond wrth fyn'd adre' o
Rhydlydan, wedi bod yn chwareu yn nhy Modryb Ann y
Green, ar ben y lôn groes, daeth boneddwr i'w gyfarfod, ag
aeth yn ymgom rhyngddynt. Gofynodd y boneddwr iddo
chware' *match* o gardiau gydag e. 'Nid oes genyf gardiau,'
meddai Bob. 'Oes, y mae genyt ddau ddec yn dy bocet,'
meddai'r boneddwr. Ag fe gytunwyd i chware' *match* ar
Bont Rhyd-y-Cae, gan ei bod yn oleu lleuad braf. Bu y
boneddwr yn daer iawn arno dd'od i Blas Iolyn, y caent
ddigon o oleu yno, er nad oedd neb yn byw yno ar y pryd.
Ond nacaodd yn lân. Aed ati o ddifrif ar y bont, R. Ll. yn
curo bob tro. Ond syrthiodd cardyn dros y bont, ac fe
edrychodd yntau i lawr. Beth welai ond carnau ceffyl gan
y boneddwr. Tyngodd ar y Mawredd na chwareuai ddim
chwaneg; ar hyn fe aeth ei bartner yn olwyn o dân rhyngddo

a Phlas Iolyn, ac aeth yntau adre' i'r Gilar." The English
of the tale is as follows :—

Robert Llwyd Hari was a servant in Gilar farm, and the
champion card player of his day. When going home from
Rhydlydan, after a game of cards in Aunty Ann's house,
called the Green, he was met at the end of the cross-lane by
a gentleman, who entered into conversation with him. The
gentleman asked him to have a game of cards, " I have no
cards," answered Bob, " Yes you have, you have two packs
in your pocket," answered the gentleman. They settled to
play a game on the bridge of Rhyd-y-Cae, as it was a
beautiful moonlight night. The gentleman was very pressing that they should go to Plas Iolyn, because they would
find there, he said, plenty of light, although no one was then
living at the place. But Bob positively refused to go there.
They commenced the game in downright good earnest on the
bridge, R. Ll. winning every game. But a card fell over the
bridge into the water, and Bob looked over, and saw that
the gentleman had hoofs like a horse. He swore by the
Great Being that he would not play any longer, and on this
his partner turned himself into *a wheel of fire*, and departed
bowling towards Plas Iolyn, and Bob went home to Gilar.

Satan Snatching a Man up into the Air.

It would appear that poor Bob was doomed to a sad end.
His last exploit is thus given :—

" Wrth fyned adre o chware cardia, ar Bont Maesgwyn
gwelai Robert Llwyd Hari gylch crwn o dân; bu agos
iddo droi yn ol, cymerodd galon eilwaith gan gofio fod
ganddo Feibl yn ei boced, ac i ffordd ag e rhyngddo a'r tân,
a phan oedd yn passio fe'i cipiwyd i fyny i'r awyr gan
y Gwr Drwg, ond gallodd ddyweyd rhiw air wrth y D——,
gollyngodd ef i lawr nes ydoedd yn disgyn yn farw mewn
llyn a elwir Llyn Hari."

Which in English is as follows :—

When going home from playing cards, on Maesgwyn Bridge Robert Llwyd Hari saw a hoop of fire ; he was half inclined to turn back, but took heart, remembering that he had a Bible in his pocket. So on he went, and when passing the fire he was snatched up into the air by the Bad Man, but he was able to utter a certain word to the D——, he was dropped down, and fell dead into a lake called Harry's Lake.

Many tales, varying slightly from the preceding three stories, are still extant in Wales, but these given are so typical of all the rest that it is unnecessary to record more.

It may be remarked that card playing was looked upon in the last century—and the feeling has not by any means disappeared in our days—as a deadly sin, and consequently a work pleasing to the Evil One, but it appears singular that the aid of Satan himself should have been invoked to put down a practice calculated to further his own interests. The incongruity of such a proceeding did not apparently enter into the minds of those who gave currency to these unequal contests. But in the tales we detect the existence of a tradition that Satan formerly joined in the pastimes of the people, and, if for card playing some other game were substituted, such as dancing, we should have a reproduction of those fabulous times, when satyrs and demigods and other prototypes of Satan are said to have been upon familiar terms with mortals, and joined in their sports.

The reader will have noticed that the poor man who lost his life in the Lake thought himself safe because he had a Bible in his pocket. This shows that the Bible was looked upon as a talisman. But in this instance its efficacy was only partial. I shall have more to say on this subject in another part of this work.

Satan in the preceding tales, and others, which shall by
and by be related, is represented as transforming himself
into a ball, or wheel of fire—into fire, the emblem of an
old religion, a religion which has its votaries in certain
parts of the world even in this century, and which, at
one period in the history of the human race, was wide-
spread. It is very suggestive that Satan should be spoken
of as assuming the form of the Fire God, when his person-
ality is detected, and the hint, conveyed by this transformation, would imply that he was himself the Fire God.

Having made these few comments on the preceding
tales, I will now record a few stories in which Satan is made
to take a role similar to that ascribed to him in the card-
playing stories.

In the following tales Satan's aid is invoked to bring
about a reformation in the observance of the Sabbath day.

Satan frightening a Man for gathering Nuts on Sunday.

The following tale was related to me by the Rev. W. E.
Jones, rector of Bylchau, near Denbigh :—

Richard. Roberts, Coederaill, Bylchau, when a young man,
worked in Flintshire, and instead of going to a place of
worship on Sunday he got into the habit of wandering
about the fields on that day. One fine autumn Sunday he
determined to go a-nutting. He came to a wood where
nuts were plentiful, and in a short time he filled his pockets
with nuts, but perceiving a bush loaded with nuts, he put
out his hand to draw the branch to him, when he observed
a hairy hand stretching towards the same branch. As soon
as he saw this hand he was terribly frightened, and without
turning round to see anything further of it, he took to his
heels, and never afterwards did he venture to go a-nutting
on Sunday.

Richard Roberts told the tale to Mr. Jones, his Rector,

who tried to convince Roberts that a monkey was in the bush, but he affirmed that Satan had come to him.

Satan taking possession of a man who fished on Sunday.

The following tale is in its main features still current in Cynwyd, a village about two miles from Corwen. The first reference to the story that I am acquainted with appeared in an essay sent in to a local Eisteddfod in 1863. The story is thus related in this essay :—

" About half a mile from Cynwyd is the ' Mill Waterfall,' beneath which there is a deep linn or whirlpool, where a man, who was fishing there on Sunday, once found an enormous fish. ' I will catch him, though the D——l take me,' said the presumptuous man. The fish went under the fall, the man followed him, and was never afterwards seen." Such is the tale, but it is, or was believed, that Satan had changed himself into a fish, and by allurement got the man into his power and carried him bodily to the nethermost regions.

Satan appearing in many forms to a Man who
Travelled on Sunday.

I received the following tale from my deceased friend, the Rev. J. L. Davies, late Rector of Llangynog, near Llanfyllin, Montgomeryshire, and he obtained it from William Davies, the man who figures in the story.

As a preface to the tale, it should be stated that it was usual, some years ago, for Welsh labourers to proceed to the harvest in England, which was earlier there than in Wales, and after that was finished, they hastened homewards to be in time for their own harvest. These migratory Welsh harvestmen are not altogether extinct in our days, but about forty years ago they were much more common than they are at present. Then respectable farmers' sons with sickles on their backs, and well filled wallets over their shoulders, went in companies to the early English Lowlands to hire themselves as harvest labourers. My tale now commences :—

William Davies, Penrhiw, near Aberystwyth, went to England for the harvest, and after having worked there about three weeks, he returned home alone, with all possible haste, as he knew that his father-in-law's fields were by this time ripe for the sickle. He, however, failed to accomplish the journey before Sunday; but he determined to travel on Sunday, and thus reach home on Sunday night to be ready to commence reaping on Monday morning. His conscience, though, would not allow him to be at rest, but he endeavoured to silence its twittings by saying to himself that he had with him no clothes to go to a place of worship. He stealthily, therefore, walked on, feeling very guilty every step he took, and dreading to meet anyone going to chapel or church. By Sunday evening he had reached the hill overlooking Llanfihangel Creuddyn, where he was known, so he determined not to enter the village until after the people had gone to their respective places of worship; he therefore sat down on the hill side and contemplated the scene below. He saw the people leave their houses for the house of God, he heard their songs of praise, and now he thinks he could venture to descend and pass through the village unobserved. Luckily no one saw him going through the village, and now he has entered a barley field, and although still uneasy in mind, he feels somewhat reassured, and steps on quickly. He had not proceeded far in the barley field before he found himself surrounded by a large number of small pigs. He was not much struck by this, though he thought it strange that so many pigs should be allowed to wander about on the Sabbath day. The pigs, however, came up to him, stared at him, grunted, and scampered away. Before he had traversed the barley field he saw approaching him an innumerable number of mice, and these, too, surrounded him, only, however, to stare at him, and then to disappear. By this Davies began to be frightened, and he was almost sorry that he had broken the Sabbath day by travelling with his pack on his back instead of keeping the day holy. He was not now very far from home, and this thought gave him courage and on he went. He had not proceeded any great distance from the spot where the mice had appeared when he saw a large greyhound walking before him on the pathway. He anxiously watched the dog, but suddenly it vanished out of his sight. By this the poor man was thoroughly frightened, and many and truly sincere were his regrets that he had broken the Sabbath ; but on he went. He passed through the village of Llanilar without any further fright. He had now gone about three miles from Llanfihangel along the road that goes to Aberystwyth, and he had begun to dispel the fear that had seized him, but to his horror he saw something approach him that made his hair stand on end. He could not at first make it out, but he soon clearly saw that it was a horse that was madly dashing towards him. He had only just time to step on to the ditch, when, horrible to relate, a headless white horse rushed past him. His limbs shook and the perspiration stood out like beads on his forehead. This terrible spectre he saw when close to Tan'rallt, but he dared not turn into the house, as he was travelling on Sunday, so on he went again, and heartily did he wish himself at home. In fear and dread he proceeded on his journey towards Penrhiw. The most direct way from Tan'rallt to Penrhiw was a pathway through the fields, and Davies took this pathway, and now he was in sight of his home, and he hastened towards the boundary fence between Tan'rallt and Penrhiw. He knew that there was a gap in the hedge that he could get through, and for this gap he aimed ; he reached it, but further progress was impossible, for in the gap was a lady lying at full length, and immovable, and stopping up the gap entirely. Poor Davies was now more thoroughly terrified than ever. He sprang aside, he screamed, and then he fainted right away. As soon as he recovered consciousness, he, on his knees, and in a loud supplicating voice, prayed for pardon. His mother and father-in-law heard him, and the mother knew the voice and said, "It is my Will ; some mishap has overtaken him." They went to him and found he was so weak that he could not move, and they were obliged to carry him home, where he recounted to them his marvellous experience.

My clerical friend, who was intimately acquainted with William Davies, had many conversations with him about his Sunday journey, and he argued the matter with him, and tried to persuade him that he had seen nothing, but that it was his imagination working on a nervous temperament that had created all his fantasies. He however failed to convince him, for Davies affirmed that it was no hallucination, but that what he had seen that Sunday was a punishment for his having broken the Fourth Commandment. It need hardly be added that Davies ever afterwards was a strict observer of the Day of Rest.

The following tale, taken from *A Relation of Apparitions*, &c., by the Rev. Edmund Jones, inculcates the same lesson as that taught by the previous tales. I will give the tale a title.

The Evil Spirit appearing to a Man who frequented
Alehouses on Sunday.

Jones writes as follows :—" W. J. was once a Sabbath-breaker at *Risca* village, where he frequently used to play and visit the alehouses on the Sabbath day, and there stay till late at night. On returning homeward he heard something walking behind him, and turning to see what it was he could see the likeness of a man walking by his side ; he could not see his face, and was afraid to look much at it, fearing it was an evil spirit, as it really was, therefore he did not wish it good night. This dreadful dangerous apparition generally walked by the left side of him. It afterwards appeared like a great mastiff dog, which terrified him so much that he knew not where he was. After it had gone about half a mile, it transformed itself into a great fire, as large as a small field, and resembled the noise which a fire makes in burning gorse."

This vision seems to have had the desired effect on W. J. for we are told that he *was once* a Sabbath breaker, the inference being, that he was not one when the Rev. Edmund Jones wrote the above narrative.

Tales of this kind could be multiplied to almost any extent, but more need not be given. The one idea that runs through them all is that Satan has appeared, and may appear again, to Sabbath breakers, and therefore those who wish to avoid coming in contact with him should keep the Sabbath day holy.

Satan Outwitted.

In the preceding tales the Evil One is depicted as an agent in the destruction of his own kingdom. He thus shows his obtuseness, or his subordination to a higher power. In the story that follows, he is outwitted by a Welshman. Many variants of this tale are found in many countries. It is evident from this and like stories, that it was believed the Spirit of Evil could easily be circumvented by an intelligent human being.

The tale is taken from *Y Brython*, vol. v., p. 192. I when a lad often heard the story related, and the scene is laid in Trefeglwys, Montgomeryshire, a parish only a few miles distant from the place where I spent my childhood. The writer in *Y Brython*, speaking of *Ffinant*, says that this farm is about a mile from Trefeglwys, on the north side of the road leading to Newtown. He then proceeds as follows:—

"Mae hen draddodiad tra anhygoel yn perthyn i'r lle hwn. Dywedir fod hen ysgubor yn sefyll yn yr ochr ddeheuol i'r brif-ffordd. Un boreu Sul, pan ydoedd y meistr yn cychwyn i'r Eglwys, dywedodd wrth un o'i weision am gadw y brain oddi ar y maes lle yr oedd gwenith wedi ei hau, yn yr hwn y safai yr hen ysgubor. Y gwas, trwy ryw foddion, a gasglodd y brain oll iddi, a chauodd arnynt; yna dilynodd ei feistr i'r Eglwys; yntau, wrth ei weled yno, a ddechreuodd ei geryddu yn llym. Y meistr, wedi clywed y fath newydd, a hwyliodd ei gamrau tua'i gartref; ac efe a'u cafodd, er ei syndod, fel y crybwyllwyd; ac fe ddywedir fod yr ysgubor yn orlawn o honynt. Gelwir y maes hwn yn *Crow-barn*, neu Ysgubor y brain, hyd heddyw. Dywedir mai enw y gwas oedd Dafydd Hiraddug, ac iddo werthu ei hun i'r diafol, ac oherwydd hyny, ei fod yn alluog i gyflawni gweithredoedd anhygoel yn yr oes hon. Pa fodd bynag, dywedir i Dafydd fod yn gyfrwysach na'r hen sarff y tro hwn, yn ol y cytundeb fu rhyngddynt. Yr ammod oedd, fod i'r diafol gael meddiant hollol o Ddafydd, os dygid ei gorff dros erchwyn gwely, neu trwy ddrws, neu os cleddid ef mewn mynwent, neu mewn Eglwys, Yr oedd Dafydd wedi gorchymyn, pan y byddai farw, am gymmeryd yr afu a'r ysgyfaint o'i gorff, a'i daflu i ben tomen, a dal sylw pa un ai cigfran ai colomen fyddai yn ennill buddugoliaeth am danynt; os cigfran, am gymmeryd ei gorff allan trwy waelod ac nid dros erchwyn y gwely; a thrwy bared ac nid trwy

ddrws, a'i gladdu, nid mewn mynwent na llan, ond o dan
fur yr Eglwys; ac i'r diafol pan ddeallodd hyn lefaru, gan
ddywedyd:—

> Dafydd Hiraddug ei ryw,
> *Ffals* yn farw, *ffals* yn fyw."

The tale in English is as follows:—

There is an incredible tradition connected with this place
Ffinant, Trefeglwys. It is said that an old barn stands on
the right hand side of the highway. One Sunday morning,
as the master was starting to church, he told one of the
servants to keep the crows from a field that had been sown
with wheat, in which field the old barn stood. The servant,
through some means, collected all the crows into the barn,
and shut the door on them. He then followed his master
to the Church, who, when he saw the servant there, began
to reprove him sharply. But the master, when he heard the
strange news, turned his steps homewards, and found to his
amazement that the tale was true, and it is said that the
barn was filled with crows. This barn, ever afterwards was
called *Crow-barn*, a name it still retains.

It is said that the servant's name was Dafydd Hiraddug,
and that he had sold himself to the devil, and that consequently, he was able to perform feats, which in this age are
considered incredible. However, it is said that Dafydd was
on this occasion more subtle than the old serpent, even
according to the agreement which was between them. The
contract was, that the devil was to have complete possession
of Dafydd if his corpse were taken over the side of the bed,
or through a door, or if buried in a churchyard, or inside a
church. Dafydd had commanded, that on his death, the
liver and lights were to be taken out of his body and thrown
on the dunghill, and notice was to be taken whether a
raven or a dove got possession of them; if a raven, then his
body was to be taken away by the foot, and not by the side

of the bed, and through the wall, and not through the door, and he was to be buried, not in the churchyard nor in the Church, but under the Church walls. And the devil, when he saw that by these arrangements he had been duped cried, saying :—

> Dafydd Hiraddug, badly bred,
> False when living, and false when dead.

Such is the tale, I now come to another series of Folk-Lore stories, which seem to imply that in ancient days rival religions savagely contended for the supremacy, and in these tales also Satan occupies a prominent position.

Satan and Churches.

The traditional stories that are still extant respecting the determined opposition to the erection of certain churches in particular spots, and the removal of the materials during the night to some other site, where ultimately the new edifice was obliged to be erected, and the many stories of haunted churches, where evil spirits had made a lodgment, and could not for ages be ousted, are evidences of the antagonism of rival forms of paganism, or of the opposition of an ancient religion to the new and intruding Christian Faith.

Brash in his *Ogam Inscribed Stones*, p. 109, speaking of Irish Churches, says :—

"It is well known that many of our early churches were erected on sites professedly pagan."

The most ancient churches in Wales have circular or ovoidal churchyards—a form essentially Celtic—and it may well be that these sacred spots were dedicated to religious purposes in pagan times, and were appropriated by the early Christians,—not, perhaps, without opposition on the part of the adherents of the old faith—and consecrated to the use of the Christian religion. In these churchyards were often to be found holy, or sacred wells, and many of them still exist, and modes of divination were practised at these wells, which have come down to our days, and which must have originated in pre-Christian or pagan times.

It is highly probable that the older faith would for a while exist concurrently with the new, and mutual contempt and annoyance on the part of the supporters of the respective beliefs would as naturally follow in those times as in any succeeding age, but this fact should be emphasised—that the modes of warfare would correspond with the civilized or uncivilized state of the opponents. This remark is general in its application, and applies to races conquered by the Celts in Britain, quite as much as to races who conquered the Celt, and there are not wanting certain indications that the tales associated with Satan belong to a period long anterior to the introduction of Christianity. Certain classes of these tales undoubtedly refer to the antagonism of beliefs more ancient than the Christian faith, and they indicate the measures taken by one party to suppress the other. Thus we see it related that the Evil Spirit is forcibly ejected from churches, and dragged to the river, and there a tragedy occurs. In other words a horrible murder is committed on the representative of the defeated religion. The very fact that he loses his life in a river— in water—in an object of wide spread worship—is not without its significance.

We have seen in the legend of the Evil Spirit in Cerrig-y-drudion Church, p. 133,—that it was ejected, after a severe struggle, from the sacred building—that it was dragged to the lake, where it lost its life, by two *Ychain Banawg*—that they, and it, perished together in the lake.— Now these *Ychain Banawg* or long-horned oxen, huge in size and strong of limb, are traditional, if not fabulous animals, and this one incident in the legend is enough to

T

prove its great antiquity. Undoubtedly it dates from remote pre-Christian times, and yet the tale is associated with modern ideas, and modes of expression. It has come down to us along the tide of time, and has received its colouring from the ages it has passed through. Yet on the very surface of this ancient legend we perceive it written that in days of old there was severe antagonism between rival forms of pagan faith, and the manner in which the weaker,—and perhaps the more ancient—is overcome, is made clear. The instrument used is brute force, and the vanquished party is *drowned* or, in the euphonius language of the tales, *is laid.*

There are many stories of spirits that have been cast out of churches, still extant in Wales, and one of the most famous of these is that of Llanfor Church, near Bala. It resembles that of Cerrig-y-drudion. I have succeeded in obtaining several versions of this legend. I am indebted for the first to Mr. R. Roberts, Clocaenog, a native of Bala.

The Ejectment of the Evil Spirit from Llanfor Church.

Mr. Roberts states that his grandmother, born in 1744, had only traditions of this spirit. He was said to have worn a three-cocked hat, and appeared as a gentleman, and whilst divine service was performed he stood up in the church. But at night the church was lit up by his presence, and the staves between the railings of the gallery were set in motion, by him, like so many spindles, although they were fast in their sockets. He is not reported to have harmed any one, neither did he commit any damage in the church. It is said, he had been seen taking a walk to the top of *Moel-y-llan,* and although harmless he was a great terror to the neighbourhood, and but few would venture to enter the church alone. Mr. Roberts was told that on a certain occasion a vestry was held in a public house, that stood on the north side of the church, not a vestige of which now remains, but no one would go to the church for the parish books. The landlady had the courage to go but no sooner had she crossed the threshold than the Evil Spirit blew the light out; she got a light again, but this also was blown out. Instead of returning for another light, she went straight to the coffer in the dark, and brought the books to the house, and that without any molestation.

Mr. Roberts states that as the Spirit of darkness became more and more troublesome, it was determined to have him removed, and two gentlemen skilled in divination were called *to offer him to Llyn-y-Geulan-Goch.* These men were procured and they entered the church in the afternoon and held a conversation with the Spirit, and in the end told him that they would call at such an hour of the night to remove him to his rest. But they were not punctual and when they entered they found him intractable, however, he was compelled to submit, and was driven out of the church in the form of a cock, and carried behind his vanquisher on horseback, and thrown into *Llyn-y-Geulan-Goch.*

According to tradition the horse made the journey from the church to the pool by two leaps. The distance was two fields' breadth.

On their arrival at the river side, a terrible struggle ensued, the Fiend would not submit to be imprisoned, and he made a most determined attempt to drag his captors into the water. He, however, by and by, agreed to enter his prison on the condition that they would lie on their faces towards the ground when he entered the river, this they did, and the Spirit with a splash jumped into the water.

Mr. Roberts further states, that there was a tradition in those parts, that the horse which carried the Devil to the river left the impression of his hoof in a stone by the river side, but Mr. Roberts assures me that he could never discover this stone, nor did he know of any one who had seen it.

The case of the imprisoned Spirit was not hopeless—tradition says he was to remain in the pool only until he counted all the sand in it. It would almost appear that he had accomplished his task, for Mr. Roberts says that he had heard that his father's eldest brother whilst driving his team in the dead of night through Llanfor village saw two pigs walking behind the waggon. He thought nothing of this, and began to apply his whip to them, but to no purpose, for they followed him to *Llyn-y-Geulan-Goch*, and then disappeared.

There was in these latter times some dispute as to the Spirit being still in the pool. This, however, has been settled in the affirmative. A wise man, in company with others, proceeded to the river, and threw a stone with writing on it into the pool, but nothing came of it, and he then affirmed there was no spirit there. This the people would not, believe, so he threw another stone into the water, and now the river boiled up and foamed. " Yes," said the sceptic, " he is there, and there he will remain for a long time."

Such is Mr. Roberts's account.

Llyn-y-Geulan-Goch is a pool in the river Dee, about a quarter of a mile from Llanfor village.

For the purpose of shewing how variously tales are nárrated, I will give another version of this haunted church, which was taken down by me from the mouth of an aged woman, a native of the village, whose life had been spent among her own people, and who at present lives in a little cottage on the road side between Llanfor Rectory and Bala. Her name is Ann Hughes, she firmly believes the story, but she could not tell how long ago the spirit was driven out of the church, though she thought it was in her grandfather's days. Her tale was as follows :—

The Evil Spirit was heard but not seen by the people, and he was in the habit of coming down the pathway leading from Rhiwlas to the church, making a great noise, as if dragging after him chains, or wheeling a wheelbarrow, and he went straight into the church, and there he stayed all night lighting up the church and making a great noise, as though engaged in manual labour. There was then a pathway leading to a row of houses situated in the church yard on the north side, and the people who occupied those cottages dared not leave them the live-long night, in fact the whole village avoided that, and every other path in the neighourhood of the church, whilst the Spirit was in the church, and every one could see when he was there. At last the disturbance was so great that the parson and another man determined to lay the Spirit, and therefore one night they walked three times round the church, and then went into it, and by and by three men were seen emerging from the church and they walked into the public house through the door that opened into the church yard and they went together into the little parlour. The parson had already given instructions that no one was to come to them on any account, nor even to try to get a glimpse of them; but there was a man in the house who went to the keyhole of the parlour and, looking into the room, saw distinctly three men sitting round the table. No sooner, however, had he done so than the parson came out and said if anyone looked through the keyhole again their plans would be frustrated. This put a stop to all further inquisitiveness, and their deliberations were not again interrupted.

Ann Hughes could not tell me what plan was adopted to get rid of the Evil Spirit, but she knew this much, that he was laid in *Llyn-y-Geulan-Goch,* and that he was to remain there until a lighted candle, which was hidden somewhere in the church, when the Spirit was overcome, should go out. Often and again had she searched for this taper, but failed to discover it, but she supposes it is still burning somewhere, for the Evil One has not yet escaped from the pool.

There is a version of the ejectment of Llanfor Spirit given in *Y Gordofigion*, p. 106, which is somewhat as follows :—

Llanfor Spirit troubled the neighbourhood of Bala, but he was particularly objectionable and annoying to the inhabitants of Llanfor, for he had taken possession of their Church. At last, the people were determined to get rid of him altogether, but they must procure a mare for this purpose, which they did. A man riding on the mare entered the Church with a friend, to exorcise the Spirit. Ere long this man emerged from the Church with the Devil seated behind him on the pillion. An old woman who saw them cried out, "Duw anwyl! Mochyn yn yr Eglwys"—"Good God! A pig in the Church." On hearing these words the pig became exceedingly fierce, because the silence had been broken, and because God's name had been used, and in his anger he snatched up both the man and the mare, and threw them right over the Church to the other side, and there is a mark to this day on a grave stone of the horse's hoof on the spot where she lit. But the Spirit's anger was all in vain, for he was carried by the mare to the river, and laid in *Llyn-y-Geulan-Goch*, but so much did the poor animal perspire whilst carrying him, that, although the distance was only a quarter of a mile, she lost all her hair.

Tales very much like the preceding are related of many churches in Wales. The details differ, but in general outlines they are alike. I will give one other story of this kind.

An Evil Spirit in Llandysilio Church, Montgomeryshire.

The history of this Spirit's proceedings is given in *Bye-*

Gones, Vol. ii, p. 179, and the writer's fictitious name is *Gypt.*

" This church," says *Gypt,* " was terribly troubled by a Spirit in times gone by, so I was informed by a person who took me over the church, and, being curious to hear the story, my guide related the following :—

" To such extremes had things come that it was resolved to send for a well known and expert person to lay the Spirit. But the Spirit nearly overcame the expert, and the fight continued hard and fast for a long time. The ghost layer came out often for fresh air and beer, and then was plainly seen, from his bared arms and the perspiration running down his face, that there was a terrible conflict going on within the church. At last success crowned the effort, and the Spirit, not unlike a large fly, was put into a bottle and thrown into a deep pool in the River Verniew, where it remains to this day, and the church was troubled no more."

Gypt adds :—" As a proof of the truth of the story, my informant showed me the beams which were cracked at the time the Spirit troubled the church."

In these tales we have a few facts common to them all. An Evil Spirit troubles the people, and makes his home nightly in the church, which he illuminates. His presence there becomes obnoxious, and ultimately, either by force or trickery, he is ejected, and loses his life, or at least he is deposited by his captors in a lake, or pool of water, and then peace and quietness ensue.

There is a good deal that is human about these stories when stripped of the marvellous, which surrounds them, and it is not unreasonable to ask whether they had, or had not, a foundation in fact, or whether they were solely the creations of an imaginative people. It is not, at least, improbable that these ghostly stories had, in long distant pre-historic times, their origin in fact, and that they have reached our days with glosses received from the intervening ages.

They seem to imply that, in ancient times, there was deadly antagonism between one form of Pagan worship and another, and, although it is but dimly hinted, it would appear that fire was the emblem or the god of one party, and water the god of the other; and that the water worshippers prevailed and destroyed the image, or *laid* the priest, of the vanquished deity in a pool, and took possession of his sacred enclosures.

It was commonly believed, within the last hundred years or so, that Evil Spirits at certain times of the year, such as St John's Eve, and May Day Eve, and All Hallows' Eve, were let loose, and that on these nights they held high revelry in churches. This is but another and more modern phase of the preceding stories. This superstitious belief was common to Scotland, and everyone who has read Burns has heard of Alloway Kirk, and of the " unco sight " which met *Tam o' Shanter's* eye there, who, looking into the haunted kirk, saw witches, Evil Spirits, and Old Nick himself. Thus sings the poet :—

> There sat auld Nick, in shape o' beast ;
> A towzie tyke, black, grim, and large,
> To gi'e them music was his charge.

But in Wales it was believed that a Spirit—an evil one—certainly not an Angel of Light, revealed, to the inquisitive, coming events, provided they went to the church porch on *Nos G'lan Geua'*, or All-Hallows' Eve, and waited there until midnight, when they would hear the Spirit announce the death roll for the coming year. Should, however, no voice be heard, it was a sign that no death would occur within the twelve succeeding months. A couple of tales shall suffice as illustrative of this superstition.

A Spirit in Ab rhafesp Church announcing the death of a person on Nos G'lan Geua.'

Mr. Breeze, late governor of the Union House at Caersws, told me that he had heard of a person going to Aberhafesp Church porch, on All-Hallows' Eve, to ascertain whether there would be a death in that parish in the coming year.

A couple of men, one of whom, I believe, Mr. Breeze said was his relative, went to the church porch before twelve o'clock at night, and sat there a length of time without hearing any sound in the church ; but about the midnight hour, one of the men distinctly heard the name of his companion uttered by a voice within the church. He was greatly terrified, and, addressing his friend, he found that he had fallen asleep, and that, therefore, fortunately he had not heard the ominous voice. Awaking his companion, he said—" Let's go away, it's no use waiting here any longer."

In the course of a few weeks, there was a funeral from the opposite parish of Penstrowed, and the departed was to be buried in Aberhafesp Church yard. The River Severn runs between these two parishes, and there is no bridge nearer than that which spans the river at Caersws, and to take the funeral that way would mean a journey of more than five miles. It was determined, therefore, to ford the river opposite Aberhafesp Church. The person who had fallen asleep in the porch volunteered to carry the coffin over the river, and it was placed on the saddle in front of this person, who, to save it from falling, was obliged to grasp it with both arms ; and, as the deceased had died of an infectious fever, the coffin bearer was stricken, and within a week he too was a dead man, and he was the first parishioner, as foretold by the Spirit, who died in the parish of Aberhafesp that year.

U

According to Croker, in *Fairy Legends of Ireland*, vol. II., p. 288, the Irish at Easter, Whitsuntide, and Christmas, after decorating the graves of their ancestors :—" Also listen at the churchdoor in the dark, when they sometimes fancy they hear the names called over in church of those who are destined shortly to join their lost relatives in the tomb."

It is not difficult to multiply instances of Spirits speaking in churches, for legendary stories of this kind were attached to, or were related of, many churches in Wales. One further tale therefore, shall suffice.

A Spirit in Llangerniew Church, Denbighshire.

There was a tradition in this parish that on All-Hallows' Eve a Spirit announced from the altar the names of those who were doomed to die in the coming year. The Spirit was locally called *Angelystor*. Those who were anxious to know whether they or their neighbours had a longer time to live stood underneath the east window on that eve, and anxiously listened for the dreaded 'revelation. It is related of a tailor, who was reckoned a wit, and affected disbelief in the Spirit story, that he announced his intention to prove the thing a myth, and so, one *Nos G'lan Geua'*, Shon Robert, as he was called, proceeded to the church just before midnight, and, to his horror, he heard his own name— "Shon ap Robert," uttered by the Spirit. "Hold, hold !" said the tailor, "I am not quite ready !" But, ready or not ready, it made no difference to the messenger of death, for that year the tailor died.

According to rustic opinion, demons were, from sinister motives, much given to frequenting churches still it was thought that as the Priest entered the sacred building by the south door these Spirits were obliged to make their exit through the north door, which was called in consequence he Devil's Door ; and this door was opened, and left open awhile, to enable these Evil Spirits to escape from the church, before divine service commenced. In agreement with this notion, the north side of church yards was designated the Domain of Demons, and, by association of ideas, no one formerly was buried in this side, but in our days the north part of the church yard—where the space in the other parts has already been occupied—is used for interments, and the north doors in most old churches have been built up.

Formerly, at baptisms, the north church door was, in Wales, left open, and that too for the same reason that it was opened before the hours of prayer. But these superstitions have departed, as intimated by the blocking up of north church doors.

Satan and Bell Ringing.

Durand, according to Bourne, in his *Antiquities of the Common People*, ed. 1725, p. 17, was of opinion that Devils were much afraid of bells, and fled away at the sound of them. Formerly, in all parts of Wales, the passing bell was tolled for the dying. This is a very ancient custom, being alluded to by the Venerable Bede—

> When the bell begins to toll,
> Lord, have mercy on the soul.

A small hand bell was also rung by the parish clerk as he preceded the funeral procession, and the church bell was tolled before, at, and after the burial. I do not know whether this was done because the people, entertaining Durand's opinion, wished to save the souls and bodies of their departed friends from Satan. Reference is often made to small handbells in parish terriers, and they are enumerated in those documents with other church property. Thus, in Llanfair Dyffryn Clwyd terrier, 1729, among the articles mentioned as belonging to the church is a small bell :—

"A little bell to be rung before the corps."

In Rhuddlan terrier, 1791, we find :—

"One small bell, and another small corps bell."

I may say that there is hardly a terrier belonging to a Church in North Wales which does not mention this portable handbell. Although the modern reason given for their use at funerals was, that all impediments might be removed from the roads before the funeral procession arrived, still it is probable that the custom at one time meant something more than this. The custom does not at present exist.

Giraldus Cambrensis thus alludes to these handbells :—

"I must not omit that the portable bells . . . . were held in great reverence by the people and clergy both in Ireland, Scotland, and Wales; insomuch that they had greater regard for oaths sworn on these than on the gospels."
—Bohn's Edition, p. 146.

As it was thought that the Passing Bell was originally intended to drive away the Evil Spirit hovering about in readiness to seize the soul of the deceased, so it might have been thought that the tolling of these handbells at funerals kept the Great Enemy away from the body about to be consigned to consecrated ground. But from a couple of lines quoted by Bourne, p. 14, from Spelman, in which all the ancient offices of bells seem to be included, it does not appear that this opinion was then current. The lines are :—

Laudo Deum verum, Plebem voco, congrego Clerum,
Defunctos ploro, pestem fugo, Festa decoro.
I praise the true God, call the people, convene the Clergy,
Lament the dead, dispel pestilence, grace Festivals.

There is nothing in these lines corroborative of Durand's opinion, but as I do not know the age of the lines I cannot controvert his opinion, but if it was believed that the tolling of a bell could drive away pestilence, well can it be understood that its sound could be credited with being inimical to Evil Spirits, and that it sent them away to other places to seek for rest.

It certainly was an opinion, according to Croker, entertained in Ireland and elsewhere, that the dwarfs or fairies, were driven away from places by the ringing of the bells of churches, and Croker in his *Fairy Legends of Ireland,* vol. ii., p. 106, states that Thiele collected traditions according to which the Troldes leave the country on the ringing of bells, and remain away.   Thus these mythic beings are confounded with Satan; indeed Croker remarks (vol. i., p. 46) "The notion of fairies, dwarfs, brownies, &c., being excluded from salvation, and of their having formed part of the crew that fell with Satan, seems to be pretty general all over Europe."   He instances Ireland, Denmark, and Spain.

Bells certainly were objects of great superstition.   In Dyer's *English Folk-Lore,* p. 264, it is stated that—Wynkin de Worde tells us that bells are rung during thunder storms, to the end that fiends and wicked Spirits should be abashed and flee and cease the moving of the tempest.

Croker also remarks in vol. ii., p. 140, of the above-named work:—"The belief in fairies and Spirits prevailed over all Europe long before the introduction of Christianity.   The teachers of the new faith endeavoured to abolish the deeply-rooted heathenish ideas and customs of the people, by representing them as sinful and connected with the Devil." In this way the Devil inherited many attributes that once belonged to the Fairies, and these beings were spoken of as Evil Spirits, Fiends, or Devils.

I now come to another kind of Welsh Folk-Lore associated with fairies, Evil Spirits, or some mysterious power, that is the removal of churches from one site to another.   The agency employed varies, but the work of the day disappeared in the night, and the materials were found, it is said, the next morning, on the spot where the church was to be erected.

Mysterious Removal of Churches.

I. LLANLLECHID CHURCH.

There was a tradition extant in the parish of Llanllechid, near Bangor, Carnarvonshire, that it was intended to build a church in a field called Cae'r Capel, not far from Plasuchaf Farm, but it was found the next morning that the labours of the previous day had been destroyed, and that the materials had been transported in the night to the site of the present church. The workmen, however, carried them all back again, and resumed their labours at Cae'r Capel, but in vain, for the next day they found their work undone, and the wood, stones, &c., in the place where they had found them when their work was first tampered with. Seeing that it was useless fighting against a superior power, they desisted, and erected the building on the spot indicated by the destroyers of their labours.

I asked the aged, what or who it was that had carried away the materials : some said it was done by Spirits, others by Fairies, but I could obtain no definite information on the point. However, they all agreed that the present site was more convenient for the parishioners than the old one.

Many legends of this kind are current in Wales. They are all much alike in general outline. A few only therefore shall be mentioned.

II. CORWEN CHURCH.

In Thomas's *History of the Diocese of St. Asaph*, p. 687, the legend connected with the erection of the present church is given as follows :—" The legend of its (Corwen Church) original foundation states that all attempts to build the church in any other spot than where stood the

Carreg y Big yn y fach rewlyd,' i.e., 'The pointed stone in the icy nook,' were frustrated by the influence of certain adverse powers."

No agency is mentioned in this narrative. When questioned on such a matter, the aged, of forty years ago, would shake their heads in an ominous kind of manner, and remain silent, as if it were wrong on their part to allude to the affair. Others, more bold, would surmise that it was the work of a Spirit, or of the Fairies. By and by I shall give Mr. A. N. Palmer's solution of the mystery.

III. Capel- Garmon Church.

A legend much like the preceding is current respecting Capel Garmon Church. I will give the story in the words of my friend, the Rev. Owen Jones, Pentrevoelas, who writes to me thus:—

"The tradition is that Capel Garmon Church was to have been built on the side of the mountain just above the present village, near the Well now called Ffynnon Armon, but the materials carried there in the daytime were in a mysterious manner conveyed by night to the present site of the church."

IV. Llanfair Dyffryn Clwyd.

For the following legend, I am indebted to Mr. R. Prys Jones, who resided for several years in the parish of Llanfair Dyffryn Clwyd. In answer to a letter from me respecting mysterious removal of churches, Mr. Jones writes as follows:—

" We have the same tradition in connection with a place not very far from Llanfair village : It was first intended to erect Llanfair Church on the spot where Jesus Chapel now stands, or very near to it. Tradition ascribes the failure of erecting the structure to a phantom in the shape of *a sow's head*, destroying in the night what had been built during the day. The farm house erected on the land is still called *Llanbenwch*"—Llan-pen-hwch, i.e., the *Llan, or church, of the Sow's Head.*

In this tale the agent is a sow, and Mr. Gomme in the *Antiquary*, vol. iii. p. 9, records a like story of Winwick Parish Church, Lancashire. He states that the founder had destined a different site for this church, "but after progress had been made at the original foundation, at night time, 'a pig' was seen running hastily to the site of the new church, crying or screaming aloud 'We-ee-wick, we-ee-wick, we-ee-wick.' Then taking up a stone in his mouth he carried it to the spot sanctified by the death of St. Oswald, and thus succeeded in removing all the stones which had been laid by the builders."

V. LLANFIHANGEL GENEU'R GLYN.

The traveller who has gone to Aberystwyth by the Cambrian Line has, most probably, noticed on the left hand side, shortly after he has left Borth, a small church, with a churchyard that enters a wood to the west of the church, the grave stones being seen among the trees. There is in connection with this church a legend much like those already given. I am indebted to the Rev. J. Felix, vicar of Gilcen, near Mold, for the following account of the transaction.

"It was intended to build Llanfihangel Church at a place called Glanfread, or Glanfread-fawr, which at present is a respectable farm house, and the work was actually commenced on that spot, but the portion built during the day was pulled down each night, till at last a Spirit spoke in these words:—

Llanfihangel Geneu'r Glyn,
Glanfread-fawr gaiff fod fan hyn.

Llanfihangel Geneu'r Glyn,
Glanfread-fawr shall stand herein,"

Intimating that the church was to be built at Geneu'r Glyn, and that Glanfreadfawr farm house was to occupy the place where they were then endeavouring to build the church. The prophecy, or warning, was attended to, and the church erection abandoned, but the work was carried out at Geneu'r Glyn, in accordance with the Spirit's direction, and the church was built in its present position.

VI. Wrexham Church.

The following extract is from Mr. A. Neobard Palmer's excellent *History of the Parish Church of Wrexham*, p. 6:—
" There is a curious local tradition, which, *as I understand it*, points distinctly to a re-erection of one of the earlier churches on a site different from that on which the church preceding it had stood."

" According to the tradition just mentioned, which was collected and first published by the late Mr. Hugh Davies, the attempt to build the church on another spot (at Bryn-y-ffynnon as 't is said), was constantly frustrated, that which was set up during the day being plucked down in the night. At last, one night when the work wrought on the day before was being watched, the wardens saw it thrown suddenly down, and heard a voice proceeding from a Spirit hovering above them which cried ever ' Bryn-y-grog !' ' Bryn-y-grog !' Now the site of the present church was at that time called ' Bryn-ŷ-grog ' (Hill of the Cross), and it was at once concluded that this was the spot on which the church should be built. The occupier of this spot, how-ever, was exceedingly unwilling to part with the inheritance of his forefathers, and could only be induced to do so when the story which has just been related was told to him, and other land given him instead. The church was then founded at ' Bryn-y-grog,' where the progress of the work suffered no interruption, and where the Church of Wrexham still stands."

Mr. Palmer, having remarked that there is a striking resemblance between all the traditions of churches removed mysteriously, proceeds to solve the difficulty, in these words :—

" The conclusions which occurred to me were, that these stories contain a record, imaginative and exaggerated, of real incidents connected with the history of the churches to which each of them belongs, and that they are *in most cases* reminiscences of *an older church which once actually stood on another site.* The destroying powers of which they all speak were probably human agents, working in the interest of those who were concerned in the transference of the site of the church about to be re-built ; while the stories, as a whole, were apparently concocted and circulated with the intention of overbearing the opposition which the proposed transference raised—an opposition due to the inconvenience of the site proposed, to sacred associations connected with the older site, or to the unwillingness of the occupier to surrender the spot selected."

This is, as everything Mr. Palmer writes, pertinent, and it is a reasonable solution, but whether it can be made to apply to *all* cases is somewhat doubtful. Perhaps we have not sufficient data to arrive at a correct explanation of this kind of myth. The objection was to the *place* selected and not to the *building* about to be erected on that spot ; and the *agents* engaged in the destruction of the proposed edifice differ in different places ; and in many instances, where these traditions exist, the land around, as regards agricultural uses, was equally useful, or equally useless, and often the distance between the two sites is not great, and the land in our days, at least, and presumably in former, belonged to the same proprietor—if indeed it had a proprietor at all. We must, therefore, I think, look

outside the occupier of the land for objections to the
surrender of the spot first selected as the site of the new
church.

Mr. Gomme, in an able article in the *Antiquary*, vol. iii.,
p. 8—13, on "Some traditions and superstitions connected
with buildings," gives many typical examples of buildings
removed by unseen agencies, and, from the fact that these
stories are found in England, Scotland, and other parts, he
rightly infers that they had a common origin, and that
they take us back to primitive times of British history.
The cause of the removal of the stones in those early times,
or first stage of their history, is simply described as
invisible agency, witches, fairies; in the second stage of
these myths, the supernatural agency becomes more clearly
defined, thus :—*doves, a pig, a cat, a fish, a bull*, do the
work of demolishing the buildings, and Mr. Gomme remarks
with reference to these animals:—" Now here we have some
glimmer of light thrown upon the subject—the introduction
of animal life leads to the subject of animal sacrifice." I
will not follow Mr. Gomme in this part of his dissertation,
but I will remark that the agencies he mentions as belonging
to the first stage are identical in Wales, England, and
Scotland, and we have an example of the second stage in
Wales, in the traditions of Llanfair Dyffryn Clwyd, and
of Llangar Church, near Corwen.

VII. Llangar Church.

"The tradition is that Llangar Church was to have been
built near the spot where the Cynwyd Bridge crosses the
Dee. Indeed, we are told that the masons set to work, but
all the stones they laid in the day were gone during the
night none knew whither. The builders were warned,
supernaturally, that they must seek a spot where on hunting
a 'Carw Gwyn' (white stag) would be started. They did

so, and Llangar Church is the result. From this cricum-
stance the church was called Llan-garw-gwyn, and from
this name the transition to Llangar is easy."—*Gossiping
Guide to Wales*, p. 128.

I find in a document written by the Rural Dean for the
guidance of the Bishop of St. Asaph, in 1729, that the stag
was started in a thicket where the Church of Llangar now
stands. "And (as the tradition is) the boundaries of the
parish on all sides were settled for 'em by this poor deer,
where he was forc'd to run for his life, there lye their
bounds.   He at last fell, and the place where he was
killed is to this day called *Moel y Lladdfa*, or the *Hill of
Slaughter*."

VIII. St. David's Church, Denbigh.

There is a tradition connected with Old St. David's
Church, Denbigh, recorded in Gee's *Guide to Denbigh*, that
the building could not be completed, because whatever
portion was finished in the day time was pulled down and
carried to another place at night by some invisible hand,
o supernatural power.

The party who malignantly frustates the builders' designs
is in several instances said to have been the Devil. "We
find," says Mr. William Crossing, in the *Antiquary*, vol. iv.,
p. 34, "that the Church of Plymton St. Mary, has connected with it the legend so frequently attached to
ecclesiastical buildings, of the removal by *the Enemy of
Mankind* of the building materials by night, from the spot
chosen for its erection to another at some distance."

And again, Mr A.N.Palmer, quoting in the *Antiquary*, vol.
iv., p. 34, what was said at the meeting of the British
Association, in 1878, by Mr. Peckover, respecting the
detached Tower of the Church of West Walton, near
Wisbech, Norfolk, writes:—"During the early days of that

Church the Fenmen were very wicked, and the *Evil Spirit* hired a number of people to carry the tower away."

Mr. W. S. Lach-Szyrma, in the *Antiquary*, vol. iii., p. 188, writes :—"Legends of *the Enemy of Mankind* and some old buildings are numerous enough—e. g., it is said that as the masons built up the towers of Towednack Church, near St. Ives, the *Devil* knocked the stones down, hence its dwarfed dimensions."

The preceding stories justify me in relegating this kind of myth to the same class as those in which spirits are driven from churches and *laid* in a neighbouring pool ; and perhaps in these latter, as in the former, is dimly seen traces of the antagonism, in remote times, between peoples holding different religious beliefs, and the steps taken by one party to seize and appropriate the sacred spots of the other.

Apparitions of the Devil.

To accomplish his nefarious designs the Evil Spirit assumed forms calculated to attain his object. The following lines from Allan Cunningham's *Traditional Tales*, p. 9, aptly describe his transformations :—

> Soon he shed
> His hellish slough, and many a subtle wile
> Was his to seem a heavenly spirit to man,
> First, he a hermit, sore subdued in flesh,
> O'er a cold cruse of water and a crust,
> Poured out meet prayers abundant. Then he changed
> Into a maid when she first dreams of man,
> And from beneath two silken eyelids sent,
> The sidelong light of two such wondrous eyes,
> That all the saints grew sinners. . . . .
> Then a professor of God's word he seemed,
> And o'er a multitude of upturned eyes
> Showered blessed dews, and made the pitchy path,
> Down which howl damnéd Spirits, seem the bright
> Thrice hallowed way to Heaven ; yet grimly through

> The glorious veil of those seducing shapes,
> Frowned out the fearful Spirit.

S. Anthony, in the wilderness, as related in his life by S. Athanasius, had many conflicts in the night with the powers of darkness, Satan appearing personally to him, to batter him from the strongholds of his faith. S. Dunstan, in his cell, was tempted by the Devil in the form of a lovely woman, but a grip of his nose with a heated tongs made him bellow out, and cease his nightly visits to that holy man. Ezra Peden, as related by Allan Cunningham, was also tempted by one who " was indeed passing fair, and the longer he looked on her she became the lovelier—" *owre lovely for mere flesh and blood,*" and poor Peden succumbed to her wiles.

From the book of Tobit it would appear that an Evil Spirit slew the first seven husbands of Sara from jealousy and lust, in the vain hope of securing her for himself. In Giraldus Cambrensis's *Itinerary through Wales*, Bohn's ed., p. 411 demons are shown to possess those qualities which are ascribed to them in the Apocryphal book of Tobit.

There is nothing new, as far as I am aware, respecting the doings of the Great Enemy of mankind in Welsh Folk-Lore. His tactics in the Principality evince no originality. They are the usual weapons used by him everywhere, and these he found to be sufficient for his purposes even in Wales.

Gladly would I here put down my pen and leave the uncongenial task of treating further about the spirits of darkness to others, but were I to do so, I should be guilty of a grave omission, for, as I have already said, ghosts, goblins, spirits, and other beings allied to Satan, occupy a prominent place in Welsh Folk-Lore.

Of a winter's evening, by the faint light of a peat fire and rush candles, our forefathers recounted the weird stories of olden times, of devils, fairies, ghosts, witches, apparitions, giants, hidden treasures, and other cognate subjects, and they delighted in implanting terrors in the minds of the listeners that no philosophy, nor religion of after years, could entirely eradicate. These tales made a strong impression upon the imagination, and possibly upon the conduct of the people, and hence the necessity laid upon me to make a further selection of the many tales that I have collected on this subject.

I will begin with a couple of stories extracted from the work of the Rev. Edmund Jones, by a writer in the *Cambro-Briton*, vol. ii., p. 276.

Satan appearing to a Man who was fetching a Load of Bibles, &c.

" A Mr. Henry Llewelyn, having been sent to Samuel Davies, of Ystrad Defodoc Parish, in Glamorganshire, to fetch a load of books, viz., Bibles, Testaments, Watts's Psalms, Hymns, and Songs for Children, said —Coming home by night towards Mynyddustwyn, having just passed by Clwyd yr Helygen ale-house, and being in a dry part of the lane—the mare, which he rode, stood still, and, like the ass of the ungodly Balaam, would go no farther, but kept drawing back. Presently he could see a living thing, round like a bowl, rolling from the right hand to the left, and crossing the lane, moving sometimes slow and sometimes very swift—yea, swifter than a bird could fly, though it had neither wings nor feet,—altering also its size. It appeared three times, less one time than another, seemed least when near him, and appeared to roll towards the mare's belly. The mare would then want to go forward, but he stopped her, to see more carefully what manner of thing it was. He staid, as he thought, about three minutes, to look at it; but, fearing to see a worse sight, he thought it high time to speak to it, and said—' What seekest thou, thou foul thing? In the name of the Lord Jesus, go away!'. And by speaking this it vanished, and sank into the ground near the mare's feet. It appeared to be of a *reddish oak colour.*"

In a footnote to this tale we are told that formerly near Clwyd yr Helygen, the Lord's Day was greatly profaned, and " it may be that the Adversary was wroth at the good books and the bringer of them; for he well knew what burden the mare carried."

The editor of the *Cambro-Briton* remarks that the superstitions recorded, if authentic, " are not very creditable to the intelligence of our lower classes in Wales ; but it is some satisfaction to think that none of them are of recent date." The latter remark was, I am sorry to say, rather premature.

One other quotation from the same book I will here make.

The Devil appearing to a Dissenting Minister at Denbigh.

" The Rev. Mr. Thomas Baddy, who lived in Denbigh Town, and was a Dissenting Minister in that place, went into his study one night, and while he was reading or writing, he heard some one behind him laughing and grinning at him, which made him stop a little—as well indeed it might. It came again, and then he wrote on a piece of paper, that devil-wounding scripture, 1st John, 3rd,—' For this was the Son of God manifested, that he might destroy the works of the Devil,'—and held it backwards from him, when the laughing ceased for ever ; for it was a melancholy word to a scoffing Devil, and enough to damp him. It would have damped him yet more, if he had shewn him James, ii. 19 —' The devils believe and tremble.' But he had enough for one time."

The following objectless tale, still extant, I believe, in the mountainous parts of Denbighshire, is another instance of the credulity in former days of the people.

Satan seen Lying right across a Road.

The story related to me was as follows :—Near Pentre-voelas lived a man called John Ty'nllidiart, who was in the habit of taking, yearly, cattle from the uplands in his neighbourhood, to be wintered in the Vale of Clwyd. Once, whilst thus engaged, he saw lying across the road right in front of him and the cattle, and completely blocking up the way, Satan with his head on one.wall and his tail on the other, moaning horribly.   John, as might be expected, hurried homewards, leaving his charge to take their chance with the Evil One, but long before he came to his house, the odour of brimstone had preceded him, and his wife was only too glad to find that it was her husband that came through the door, for she thought that it was someone else that was approaching.

The Devil's Tree by Eglwys Rhos, near Llandudno.

At the corner of the first turning after passing the village of Llanrhos, on the left hand side, is a withered oak tree, called by the natives of those parts the Devil's Tree, and it was thought to be haunted, and therefore the young and timid were afraid to pass it of a dark night.

The Rev. W. Arthur Jones, late Curate of the parish, told me that his horse was in the habit of shying whenever it came opposite this blighted tree, and his servant accounted for this by saying that the horse saw something there which was invisible to the sight of man.   Be this as it may, the tree has an uncanny appearance and a bad reputation, which some years ago was greatly increased by an occurrence that happened there to Cadwaladr Williams, a shoe-maker, who lived at Llansantffraid Glan Conway.

W

Cadwaladr was in the habit of carrying his work home to Llandudno to his customers every Saturday night in a wallet, and with the money which they paid him he bought eatables for the coming week, and carried shoes to be patched in one end of the wallet, and groceries, &c., in the other end, and, by adjusting the wallet he balanced it, and carried it, over his shoulders, home again.

This shoemaker sometimes refreshed himself too freely before starting homewards from Llandudno, and he was in the habit of turning into the public house at Llanrhos to gain courage to pass the Devil's Tree.

One Saturday night instead of quietly passing this tree on the other side, he walked fearlessly up to it, and defied the Evil One to appear if he were there. No sooner had he uttered the defiant words than something fell from the tree, and lit upon his shoulders, and grasped poor Cadwaladr's neck, with a grip of iron. He fought with the incubus savagely to get rid of it, but all his exertions were in vain, and so he was obliged to proceed on his journey with this fearful thing clinging to him, which became heavier and heavier every step he took. At last, thoroughly exhausted, he came to Towyn, and, more dead than alive, he reached a friend's door and knocked, and, oh, what pleasure, before the door was opened the weight on his back had gone, but his friend knew who it was that Cadwaladr had carried from the Devil's Tree.

Satan appearing as a Lovely Maiden.

The following story I received from the Rev. Owen Jones, Pentrevoelas. As regards details it is a fragment.

A young man who was walking from Dyserth to Rhyl was overtaken by a lovely young lady dressed in white. She invited conversation; and they walked together awhile talking kindly, but, when they came opposite a pool on the road side she disappeared, in the form of a ball of fire, into the water.

All that has reached our days, in corroboration of this tale, is the small pool.

The next tale was told me by the Rev. R. Jones, Rector of Llanycil. Mr. Jones gave names and localities, which I have indicated by initials.

A Man carried away by the Evil One.

W. E., of Ll—— M——, was a very bad man; he was a brawler, a fighter, a drunkard. He is said to have spat in the parson's face, and to have struck him, and beaten the parish clerk who interfered. It was believed that he had sold himself to work evil, and many foul deeds he committed, and, what was worse, he gloried in them.

People thought that his end would be a shocking one, and they were not disappointed. One night this reprobate and stubborn character did not return home. The next day search was made for him, and his dead body was found on the brink of the river. Upon inspecting the ground, it became evident that the deceased had had a desperate struggle with an unknown antagonist, and the battle commenced some distance above the *ceunant*, or *dingle*, where the body was discovered. It was there seen that the man had planted his heels deep into the ground, as if to resist a superior force, intent upon dragging him down to the river. There were indications that he had lost his footing; but a few yards lower down it was observed that his feet had ploughed the ground, and every step taken from this spot was traceable all down the declivity to the bottom of the ravine, and every yard gave proof that a desperate and prolonged struggle had taken place along the whole course. In one place an oak tree intercepted the way, and it was seen that a bough had its bark peeled off, and evidently the wretched man had taken hold of this bough and did not let go until the bark came off in his hands, for in death he still clutched the bark. The last and most severe struggle took place close to the river, and here the body was dragged underneath the roots of a tree, through a hole not big enough for a child to creep through, and this ended the fight.

Mr. Jones stated that what was most remarkable and ominous in connection with this foul work was the fact that, although footprints were seen in the ground, they were all those of the miserable man, for there were no other marks visible. From this fact and the previous evil life of this wretched creature, the people in those parts believed that the fearful struggle had taken place between W. E. and the Evil One, and that he had not been murdered by any man, but that he was taken away by Satan.

The next tale is a type of many once common in Wales, and as in one respect it connects these tales, or at least this particular one, with Fairy stories, I will relate it.

Satan appearing to a Young Man.

A young man, who had left Pentrevoelas to live in a farm house called Hafod Elwy, had to go over the hills to Denbigh on business. He started very early, before the cock crew, and as it was winter, his journey over the bleak moorlands was dismal and dreary. When he had proceeded several miles on his journey an unaccountable dread crept over him. He tried to dispel his fear by whistling and by knocking the ground with his walking stick, but all in vain. He stopped, and thought of returning home, but this he could not do, for he was more afraid of the ridicule of his friends than of his own fear, and therefore he proceeded on his journey and reached Pont Brenig, where he stopped awhile, and listened, thinking he might see or hear someone approaching. To his horror, he observed, through the glimmering light of the coming day, a tall gentleman approaching, and by a great exertion he mastered his feelings so far as to enable him to walk towards the stranger, but when within a few yards of him he stood still, for from fright he could not move. He noticed that the gentleman wore grey clothes, and breeches fastened with yellow buckles, on his coat were two rows of buttons like gold, his shoes were low, with bright clasps to them. Strange to say, this gentleman did not pass the terrified man, but stepped into the bog and disappeared from view.

Ever afterwards, when this man passed the spot where he had met the Evil One, he found there money or other valuables. This latter incident connects this tale with Fairy Folk-Lore, as the Fair People were credited with bestowing gifts on mortals.

Satan appearing to a Collier.

John Roberts of Colliers' Row, Cyfartha, Merthyr, was once going to Aberdare over the mountain. On the top of the hill he was met by a handsome gentleman, who wore a three-cocked hat, a red waistcoat, and a blue coat. The appearance of this well dressed man took John Roberts's fancy; but he could not understand why he should be alone on Aberdare mountain, and, furthermore, why he did not know the way to Aberdare, for he had asked Roberts to direct him to the town. John stared at the gentleman, and saw clearly a cloven foot and a long tail protruding underneath the blue coat, and there and then the gentleman changed himself into a *pig*, which stood before John, gave a big grunt, and then ran away.

I received the story from a lady to whom Roberts related it.

All these tales belong to modern times, and some of them appear to be objectless as well as ridiculous.

There are a few places in Wales which take their names from Satan. The *Devil's Bridge* is so called from the tradition that it was erected by him upon the condition that the first thing that passed over it should be his. In his design he was balked, for his intended victim, who was accompanied by his faithful dog, threw a piece of bread across the bridge after which the dog ran, and thus became the Devil's property, but this victim Satan would not take.

The Devil's Kitchen is a chasm in the rock on the west side of Llyn Idwal, Carnarvonshire. The view through this opening, looking downwards towards Ogwen Lake, is sublime, and, notwithstanding its uncanny name, the Kitchen is well worthy of a visit from lovers of nature.

From the following quotation, taken from *Y Gordofigion*, p. 110, it would appear that there is a rock on the side of Cader Idris called after the Evil One. The words are:—

"Mae ar dir Rhiwogo, ar ochr Cader Idris, graig a elwir. 'Careg-gwr-drwg,' byth ar ol y Sabboth hwnw pan ddaeth yno at drigolion plwyfydd Llanfihangel Pennant ac Ystradgwyn, pan oeddynt wedi ymgasglu i chwareu cardiau, a dawnsio; ac y rhoddodd dro o amgylch y graig gan ddawnsio, ac y mae ol ei draed ar y graig eto."

This in English is as follows:—There is on the land belonging to Rhiwogo, on the side of Cader Idris, a rock called *The Rock of the Evil One*, so named ever after that Sabbath, when he came there to join the parishioners of Llanfihangel Pennant and Ystradgwyn, who had gathered together to play cards and dance, and there he danced around the rock, and to this day the marks of his feet are to be seen in the rock.

There were, perhaps are, in Pembrokeshire, two stones, called the Devil's Nags, which were haunted by Evil Spirits, who troubled the people that passed that way.

Ceubren yr Ellyll, the Hobgoblin's Hollow Tree, a noble oak, once ornamented Nannau Park, Merionethshire. Tradition says that it was within the trunk of this tree that Glyndwr buried his cousin, Howel Sele, who fell a victim to the superior strength and skill of his relative. Ever after that sad occurrence the place was troubled, sounds proceeded out of the tree, and fire hovered over it, and, according to a writer in *The Cambro-Briton*, vol. i., p. 226:—

> E'en to this day, the peasant still
> With cautious fear treads o'er the ground ;
> In each wild bush a spectre sees,
> And trembles at each rising sound.

One of the caves in Little Orme's Head, Llandudno, is known as *Ogof Cythreuliaid*, the Cave of Devils.

From the preceding names of places, which do not by any means exhaust the list, it will be seen that many romantic spots in Wales are associated with Demons.

There are also sayings in Welsh connected with the Evil One. Thus, in our days may be heard, when it rains and the sun shines at the same time, the expression, "*Mae'r Gwr Drwg yn waldio'i wraig*"—the Devil is beating his wife.

Besides the Biblical names, by which Satan is known, in Wales, there are several others in use, not to be found in the Bible, but it would seem that these names are borrowed being either importations or translations ; in fact, it is doubtful, whether we possess any exclusively Welsh terms applied solely to the Devil. *Andras* or Andros is common in North Wales for the Evil One. Canon Silvan Evans in his Welsh Dictionary derives this word from *an*, without, and *gras*, grace; thus, the word becomes synonymous with gracelessness, and

he remarks that, although the term is generally rendered
devil, it is much softer than that term, or its Welsh equivalent *diawl*.

Y Fall is another term applied to Satan in Wales.
Dr. Owen Pugh defines the word as what is squabby, bulky.
The most common expressions for the devil, however, are
Cythraul, and *diawl*, or *diafol*, but these two last named
words are merely forms of Diabolos. Other expressions,
such as Old Nick, Old Harry, have found a home in Wales.
Y gwr drwg, the bad man, *Gwas drwg*, the wicked servant,
Yr yspryd drwg, the wicked spirit, *Yr hen fachgen*, the old
boy, and such like expressions, are also common. Silly
women frighten small children by telling them that the
Bo, the *bogey*, the *bogey bo*, or *bolol*, &c., will take them away
if they are not quiet.

Ghosts, or Spirits.

Ghosts, or Spirits, were supposed to be the shades of
departed human beings. who, for certain reasons, were permitted to visit either nightly, or periodically, this upper world.

The hour that Spirits came to the earth was mid-night, and
they remained until cock-crowing, when they were obliged
to depart. So strongly did the people believe in the hours
of these visits, that formerly no one would stay from home
later than twelve o'clock at night, nor would any one proceed on a journey, until chanticleer had announced that the
way was clear. Christmas Eve, however, was an exception,
for during that night, no evil Spirit could appear.

It was thought that if two persons were together, one
only could see the Spirit, to the other he was invisible, and
to one person only would the Spirit speak, and this he
would do when addressed ; otherwise, he remained silent.

Ghosts re-visited the world to reveal hidden treasures,
and the murdered haunted the place where their unburied

bodies lay, or until vengeance overtook the murderer, and
the wicked were doomed to walk the earth until they were
laid in lake, or river, or in the Red Sea.

The presence of Spirits was announced by a clanking of
chains, by shrieks, or other horrible noises, and dogs, and
horses, were credited with the power of seeing Spirits.
Horses trembled and perspired at their presence, and dogs
whined and crouched at their approach.

The tales which I shall now relate throw a glimmering
light on the subject now under consideration.

The Gloddaeth Ghost.

The following tale was told the Rev. Owen Jones, Pentrevoelas, by Thomas Davies, Tycoch, Rhyl, the hero in the story.

I may say that Gloddaeth Wood is a remnant of the
primæval forest that is mentioned by Sir John Wynn, in his
History of the Gwydir Family, as extending over a large
tract of the country. This wood, being undisturbed and in
its original wild condition, was the home of foxes and other
vermin, for whose destruction the surrounding parishes
willingly paid half-a-crown per head. This reward was an
inducement to men who had leisure, to trap and hunt these
obnoxious animals. Thomas Davies was engaged in this
work, and, taking a walk through the wood one day for the
purpose of discovering traces of foxes, he came upon a fox's
den, and from the marks about the burrow he ascertained
that there were young foxes in the hole. This was to him
a grand discovery, for, in anticipation, cubs and vixen were
already his. Looking about him, he noticed that there was
opposite the fox's den a large oak tree with forked branches,
and this sight settled his plan of operation. He saw that
he could place himself in this tree in such a position that
he could see the vixen leave, and return to her den, and,
from his knowledge of the habits of the animal, he knew

X

she would commence foraging when darkness and stillness prevailed. He therefore determined to commence the campaign forthwith, and so he went home to make his preparations.

I should say that the sea was close to the wood, and that small craft often came to grief on the coast. I will now proceed with the story.

Davies had taken his seat on a bough opposite the fox's den, when he heard a horrible scream in the direction of the sea, which apparently was that of a man in distress, and the sound uttered was " Oh, Oh." Thus Davies's attention was divided between the dismal, " Oh." and his fox. But, as the sound was a far way off, he felt disinclined to heed it, for he did not think it incumbent on him to ascertain the cause of that distressing utterance, nor did he think it his duty to go to the relief of a suffering fellow creature. He therefore did not leave his seat on the tree. But the cry of anguish, every now and again, reached his ears, and evidently, it was approaching the tree on which Davies sat. He now listened the more to the awful sounds, which at intervals reverberated through the wood, and he could no longer be mistaken—they were coming in his direction. Nearer and nearer came the dismal " Oh! Oh! " and with its approach, the night became pitch dark, and now the " Oh! Oh! Oh! " was only a few yards off, but nothing could be seen in consequence of the deep darkness. The sounds however ceased, but a horrible sight was presented to the frightened man's view. There, he saw before him, a nude being with eyes burning like fire, and these glittering balls were directed towards him. The awful being was only a dozen yards or so off. And now it crouched, and now it stood erect, but it never for a single instant withdrew its terrible eyes from the miserable man in the tree, who would have fallen to the ground were it not for the protecting boughs. Many times Davies thought that his last moment had come, for it seemed that the owner of those fiery eyes was about to spring upon him. As he did not do so, Davies somewhat regained his self possession, and thought of firing at the horrible being; but his courage failed, and there he sat motionless, not knowing what the end might be. He closed his eyes to avoid that gaze, which seemed to burn into him, but this was a short relief, for he felt constrained to look into those burning orbs, still it was a relief even to close his eyes, and so again and again he closed them, only, however, to open them on those balls of fire. About 4 o'clock in the morning, he heard a cock crow at Penbryn farm, and at the moment his eyes were closed, but at the welcome sound he opened them, and looked for those balls of fire, but, oh ! what pleasure, they were no longer before him, for, at the crowing of the cock, they, and the being to whom they belonged, had disappeared.

Tymawr Ghost, Bryneglwys.

This Ghost plagued the servants, pinched and tormented them, and they could not get rest day nor night; such was the character of this Ghost as told me by Mr. Richard Jones, Ty'n-y-wern. But, said I, what was the cause of his acts, was it the Ghost of anyone who had been murdered ? To this question, Jones gave the following account of the Ghost's arrival at Tymawr. A man called at this farm, and begged for something to eat, and as he was shabbily dressed, the girls laughed at him, and would not give him anything, and when going away, he said, speaking over his shoulder, "You will repent your conduct to me." In a few nights afterwards the house was plagued, and the servants were pinched all night. This went on days and days, until the people were tired of their lives. They, however, went to Griffiths, Llanarmon, a minister, who was celebrated as a Layer of Ghosts, and he came, and succeeded in capturing the Ghost in the form of a spider, and shut him up in his tobacco box and carried him away, and the servants were never afterwards plagued.

Ffrith Farm Ghost.

I am indebted to Mr. Williams, schoolmaster, Bryneglwys, for the history of this Ghost.

It was not known why Ffrith farm was troubled by a Ghost; but when the servants were busily engaged in cheese making the Spirit would suddenly throw mortar, or filthy matter, into the milk, and thus spoil the curds. The dairy was visited by the Ghost, and there he played havoc with the milk and dishes. He sent the pans, one after the other, around the room, and dashed them to pieces. The terrible doings of the Ghost was a topic of general conversation in those parts. The farmer offered a reward of five pounds to anyone who would lay the Spirit. One Sunday afternoon, about 2 o'clock, an aged priest visited the farm yard, and in the presence of a crowd of spectators exorcised the Ghost, but without effect. In fact, the Ghost waved a woman's bonnet right in the face of the priest. The farmer then sent for Griffiths, an Independent minister at Llanarmon, who enticed the Ghost to the barn. Here the Ghost appeared in the form of a lion, but he could not touch Griffiths, because he stood in the centre of a circle, which the lion could not pass over. Griffiths persuaded the Ghost to appear in a less formidable shape, or otherwise he would have nothing to do with him. The Ghost next came in the form of a mastiff, but Griffiths objected even to this appearance; at last, the Ghost appeared as a fly, which was captured by Griffiths and secured in his tobacco box, and carried away. Griffiths acknowledged that this Ghost was the most formidable one that he had ever conquered.

From this tale it would appear that some ghosts were more easily overcome than others.

Pont-y-Glyn Ghost.

There is a picturesque glen between Corwen and Cerrig-y-Drudion, down which rushes a mountain stream, and over this stream is a bridge, called Pont-y-Glyn. On the left hand side, a few yards from the bridge, on the Corwen side, is a yawning chasm, through which the river bounds. Here people who have travelled by night affirm that they have seen ghosts—the ghosts of those who have been murdered in this secluded glen.

A man who is now a bailiff near Ruthin, but at the time of the appearance of the Ghost to him at Pont-y-Glyn was a servant at Garth Meilio—states that one night, when he was returning home late from Corwen, he saw before him, seated on a heap of stones, a female dressed in Welsh costume. He wished her good night, but she returned him no answer. She, however, got up and proceeded down the road, which she filled, so great were her increased dimensions.

Other Spirits are said to have made their homes in the hills not far from Pont-y-Glyn. There was the Spirit of Ystrad Fawr, a strange Ghost that transformed himself into many things. I will give the description of this Ghost in the words of the author of *Y Gordofigion.*

Ysbryd Ystrad Fawr.

"Yr oedd Ysbryd yn Ystrad Fawr, ger Llangwm, yn arfer ymddangos ar brydiau ar lun twrci, a'i gynffon o'i amgylch fel olwyn troell. Bryd arall, byddai yn y coed, nes y byddai y rhai hyny yn ymddangos fel pe buasent oll ar dân ; bryd arall, byddai fel ci du mawr yn cnoi asgwrn."—*Y Gordofigion*, p. 106.

Ystrad Fawr Ghost in English is as follows :—

There was a Ghost at Ystrad Fawr, near Llangwm, that was in the habit of appearing like a turkey with his tail spread out like a spinning wheel. At other times he appeared in the wood, when the trees would seem as if they were on fire, again he would assume the shape of a large black dog gnawing a bone.

Ty Felin Ghost, Llanynys.

An exciseman, overtaken by night, went to a house called Ty Felin, in the parish of Llanynys, and asked for lodgings. Unfortunately the house was a very small one, containing only two bedrooms, and one of these was haunted, consequently no one dared sleep in it. After awhile, however, the stranger induced the master to allow him to sleep in this haunted room ; he had not been there long before a Ghost entered the room in the shape of a travelling Jew, and the Spirit walked around the room. The exciseman tried to catch him, and gave chase, but he lost sight of the Jew in the yard. He had scarcely entered the room, a second time, when he again saw the Ghost. He again chased him, and lost sight of him in the same place. The third time he followed the Ghost, he made a mark on the yard, where the Ghost vanished and went to rest, and was not again troubled. He got up early and went his way, but, before long, he returned to Ty Felin accompanied by a policeman, whom he requested to dig in the place where his mark was. This was done, and, underneath a superficial covering, a deep well was discovered, and in it a corpse. On examining the tenant of the house, he confessed that a travelling Jew, selling jewelry, &c., once lodged with him, and that he had murdered him, and cast his body in the well.

Llandegla Spirit.

The tale of this Spirit was given me by Mr. Roberts, late Schoolmaster of Llandegla. A small river runs close to the secluded village of Llandegla, and in this mountain stream under a huge stone lies a wicked Ghost. The tale is as follows :—

The old Rectory at Llandegla was haunted; the Spirit was very troublesome; no peace was to be got because of it; every night it was at its work. A person of the name of Griffiths, who lived at Graianrhyd, was sent for to lay the Ghost. He came to the Rectory, but the Spirit could not be overcome. It is true Griffiths saw it, but in such a form that he could not approach it; night after night, the Spirit appeared in various forms, but still the conjurer was unable to master it. At last it came to the wise man in the form of a fly, which Griffiths immediately captured, and placed in a small box. This box he buried under a large stone in the river, just below the bridge, near the Llandegla Mills, and there the Spirit is to remain until a certain tree, which grows by the bridge, reaches the height of the parapet, and then, when this takes place, the Spirit shall have power to regain his liberty. To prevent this tree from growing, the school children, even to this day, nip the upper branches, and thus retard its upward growth. Mr. Roberts received the story I have given, from the old Parish Clerk, John Jones the weaver, who died a few years ago.

Lady Jeffrey's Spirit.

This lady could not rest in her grave because of her misdeeds, and she troubled people dreadfully; at last she was persuaded or enticed to contract her dimensions, and enter into a bottle. She did so, after appearing in a good many hideous forms; but when she got into the bottle, it was corked down securely, and the bottle was cast into the pool

underneath the Short bridge, Llanidloes, and there the lady
was to remain until the ivy that grew up the buttresses
should overgrow the sides, of the bridge, and reach the
parapet. The ivy was dangerously near the top of the
bridge when the writer was a schoolboy, and often did he
and his companions crop off its tendrils as they neared the
prescribed limits for we were all terribly afraid to release
the dreaded lady out of the bottle. In the year 1848, the
old bridge was blown up, and a new one built instead of it.
A schoolfellow, whom we called Ben, was playing by the
aforesaid pool when the bridge was undergoing reconstruc-
tion, and he found by the river's side a small bottle, and in
the bottle was a little black thing, that was never quiet, but
it kept bobbing up and down continually, just as if it wanted
to get out. Ben kept the bottle safely for a while, but ere
long he was obliged to throw it into the river, for his
relations and neighbours came to the conclusion that that
was the very bottle that contained Lady Jeffrey's Spirit, and
they also surmised that the little black restless thing was
nothing less than the lady herself. Ben consequently
resigned the bottle and its contents to the pool again, there
to undergo a prolonged, but unjust, term of imprisonment.

Pentrevoelas.—Squire Griffith's Ghost.

A couple of workmen engaged at Foelas, the seat of the
late Squire Griffiths, thought they would steal a few apples
from the orchard for their children, and for this purpose
one evening, just before leaving off work, they climbed up a
tree, but happening to look down, whom should they see
but the Squire, wearing his three-cornered hat, and dressed
in the clothes he used to wear when alive, and he was leaning against the trunk of the tree on which they were
perched. In great fright they dropped to the ground
and took to their heels. They ran without stopping

to Bryn Coch, but there, to their horror, stood the Squire in the middle of the road quietly leaning on his staff. They again avoided him and ran home every step, without looking behind them. The orchard robbers never again saw their late master, nor did they ever again attempt to rob the orchard.

David Salisbury's Ghost.

I will quote from *Bye-Gones*, vol. iii., p. 211, an account of this Spirit.

" There was an old Welsh tradition in vogue some fifty years ago, that one David Salisbury, son of *Harri Goch* of Llanrhaiadr, near Denbigh, and grandson to Thomas Salisbury hên of Lleweni, had given considerable trouble to the living, long after his remains had been laid in the grave. A good old soul, Mr. Griffiths of Llandegla, averred that he had seen his ghost, mounted upon a white horse, galloping over hedges and ditches in the dead of night, and had heard his ' terrible groans,' which, he concluded, proceeded from the weight of sin troubling the unhappy soul, which had to undergo these untimely and unpleasant antics. An old Welsh ballad entitled ' Ysbryd Dafydd Salbri,' professed to give the true account of the individual in question, but the careful search of many years has failed me in securing a copy of that horrible song.

GORONWY IFAN."

This Spirit fared better than most of his compeers, for they, poor things, were, according to the popular voice, often doomed to ride headless horses, which madly galloped, the livelong night, hither and thither, where they would, to the great terror of the midnight traveller who might meet this mad unmanageable creature, and also, as it would seem, to the additional discomfort of the unfortunate rider.

Y

It is, or was believed in Gyffylliog parish, which is in the recesses of the Denbighshire mountains, four or five miles to the west of Ruthin, that the horses ridden by Spirits and goblins were real horses, and it was there said when horses were found in their stables at dawn in a state of perspiration that they had been taken out in the night and ridden by Spirits about the country, and hence their jaded condition in the morning.

It was also thought that the horses found in the morning in their pasture ground with tangled manes and tails, and bodies covered with mud, had been during the night used by Spirits, who rushed them through mire and brier, and that consequently they presented the appearance of animals who had followed the hounds in a long chase through a stiff country.

There is a strong family likeness between all Ghost stories, and a lack of originality in their construction, but this suggests a common source from which the majority of these fictions are derived.

I now come to another phase of Spirit Folk-Lore, which has already been alluded to, viz., the visits of Ghosts for the purpose of revealing hidden treasures. The following tale, which I took down from the mouth of John Rowland, at one time the tenant of Plas-yn-llan, Efenechtyd, is an instance of this kind of story.

A Ghost Appearing to point out Hidden Treasures.

There is a farm house called Clwchdyrnog in the parish of Llanddeusant, Anglesey, which was said to have been haunted by a Spirit. It seems that no one would summon courage to speak to the Ghost, though it was seen by several parties; but one night, John Hughes, Bodedern, a widower, who visited the house for the purpose of obtaining a second Mrs. Hughes from among the servant girls there, spoke to the Ghost. The presence of the Spirit was indicated by a great noise in the room where Hughes and the girl were. In great fright Hughes invoked the Spirit, and asked why he troubled the house. " Have I done any wrong to you," said he, addressing the Spirit. " No," was the answer. Then he asked if the girl to whom he was paying his attentions was the cause of the Spirit's visit, and again he received the answer, " No." Then Hughes named individually all the inmates of the house in succession, and inquired if they were the cause of the Spirit's visits, and again he was answered in the negative. Then he asked why, since no one in the house had disturbed the Spirit, he came there to disturb the inmates. To this pertinent question the Spirit answered as follows :—" There are treasures hidden on the south side of Ffynnon Wen, which belong to, and are to be given to, the nine months old child in this house : when this is done, I will never disturb this house any more."

The spot occupied by the treasure was minutely described by the Spirit, and Hughes promised to go to the place indicated. The next day, he went to the spot, and digging into the ground, he came upon an iron chest filled with gold, silver, and other valuables, and all these things he faithfully delivered up to the parents of the child to be kept by them for him until he should come of age to take possession of them himself. This they faithfully did, and the Spirit never again came to the house.

John Rowland, my informant, was a native of Anglesey, and he stated that all the people of Llanddeusant knew of the story which he related to me. He was eighty-three years old at the time he told me the tale, and that was in October, 1882.

But one of the most singular tales of the appearance of a Ghost is recorded in the autobiography of the grandfather of the late Mr. Thomas Wright, the well-known Shropshire antiquary. Mr. Wright's grandfather was a Methodist, and in the early days of that body the belief in apparitions was was not uncommon amongst them. The story was told Mr. Wright, sen., in 1780, at the house, in Yorkshire, of Miss Bosanquet (afterwards the wife of Fletcher of Madeley), by Mr. John Hampson, sen., a well-known preacher among the Methodists, who had just arrived from Wales.

As the scene of the tale is laid in Powis Castle, I will call this visitation

The Powis Castle Ghost revealing a Hidden Box
to a Woman.

The following is the narrative :—It had been for some time reported in the neighbourhood that a poor unmarried woman, who was a member of the Methodist Society, and had become serious under their ministry, had seen and conversed with the apparition of a gentleman, who had made a strange discovery to her. Mr. Hampson, being desirous to ascertain if there was any truth in the story, sent for the woman, and desired her to give him an exact relation of the whole affair from her own mouth, and as near the truth as she possibly could. She said she was a poor woman, who got her living by spinning hemp and line; that it was customary for the farmers and gentlemen of that neighbourhood to grow a little hemp or line in a corner of their fields for their own home consumption, and as she was a good hand at spinning the materials, she used to go from house to house to inquire for work; that her method was, where they employed her, during her stay to have meat, and drink, and lodging (if she had occasion to sleep with them), for her work, and what they pleased to give her besides. That, among other places, she happened to call one day at the Welsh Earl of Powis's country seat, called Redcastle, to inquire for work, as she usually had done before. The quality were at this time in London, and had left the steward and his wife, with other servants, as usual, to take care of their country residence in their absence. The steward's wife set her to work, and in the evening told her that she must stay all night with them, as they had more work for her to do next day. When bedtime arrived, two or three of the servants in company, with each a lighted candle in her hand, conducted her to her lodging. They led her to a ground room, with a boarded floor, and two sash windows. The room was grandly furnished, and had a genteel bed in one corner of it. They had made her a good fire, and had placed her a chair and a table before it, and a large lighted candle upon the table. They told her that was her bedroom, and she might go to sleep when she pleased. They then wished her a good night and withdrew altogether, pulling the door quickly after them, so as to hasp the spring-sneck in the brass lock that was upon it. When they were gone, she gazed awhile at the fine furniture, under no small astonishment that they should put such a poor person as her in so grand a room and bed, with all the apparatus of fire, chair, table, and candle. She was also surprised at the circumstance of the servants coming so many together, with each of them a candle. However, after gazing about her some little time, she sat down and took a small Welsh Bible out of her pocket, which she always carried about with her, and in which she usually read a chapter—chiefly in the New Testament—before she said her prayers and went to bed. While she was reading she heard the room door open, and turning her head, saw a gentleman enter in a gold-laced hat and waistcoat, and the rest of his dress corresponding therewith. (I think she was very particular in describing the rest of his dress to Mr. Hampson, and he to me at the time, but I have now forgot the other particulars).

He walked down by the sash-window to the corner of the room and then returned. When he came to the first window in his return (the bottom of which was nearly breast-high), he rested his elbow on the bottom of the window, and the side of his face upon the palm of his hand, and stood in that leaning posture for some time, with his side partly towards her. She looked at him earnestly to see if she knew him, but, though from her frequent intercourse with them, she had a personal knowledge of all the present family, he appeared a stranger to her. She supposed afterwards that he stood in this manner to encourage her to speak; but as she did not, after some little time he walked off, pulling the door after him as the servants had done before.

She began now to be much alarmed, concluding it to be an apparition, and that they had put her there on purpose. This was really the case. The room, it seems, had been disturbed for a long time, so that nobody could sleep peaceably in it, and as she passed for a very serious woman, the servants took it into their heads to put the Methodist and Spirit together, to see what they would make of it.

Startled at this thought, she rose from her chair, and kneeled down by the bedside to say her prayers. While she was praying he came in again, walked round the room, and came close behind her. She had it on her mind to speak, but when she attempted it she was so very much agitated that she could not utter a word. He walked out of the room again, pulling the door after him as before.

She begged that God would strengthen her and not suffer her to be tried beyond what she was able to bear. She recovered her spirits, and thought she felt more confidence and resolution, and determined if he came in again she would speak to him, if possible.

He presently came in again, walked round, and came behind her as before; she turned her head and said, " Pray, sir, who are you, and what do you want?" He put up his finger, and said, " Take up the candle and follow me, and I will tell you." She got up, took up the candle, and followed him out of the room. He led her through a long boarded passage till they came to the door of another room, which he opened and went in. It was a small room, or what might be called a large closet. "As the room was small, and I believed him to be a Spirit," she said, " I stopped at the door; he turned and said, ' Walk in, I will not hurt you.' So I walked in. He said. ' Observe what I do.' I said, ' I will.' He stooped, and tore up one of the boards of the floor, and there appeared under it a box with an iron handle in the lid. He said, ' Do you see that box ? ' I said, ' Yes, I do.' He then stepped to one side of the room, and showed me a crevice in the wall, where, he said, a key was hid that would open it. He said, ' This box and key must be taken out, and sent to the Earl in London' (naming the Earl, and his place of residence in the city). He said, ' Will you see it done ?' I said, ' I will do my best to get it done.' He said, ' Do, and I will trouble the house no more.' He then walked out of the room and left me. (He seems to have been a very civil Spirit, and to have been very careful to affright her as little as possible). I stepped to the room door and set up a shout. The steward and his wife, and the other servants came to me immediately, all clung together, with a number of lights in their hands. It seems they had all been waiting to see the issue of the interview betwixt me and the apparition. They asked me what was the matter? I told them the foregoing circumstances, and showed them the box. The steward durst not meddle with it, but his wife had more courage, and, with the help of the other servants, lugged it out, and found the key." She said by their lifting it appeared to be pretty heavy, but that she did not see it opened, and therefore did not know what it contained; perhaps money, or writings of consequence to the family, or both.

They took it away with them, and she then went to bed and slept peaceably till the morning.

It appeared afterwards that they sent the box to the Earl in London, with an account of the manner of its discovery and by whom; and the Earl sent down orders immediately to his steward to inform the poor woman who had been the, occasion of this discovery, that if she would come and reside in his family, she should be comfortably provided for for the remainder of her days; or, if she did not choose to reside constantly with them, if she would let them know when she wanted assistance, she should be liberally supplied at his Lordship's expense as long as she lived. And Mr. Hampson said it was a known fact in the neighbourhood that she had been so supplied from his Lordship's family from the time the affair was said to have happened, and continued to be so at the time she gave Mr. Hampson this account.

Such is the tale. I will make no comments on it. Many similar stories are extant. After one more tale, I will leave these Spirit stories, and I will then relate how troublesome Ghosts were laid.

The Spirits of the preceding tales were sent from the unseen world to do good, but the Spirit of the maiden who gives a name to a Welsh lake, cried out for vengeance; but

history does not inform us that she obtained satisfaction.
There is a lake in Carnarvonshire called *Llyn-Nâd-y-Forwyn*, or the Lake of the Maiden's Cry, to which is
attached the following tale. I will call the tale—

The Spirit of Llyn-Nâd-y-Forwyn.

It is said that a young man was about to marry a young
girl, and on the evening before the wedding they were ram-
bling along the water's side together, but the man was false,
and loved another better than the woman whom he was about
to wed. They were alone in an unfrequented country, and
the deceiver pushed the girl into the lake to get rid of her to
marry his sweetheart. She lost her life. But ever afterwards
her Spirit troubled the neighbourhood, but chiefly the scene
of her murder. Sometimes she appeared as a ball of fire,
rolling along the river Colwyn, at other times she appeared
as a lady dressed in silk, taking a solitary walk along the
banks of the river. At other times, groans and shrieks were
heard coming out of the river—just such screams as would
be uttered by a person who was being murdered. Sometimes
a young maiden was seen emerging out of the waters, half
naked, with dishevelled hair, that covered her shoulders,
and the country resounded with her heart-rending crying
as she appeared in the lake. The frequent crying of the
Spirit gave to the lake its name, Llyn-Nâd-y-Forwyn.

Spirit Laying.

It must have been a consolation to those who believed in
the power of wicked Spirits to trouble people, that it was
possible to lay these evil visitors in a pool of water, or to
drive them away to the Red Sea, or to some other distant
part of the world. It was generally thought that Spirits
could be laid by a priest; and there were particular forms
of exorcising these troublesome beings. A conjuror, or
Dyn Hysbys, was also credited with this power, and it was

z

thought that the prayer of a righteous man could overcome these emissaries of evil.

But there was a place for hope in the case of these transported or laid Spirits. It was granted to some to return from the Red Sea to the place whence they departed by the length of a grain of wheat or barley corn yearly. The untold ages that it would take to accomplish a journey of four thousand miles thus slowly was but a very secondary consideration to the annihilation of hope. Many were the conditions imposed upon the vanquished Spirits by their conquerors before they could be permitted to return to their old haunts, and well might it be said that the conditions could not possibly be carried out; but still there was a place for hope in the breast of the doomed by the imposition of any terminable punishment.

The most ancient instance of driving out a Spirit that I am acquainted with is to be found in the Book of Tobit. It seems to be the prototype of many like tales. The angel Raphael and Tobias were by the river Tigris, when a fish jumped out of the river, which by the direction of the angel was seized by the young man, and its heart, and liver, and gall extracted, and at the angel's command carefully preserved by Tobias. When asked what their use might be, the angel informed him that the smoke of the heart and liver would drive away a devil or Evil Spirit that troubled anyone. In the 14th verse of the sixth chapter of Tobit we are told that a devil loved Sara, but that he did no harm to anyone, excepting to those who came near her. Knowing this, the young man was afraid to marry the woman; but remembering the words of Raphael, he went in unto his wife, and took the ashes of the perfumes as ordered, and put the heart and liver of the fish thereupon, and made a smoke therewith, the which smell, when the Evil Spirit had smelled, he fled into the utmost parts of Egypt, and the angel bound him. Such is the story, many variants of which are found in many countries.

I am grieved to find that Sir John Wynne, who wrote the interesting and valuable *History of the Gwydir Family*, which ought to have secured for him kindly recognition from his countrymen, was by them deposited after death, for troubling good people, in Rhaiadr y Wenol. The superstition has found a place in Yorke's *Royal Tribes of Wales.*

The following quotation is from the *History of the Gwydir Family*, Oswestry Edition, p. 7 :—

"Being shrewd and successful in his dealings, people were led to believe he oppressed them," and says Yorke in his *Royal Tribes of Wales*, " It is the superstition of Llanrwst to this day that the Spirit of the old gentleman lies under the great waterfall, Rhaiadr y Wennol, there to be punished, purged, spouted upon and purified from the foul deeds done in his days of nature."

This gentleman, though, is not alone in occupying, until his misdeeds are expiated, a watery grave. There is hardly a pool in a river, or lake in which Spirits have not, according to popular opinion, been laid. In our days though, it is only the aged that speak of such matters.

A Spirit could in part be laid. It is said that Abel Owen's Spirit, of Henblas, was laid by Gruffydd Jones, Cilhaul, in a bottle, and buried in a *gors* near Llanrwst.

This Gruffydd Jones had great trouble at Hafod Uch a between Llanrwst and Conway, to lay a Spirit. He began in the afternoon, and worked hard the whole night and the next day to lay the Spirit, but he succeeded in overcoming a part only of the Spirit. He was nearly dead from exhaustion and want of food before he could even master a portion of the Spirit.

The preceding is a singular tale, for it teaches that Spirits are divisible. A portion of this Spirit, repute says, is still at large, whilst a part is undergoing purification.

The following tale was told me by my friend, the Rev. T. H. Evans, Vicar of Llanwddyn.

Cynon's Ghost.

One of the wicked Spirits which plagued the secluded Valley of Llanwddyn long before it was converted into a vast reservoir to supply Liverpool with water was that of *Cynon*. Of this Spirit Mr. Evans writes thus:—" *Yspryd Cynon* was a mischievous goblin, which was put down by *Dic Spot* and put in a quill, and placed under a large stone in the river below Cynon Isaf. The stone is called ' *Careg yr Yspryd*,' the Ghost Stone. This one received the following instructions, that he was to remain under the stone until the water should work its way between the stone and the dry land."

The poor Spirit, to all appearance, was doomed to a very long imprisonment, but *Dic Spot* did not foresee the wants and enterprise of the people of Liverpool, who would one day convert the Llanwddyn Valley into a lake fifteen miles in circumference, and release the Spirit from prison by the process of making their Waterworks.

I might here say that there is another version current in the parish besides that given me by Mr. Evans, which is that the Spirit was to remain under the stone until the river was dried up. Perhaps both conditions were, to make things safe, imposed upon the Spirit.

Careg yr Yspryd and Cynon Isaf were at the entrance to the Valley of Llanwddyn, and down this opening, or mouth of the valley, rushed the river—the river that was to be dammed up for the use of Liverpool. The inhabitants of the valley knew the tradition respecting the Spirit, and they much feared its being disturbed. The stone was a large boulder, from fifteen to twenty tons in weight, and it was evident that it was doomed to destruction, for it stood in the river Vyrnwy just where operations were to commence. There was no small stir among the Welsh inhabitants when preparations were made to blast the huge Spirit-stone. English and Irish workmen could not enter into the feeling of the Welsh towards this stone, but they had heard what was said about it. They, however, had no dread of the imprisoned Spirit. In course of time the stone was bored and a load of dynamite inserted, but it was not shattered at the first blast. About four feet square remained intact, and underneath this the Spirit was, if it was anywhere. The men were soon set to work to demolish the stone. The Welshmen expected some catastrophe to follow its destruction, and they were even prepared to see the Spirit bodily emerge from its prison, for, said they, the conditions of its release have been fulfilled—the river had been diverted from its old bed into an artificial channel, to facilitate the removal of this and other stones—and there was no doubt that both conditions had been literally carried out, and consequently the Spirit, if justice ruled, could claim its release. The stone was blasted, and strange to relate, when the smoke had cleared away, the water in a cavity where the stone had been was seen to move; there was no apparent reason why the water should thus be disturbed, unless, indeed, the Spirit was about to appear. The Welsh workmen became alarmed, and moved away from the place, keeping, however, their eyes fixed on the pool. The mystery was soon solved, for a large frog made its appearance, and, sedately sitting on a fragment of the shattered stone, rubbed its eyes with its feet, as if awaking from a long sleep. The question was discussed, "Is it a frog, or the Spirit in the form of a frog; if it is a frog, why was it not killed when the stone was blasted?" And again, "Who ever saw a frog sit up in that fashion and rub the dust out of its eyes? It must be the Spirit." There the workmen stood, at a respectful distance from the frog, who, heedless of the marked attention paid to it, continued sitting up and rubbing its eyes. They would not approach it, for it must be the Spirit, and no one knew what its next movement or form might be. At last, however, the frog was driven away, and the men re-commenced their labours But for nights afterwards people passing the spot heard a noise as of heavy chains being dragged along the ground where the stone once stood.

Caellwyngrydd Spirit.

This was a dangerous Spirit. People passing along the road were stoned by it; its work was always mischievous and hurtful. At last it was exorcised and sent far away to the Red Sea, but it was permitted to return the length of a barley corn every year towards its lost home.

From the tales already given, it is seen that the people believed in the possibility of getting rid of troublesome Spirits, and the person whose aid was sought on these occasions was often a minister of religion. We have seen how Griffiths of Llanarmon had reached notoriety in this direction, and he lived in quite modern times. The clergy were often consulted in matters of this kind, and they were commonly believed to have power over Spirits. The Rev. Walter Davies had great credit as a Spirit layer, and he lived far into the present century. Going further back, I find that Archdeacon Edmund Prys, and his contemporary and friend, Huw Llwyd, were famous opponents of Evil Spirits, and their services are said to have been highly appreciated, because always successful. The manner of laying Spirits differed. In this century, prayer and Bible reading were usually resorted to, but in other days, incantation was employed. We have seen how Griffiths surrounded himself with an enchanted circle, which the Spirit could not break through. This ring was thought to be impervious to the Ghost tribe, and therefore it was the protection of the person whom it surrounded. The Spirit was invoked and commanded to depart by the person within the magic ring, and it obeyed the mandate. Sometimes it was found necessary to conduct a service in Church, in Latin by night, the Church being lit up with consecrated candles, ere the Ghost could be overcome.

When Spirits were being laid, we are told that they presented themselves in various forms to the person engaged in laying them, and that ultimately they foolishly came transformed into some innocuous insect or animal, which he was able to overcome. The simplicity of the Ghosts is ridiculous, and can only be understood by supposing that the various steps in the contest for the mastery are not forthcoming, that they have been lost.

These various metamorphoses would imply that transmigration was believed in by our forefathers.

Ghost Raising.

If the possibility of Ghost Laying was believed in, so also was the possibility of raising Evil Spirits. This faith dates from olden times. Shakespeare, to this, as to most other popular notions, has given a place in his immortal plays. Speaking rightly in the name of "Glendower," a Welshman, conversant with Ghosts and Goblins, the poet makes him say :—

" I can call Spirits from the vasty deep."

Henry the Fourth, Act III., S. 1.

And again in the same person's mouth are placed these words :—

"Why, I can teach you, cousin, *to command the devil.*"

The witches in *Macbeth* have this power ascribed to them:

> I'll catch it ere it come to ground :
> And that, distilled by magic sleights,
> *Shall raise such artificial Sprites,*
> *As by the strength of their illusion*
> Shall draw him on to his confusion.
>
> *Macbeth*, Act III., S. 5.

This idea has continued right to our own days, and adepts in the black art have affirmed that they possess this power.

Doctor Bennion, a gentleman well known in his lifetime in and about Oswestry, was thought to be able to raise Devils. I find in the history of *Ffynnon Elian*, p. 12, that the doctor visited John Evans, the last custodian of the well, and taught him how to accomplish this feat. For the benefit of those anxious to obtain this power, I will give the doctor's recipe :—"Publish it abroad that you can raise the Devil, and the country will believe you, and will credit you with many miracles. All that you have to do afterwards is to be silent, and you will then be as good a raiser of Devils as I am, and I as good as you."

Evans confesses that he acted according to the astute doctor's advice, and he adds—"The people in a very short time spoke much about me, and they soon came to intrust everything to me, their conduct frightened me, for they looked upon me as if I were a god." This man died August 14th, 1858.

Witches and Conjurors.

From and before the days of King Saul, to the present moment, witches have held dreaded sway over the affairs of man. Cruel laws have been promulgated against them, they have been murdered by credulous and infuriated mobs, they have lost their lives after legal trial, but still, witches have lived on through the dark days of ignorance, and even in these days of light and learning they have their votaries. There must be something in the human constitution peculiarly adapted to the exercise of witchcraft, or it could not have lived so long, nor could it have been so universal, as it undoubtedly is, unless men lent themselves willingly to its impositions.

It is curious to notice how good and enlightened men have clung to a belief in witchcraft. It is, consequently, not to be wondered at that the common people placed faith in witches and conjurors when their superiors in learning professed a like faith.

I have often spoken to intelligent men, who did not scruple to confess that they believed in witches and conjurors, and they adduced instances to prove that their faith had a foundation in fact.

Almost up to our days, the farmer who lost anything valuable consulted a conjuror, and vowed vengeance on the culprit if it were not restored by such and such a time, and invariably the stolen property was returned to its owner before the specified period had expired. As detectives, the conjurors, therefore, occupied a well-defined and useful place in rural morality, and witches, too, were indirectly teachers of charity, for no farm wife would refuse refreshments to the destitute lest vengeance should overtake her. In this way the deserving beggar obtained needed assistance from motives of self-preservation from benefactors whose fears made them charitable.

But, if these benefits were derived from a false faith, the evils attending that faith were nevertheless most disastrous to the community at large, and many inhuman Acts were passed in various reigns to eradicate witchcraft. From the

wording of these Acts it will be seen what witches were
credited with doing.

An Act passed 33 Henry VIII. adjudged all witchcraft
and sorcery to be felony. A like Act was passed 1 James,
c. 12, and also in the reign of Philip and Mary. The
following is an extract :—

"All persons who shall practise invocation, or conjura-
tion, of wicked spirits, any witchcraft, enchantment, charm,
or sorcery, whereby any person shall happen to be killed,
or destroyed, shall, with their aiders, and abettors, be
accounted felons, without benefit of clergy ; and all persons
practising any witchcraft, &c., whereby any person shall
happen to be wasted, consumed, or lamed in his or her
body, or members, or whereby any goods, or chattels, shall
be destroyed, wasted, or impaired, shall, with their coun-
sellors, and aiders, suffer for the first offence one year's
imprisonment and the pillory, and for the second the punishment of felony without the clergy." . . . . "If any
person shall consult, covenant with, entertain, employ, feed,
or reward any evil or wicked spirit, or *take up any dead
man, woman, or child out of his, her, or their grave*; or,
the skin, bone, or any other part of any dead person to be
employed in any manner of witchcraft, sorcery, charm, or
enchantment, &c., *he shall suffer death as a felon*, without
benefit of clergy."

The law of James I. was repealed in George II's. reign, but
even then persons pretending to use witchcraft, tell fortunes,
or discover stolen goods, by skill in the occult sciences, were
to be punished by a year's imprisonment ; and by an Act, 5
George IV., c. 83, any person or persons using any subtle art,
means, or device, by palmistry, or otherwise, to deceive his
Majesty's subjects, were to be deemed rogues and vagabonds,
and to be punished with imprisonment and hard labour.

Acts of Parliament did not succeed in eradicating witch-craft. Its power has waned, but it still exercises an influence, shadowy though it be, on certain minds, though in its grosser forms it has disappeared.

Formerly, ailments of all kinds, and misfortunes of every description, were ascribed to the malignant influence of some old decrepit female, and it was believed that nature's laws could be changed by these witches, that they could at will produce tempests to destroy the produce of the earth, and strike with sickness those who had incurred their displeasure. Thus Lady Macbeth, speaking of these hags, says:—

" I have learned by the perfectest report, they have
more in them than mortal knowledge. When I burned
in desire to question them further they made themselves air, into which they vanished."

Macbeth, Act. i., S. 5.

The uncanny knowledge possessed by witches was used, it was thought, to injure people, and their malice towards good, hard-working, honest folk was unmistakable. They afflicted children from sheer love of cruelty, and bewitched animals gratuitously, or for slights which they supposed their owners had shown towards them ; consequently their knowledge was considered to be greatly inimical to others, and particularly baneful to the industrious, whom witches hated.

There was hardly a district that had not its witches. Children ran away when they saw approaching them an aged woman, with a red shawl on, for they believed she was a witch, who could, with her evil eye, injure them. It was, however, believed that the machinations of witches could be counteracted in various ways, and by and by some of these charms shall be given. Life would have been intolerable but for these antidotes to witchcraft.

Shakespeare's knowledge of Welsh Folk-lore was exten-
sive and peculiarly faithful, and what he says of witches in
general agrees with the popular opinion respecting them in
Wales. I cannot do better than quote from this great
Folk-lorist a few things that he tells us about witches.

Mention has been made of witches taking dead bodies
out of their graves to make use of them in their enchant-
ments, and Shakespeare, in his description of the witches'
cauldron, shows that they threw into the seething pot many
portions of human beings. The first witch in *Macbeth*
says :—

> Round about the cauldron go,
> In the poisoned *entrails* throw.

The third witch mentions other things that are thrown
into the pot, as :—

> Scale of dragon tooth of wolf,
> Witches' mummy, maw and gulf
> Of the ravin'd salt-sea shark,
> Root of hemlock digged i' the dark,
> *Liver of blaspheming Jew,*
> Gall of goat, and slips of yew
> Sliver'd in the moon's eclipse,
> *Nose of Turk, and Tartar's lips,*
> Finger of birth-strangled babe
> Ditch-delivered by a drab.
>   *Macbeth*, A. IV., S. 1.

It was thought that witches could change themselves,
and other people, into the form of animals. In Wales, the
cat and the hare were the favourite animals into which
witches transformed themselves, but they did not necessarily
confine themselves to these animals. They were able to
travel in the air on a broom-stick ; make children ill ; give
maids the nightmare ; curse with madness, animals ; bring
misfortune on families ; hinder the dairy maid from making

butter; and many more imaginary things were placed to
their credit.

The personal appearance of witches, as given by Shakespeare, corresponds exactly with the Welsh idea of these
hags. On this subject the poet writes :—

> What are these
> *So wither'd and so wild in their attire*
> That look not like the inhabitants o' the earth,
> And yet are on't? Live you? Or are you ought
> That man may question? You seem to understand me,
> By each at once her chappy fingers laying
> Upon her skinny lips: You should be women,
> And yet your beards forbid me to interpret
> That you are so.
>
> *Macbeth,* Act I., S. 3.

A striking and pathetic portrait of a witch, taken from
Otway's Orphan, Act. II., is given in No. 117 of the *Spectator.*
It is so true to life and apposite to our subject that I will
quote it :—

> In a close lane, as I pursu'd my journey,
> I spy'd a wrinkled hag, with age grown double,
> Picking dry sticks, and mumbling to herself.
> Her eyes with scalding rheum were gall'd, and red,
> Cold palsy shook her head, her hands seemed wither'd,
> And on her crooked shoulders had she wrapt
> The tatter'd remnant of an old striped hanging,
> Which served to keep her carcass from the cold ;
> So there was nothing of a piece about her.
> Her lower weeds were all o'er coarsely patched,
> With different colour'd rags, black, red, white, yellow.
> And seem'd to speak variety of wretchedness.

A picture such as this is enough to create sympathy
and charity in a selfish heart, but in those dark days, when
faith in witchcraft prevailed, such a poor old decrepit
woman inspired awe, and was shunned as a malicious evil-
doer by all her neighbours.

Llanddona Witches.

There is a tradition in the parish of Llanddona, Anglesey, that these witches, with their husbands, had been expelled from their native country, wherever that was, for practising witchcraft. They were sent adrift, it is said, in a boat, without rudder or oars, and left in this state to the mercy of the wind and the wave. When they were first discovered approaching the Anglesey shore, the Welsh tried to drive them back into the sea, and even after they had landed they were confined to the beach. The strangers, dead almost from thirst and hunger, commanded a spring of pure water to burst forth on the sands. This well remains to our days. This miracle decided their fate. The strangers were allowed, consequently, to land, but as they still practised their evil arts the parish became associated with their name, and hence the *Witches of Llanddona* was a term generally applied to the female portion of that parish, though in reality it belonged to one family only within its boundaries.

The men lived by smuggling and the women by begging and cursing. It was impossible to overcome these daring smugglers, for in their neckerchief was a fly, which, the moment the knot of their cravats was undone, flew right at the eye of their opponents and blinded them, but before this last remedy was resorted to the men fought like lions, and only when their strength failed them did they release their familiar spirit, the fly, to strike with blindness the defenders of the law.

The above-mentioned tradition of the coming of these witches to Anglesey is still current in the parish of Llanddona, which is situated on the north coast of Anglesey.

It was thought that the witching power belonged to families, and descended from mothers to daughters. This was supposed to be the case with the witches of Llanddona.

This family obtained a bad report throughout the island. The women, with dishevelled hair and bared breasts, visited farm houses and requested charity, more as a right than a favour, and no one dared refuse them. *Llanddona Witches* is a name that is not likely soon to die. Taking advantage of the credulity of the people they cursed those whom they disliked, and many were the endeavours to counteract their maledictions. The following is one of their curses, uttered at *Y Ffynon Oer*, a well in the parish of Llanddona, upon a man who had offended one of these witches:—

> Crwydro y byddo am oesoedd lawer;
> Ac yn mhob cam, camfa;
> Yn mhob camfa, codwm;
> Yn mhob codwm, tori asgwrn;
> Nid yr asgwrn mwyaf na'r lleiaf,
> Ond asgwrn chwil corn ei wddw bob tro.

The English is as follows, but the alliteration and rhythm of the Welsh do not appear in the translation:—

> May he wander for ages many;
> And at every step, a stile;
> At every stile, a fall;
> At every fall, a broken bone;
> Not the largest, nor the least bone,
> But the chief neck bone, every time.

This curse seemed to be a common imprecation, possibly belonging to that family. Such was the terror of the *Llanddona Witches* that if any of them made a bid for a pig or anything else, in fair or market, no one else dared bid against them, for it was believed they would witch the animal thus bought. There were also celebrated witches at Denbigh. *Bella Fawr* (Big Bella) was one of the last and most famous of her tribe in that town, and many other places were credited with possessing persons endowed with witching powers, as well as those who could break spells.

The following tales of the doings of witches will throw light upon the matter under consideration.

Witches transforming themselves into Cats.

One of the forms that witches were supposed to change themselves into was that of a cat. In this metamorphosed state they were the more able to accomplish their designs. The following tale, illustrative of this belief, was told me by the Rev. R. Jones, Rector of Llanycil, Bala.

On the side of the old road, between Cerrigydrudion and Bettws-y-Coed—long before this latter place had become the resort of artists—stood an inn, which was much resorted to, as it was a convenient lodging house for travellers on their way to Ireland. This inn stood near the present village of Bettws-y-Coed. Many robberies occurred here. Travellers who put up there for the night were continually deprived of their money, and no one could tell how this occurred, for the lodgers were certain that no one had entered their rooms, as they were found locked in the morning just as they were the night before. The mystery was, therefore, great. By and by, one of those who had lost his money consulted *Huw Llwyd*, who lived at Cynvael, in the parish of Festiniog, and he promised to unravel the mystery. Now, Huw Llwyd had been an officer in the army, and, equipped in his regimentals, with sword dangling by his side, he presented himself one evening at the suspected inn, and asked whether he could obtain a room and bed for the night; he represented himself as on his way to Ireland, and he found no difficulty in obtaining a night's lodging. The inn was kept by two sisters of prepossessing appearance, and the traveller made himself most agreeable to these ladies, and entertained them with tales of his travels in foreign parts. On retiring for the night he stated that it was a habit with him to burn lights in his room all night, and he was supplied with a sufficient quantity of candles to last through the night. The request, as Hugh Llwyd was a military man, did not arouse suspicion. Huw retired, and made his arrangements for a night of watching. He placed his clothes on the floor within easy reach of his bed, and his sword unsheathed lay on the bed close to his right hand. He had secured the door, and now as the night drew on he was all attention; ere long two cats stealthily came down the partition between his room and the next to it. Huw feigned sleep, the cats frisked here and there in the room, but the sleeper awoke not; they chased each other about the room, and played and romped, and at last they approached Huw's clothes and played with them, and here they seemed to get the greatest amusement; they turned the clothes about and over, placing their paws now on that string, and now on that button, and ere long their paws were inserted into the pockets of his clothes, and, just as one of the cats had her paw in the pocket that contained Huw Llwyd's purse, he like lightning struck the cat's paw with his sword. With terrible screams they both disappeared, and nothing further was seen of them during the night.

Next morning, only one of the sisters appeared at the breakfast table. To the traveller's enquiry after the absent lady of the house, her sister said that she was slightly indisposed, and could not appear.

Huw Llwyd expressed regret at this, but, said he—"I must say good-bye to her, for I greatly enjoyed her company last night." He would not be refused, so ultimately he was admitted to her presence. After expressing his sympathy and regret at her illness, the soldier held out his hand to bid good-bye to the lady. She put out her left hand; this Huw refused to take, averring that he had never taken a left hand in his life, and that he would not do so now. Very reluctantly, and with evident pain, she put out her right hand, which was bandaged, and this fact cleared up the mystery connected with the robberies. These two ladies were two witches, who in the form of cats had robbed travellers who lodged under their roof. Huw, when he made this discovery said—"I am Huw Llwyd of Cynvael, and I warn you of the risk you have incurred by your thefts, and I promise you I will not let you off so easily the next time I have need to visit you."

The preceding tale is circumstantial, but unfortunately similar tales are current in other places, as shown by the following quotation :—

"The last instance of national credulity on this head was the story of the witches of Thurso, who, tormenting for a long time an honest fellow under the usual form of a cat, at last provoked him so that one night he put them to flight with his broad sword and *cut off the leg* of one less nimble than the rest. On his taking it up, to his amazement *he found it belonged to a female of his own species,* and next morning discovered the owner, an old hag, with only the companion leg to this."

Brand's Popular Antiquities, pp. 318-319.

The Witches' Revenge on Huw Llwyd.

Several months after the occurrence recorded above of Huw Llwyd, when he had just started from his home one Sunday morning to go to his Church to officiate there, for he was the parson of Llan Festiniog, he observed that the Bettws-y-Coed ladies were approaching his house, and he perceived that their object was to witch him. He knew full well that as long as his back was turned towards them he was in their power, but that when he faced them they could do him no harm, so, to avoid their evil influence, and to frustrate their designs, he faced them, and walked backwards every step from Cynvael to the Llan, and in this way he escaped being injured by his female enemies. But this was not all. Huw Llwyd knew that when he reached the Church porch he was beyond witchcraft's reach. Having arrived there he shouted out—"I defy you now, and before I leave the Church I will make you that you can never again witch anyone." He was as good as his word, for by his skill in the black art, he deprived those two ladies, ere he left the Church, of their power to witch people, and during the rest of their lives they were like other women.

Huw Llwyd, who was born 1533, and died 1620, was a clergyman, and it was generally believed that priests could counteract the evils of the enemy of mankind.

The wide-spread belief of witches being able to transform themselves into animals is shown in the legends of many countries, and, as in the case of fairy stories, the same tale, slightly changed, may be heard in various places. The possibility of injuring or *marking* the witch in her assumed form so deeply that the bruise remained a mark on her in her natural form was a common belief. A tale in certain points like the one recorded of Huw Llwyd and the witches who turned themselves into cats is to be heard in many parts of Wales. It is as follows. I quote the main facts from my friend Mr. Hamer's account of Llanidloes, published in the *Montgomeryshire Collections*, vol. x., p. 243:—

A Witch transformed into a Hare injured by one whom she tormented.

"An old woman, thought to be a witch, was said by a neighbour to be in the habit of visiting her nightly in the shape of a hare, and that in consequence she was deprived of her rest. The witch came to her bed, as a hare, and

crossed it, and the tormented one was determined to put an
end to this persecution. For this purpose she procured a
hammer, which she placed under her pillow when she
retired to rest. That night the old witch, unaware of the
reception awaiting her, paid her usual visit to her victim.
But the instant she jumped on the bed she received a
stunning blow on the head, and, it need not be added, disappeared. Next morning, a friend of the persecuted
woman, who was in the secret of the whole case, on some
pretext paid the old woman, the supposed witch, a visit, and
she was greatly astonished to find her laid up, suffering
from a frightful black eye, which her visitor believed to be
the result of the blow dealt her with the hammer on the
previous night."

A Witch shot when in the form of a Hare.

The following tale was told me by the Rev. R. Jones,
Rector of Llanycil :—

An old woman was evicted from a small farm, which
she and her family had held for many years. She was
naturally greatly annoyed at such conduct on the part of
the landlord, and of the person who supplanted her. However, she procured a small cottage close by her late home,
and there she lived. But the interloper did not get on, for
she was troubled by a hare that came nightly to her house.
A labouring man, when going to his work early in the
morning, time after time saw a hare going from the farm
towards the cottage occupied by this old woman, and he
determined to shoot this hare. He procured an old gun,
and loaded it with pebbles instead of shot, and awaited the
approach of the hare. It came as usual, the man fired,
and the hare rolled over and over, screaming and making a
terrible noise. He, however, did not heed this much, for
hares, when shot, do scream, and so he went to secure the

hare, but when he attempted to seize it, it changed into all shapes, and made horrible sounds, and the man was so terrified that he ran away, and he was very glad to get away from the scene of this shocking occurrence. In a few days afterwards the old woman who occupied the cottage was found dead, and it was noticed by the woman who laid her out that her arm and shoulder were riddled with pebbles. It was thought that she was a witch, and that she had troubled the people who had deprived her of her farm, and that she did so in the shape of a hare, and no one doubted that the injury inflicted on the old woman was anything more than the shot of the man, who supposed that he had killed a hare, when in reality he shot and killed the old woman. The farmer was never troubled after the death of the woman whom he had supplanted.

Many variants of this tale are still extant. The parish clerk of Llangadfan, a mountainous parish in Montgomeryshire, gave me one, which he located in Nant-yr-eira, but as it is in its main points much like the preceding, I will not relate it.

A Witch in the form of a Hare in a Churn.

In the *Spectator*, No. 117, are these words :—

" If the dairy-maid does not make her butter come so soon as she would have it, *Moll White* (a supposed witch) is at the bottom of the churn."

Until very lately I had thought that the milk only was considered bewitched if it could not be churned, and not that the witch herself was at the bottom of the churn. But I have been disabused of this false notion, for the Rector of Llanycil told me the following story, which was told him by his servant girl, who figures in the tale. When this girl was servant at Drws-y-nant, near Dolgelley, one day, the milk would not churn. They worked a long time at it to no purpose. The girl thought that she heard something knocking up and down in the churn, and splashing about. She told her master there was something in the churn, but he would not believe her; however, they removed the lid, and out jumped a large hare, and ran away through the open door, and this explained all difficulties, and proved that the milk was bewitched, and that the witch herself was in the churn in the shape of a hare.

This girl affirmed that she had seen the hare with her own eyes.

As the hare was thought to be a form assumed by witches it was impossible for ordinary beings to know whether they saw a hare, or a witch in the form of a hare, when the latter animal appeared and ran before them along the road, consequently the hare, as well as the witch, augured evil. An instance of this confusion of ideas was related to the writer lately by Mr. Richard Jones, Tyn-y-wern, Bryneglwys.

A Hare crossing the Road.

Mr. Jones said that when he was a lad, he and his mother went to Caerwys fair from the Vale of Clwyd, intending to sell a cow at the fair. They had not gone far on their way before a large hare crossed the road, hopping and halting and looking around. His mother was vexed at the sight, and she said—"We may as well go home, Dick, for no good will come of our journey since that old witch crosses our path." They went on, though, and reached Caerwys in safety, but they got no bid for the cow, although they stayed there all day long.

A Witch in the form of a Hare hunted by a Black Greyhound.

The writer has heard variants of the following tale in several parts of Wales :—

An old woman, credited to be a witch, lived on the

confines of the hills in a small hut in south Carnarvonshire. Her grandson, a sharp intelligent lad, lived with her. Many gentlemen came to that part with greyhounds for the purpose of coursing, and the lad's services were always in requisition, for he never failed in starting a hare, and whenever he did so he was rewarded with a shilling. But it was noticed that the greyhounds never caught the hare which the lad started. The sport was always good, the race long and exciting, but the hare never failed to elude her pursuers. Scores of times this occurred, until at last the sportsmen consulted a wise man, who gave it as his opinion that this was no ordinary hare, but a witch, and, said he— "She can never be caught but by a black greyhound." A dog of this colour was sought for far and near, and at last found and bought. Away to the hills the coursers went, believing that now the hare was theirs. They called at the cottage for the lad to accompany them and start the prey. He was as ready as ever to lead them to their sport. The hare was soon started, and off the dog was slipped and started after it, and the hare bounded away as usual, but it is now seen that her pursuer is a match for her in swiftness, and, notwithstanding the twistings and windings, the dog was soon close behind the distressed hare.

The race became more and more exciting, for hound and hare exerted themselves to their very utmost, and the chase became hot, and still hotter. The spectators shout in their excitement—"*Hei! ci du*" ("*Hi! black dog*") for it was seen that he was gaining on his victim. "*Hei! Mam gu*" ("*Hei! grandmother, dear*") shouted the lad, forgetting in his trouble that his grandmother was in the form of a hare. His was the only encouraging voice uttered on behalf of the poor hunted hare. His single voice was hardly heard amidst the shouts of the many. The

pursuit was long and hard, dog and hare gave signs of
distress, but shouts of encouragement buoyed up the
strength of the dog. The chase was evidently coming to a
close, and the hare was approaching the spot whence it
started. One single heart was filled with dread and dismay
at the failing strength of the hare, and from that heart came
the words—" *Hei ! Mam gu* " (" *Hi ! grandmother, dear.*")
All followed the chase, which was now nearing the old
woman's cottage, the window of which was open. With a
bound the hare jumped through the small casement into
the cottage, but the black dog was close behind her, and
just as she was disappearing through the window, he bit the
hare and retained a piece of her skin in his mouth, but he
could not follow the hare into the cottage, as the aperture
was too small. The sportsmen lost no time in getting into
the cottage, but, after much searching, they failed to discover puss. They, however, saw the old woman seated by
the fire spinning. They also noticed that there was blood
trickling from underneath her seat, and this they considered
sufficient proof that it was the witch in the form of a hare
that had been coursed and had been bitten by the dog just
as she bounded into the cottage.

It was believed in England, as well as in Wales, that
witches were often hunted in the shape of hares. Thus in
the *Spectator*, No. 117, these words occur :—

" If a hare makes an unexpected escape from the hounds
the huntsman curses *Moll White* (the witch) !" " Nay "
(says Sir Roger) " I have known the master of the pack,
upon such an occasion, send one of his servants to see if
Moll White had been out that morning."

In *Yorkshire Legends and Traditions*, p. 160, is a tale very
much like the one which is given above. It is as follows :—

" There was a hare which baffled all the greyhounds that

were slipped at her. They seemed to have no more chance with her than if they coursed the wind. There was, at the time, a noted witch residing near, and her advice was asked about this wonderful hare. She seemed to have little to say about it, however, only she thought they had better let it be, but, above all, they must take care how they slipped a *black* dog at it. Nevertheless, either from recklessness or from defiance, the party did go out coursing, soon after, with a black dog. The dog was slipped, and they perceived at once that puss was at a disadvantage. She made as soon as possible for a stone wall, and endeavoured to escape through a sheep-hole at the bottom. Just as she reached this hole the dog threw himself upon her and caught her in the haunch, but was unable to hold her. She got through and was seen no more. The sportsmen, either in bravado or from terror of the consequences, went straight to the house of the witch to inform her of what had happened. They found her in bed, hurt, she said, by a fall; but the wound looked very much as if it had been produced by the teeth of a dog, and it was on a part of the woman corresponding to that by which the hare had been seized by the black hound before their eyes."

Early reference to Witches turning themselves into Hares.

The prevalence of the belief that witches could transform themselves into hares is seen from a remark made by *Giraldus Cambrensis* in his topography of Ireland. He writes:—

"It has also been a frequent complaint, from old times, as well as in the present, *that certain hags in Wales*, as well as in Ireland and Scotland, *changed themselves into the shape of hares*, that, sucking teats under this counterfeit, they might stealthily rob other people's milk."

Giraldus Cambrensis, Bohn's Edition, p. 83.

cc

This remark of the Archdeacon's gives a respectable antiquity to the metamorphosis of witches, for it was in 1185 that he visited Ireland, and he tells us that what he records had descended from " old times."

The transformation fables that have descended to us would seem to be fossils of a pagan faith once common to the Celtic and other cognate races. It was not thought that certain harmless animals only could become the temporary abode of human beings. Even a wolf could be human under an animal form. Thus *Giraldus Cambrensis* records that a priest was addressed in Ireland by a wolf, and induced to administer the consolations of his priestly office to his wife, who, also, under the shape of a she-wolf, was apparently at the point of death, and to convince the priest that she was really a human being the he-wolf, her husband, tore off the skin of the she-wolf from the head down to the navel, folding it back, and she immediately presented the form of an old woman to the astonished priest. These people were changed into wolves through the curse of one Natalis, Saint and Abbot, who compelled them every seven years to put off the human form and depart from the dwellings of men as a punishment for their sins. (See *Giraldus Cambrensis*, Bohn's Edition, pp. 79-81.)

Ceridwen and Gwion (Gwiawn) Bach's Transformation.

But a striking instance of rapid transition from one form to another is given in the *Mabinogion*. The fable of Ceridwen's cauldron is as follows :—

"Ceridwen was the wife of Tegid Voel. They had a son named Morvran, and a daughter named Creirwy, and she was the most beautiful girl in the world, and they had another son named Avagddu, the ugliest man in the world. Ceridwen, seeing that he should not be received amongst gentlemen because of his ugliness, unless he should be

possessed of some excellent knowledge or strength. . . .
ordered a cauldron to be boiled of knowledge and inspiration for her son. The cauldron was to be boiled unceasingly for one year and a day until there should be in it three blessed drops of the spirit's grace.

"These three drops fell on the finger of Gwion Bach of Llanfair Caereinion in Powis, whom she ordered to attend to the cauldron. The drops were so hot that Gwion Bach put his finger to his mouth; no sooner done, than he came to know all things. Now he *transformed himself into a hare*, and ran away from the wrath of Ceridwen. She also *transformed herself into a greyhound*, and went after him to the side of a river. Gwion on this jumped into the river and transformed himself into a fish. She also transformed herself into an otter-bitch, and chased him under the water until he was fain to turn himself into a bird of the air; she, as a hawk, followed him, and gave him no rest in the sky. And just as she was about to swoop upon him, and he was in fear of death, he espied a heap of winnowed wheat on the floor of a barn, and he dropped among the wheat and buried himself into one of the grains. Then she transformed herself into a high-crested black hen, and went to the wheat and scratched it with her feet, and found him and swallowed him."

The tale of Ceridwen, whose fame was such that she can without exaggeration be styled the goddess of witches, resembles in part the chase of the witch-hare by the black dog, and probably her story gave rise to many tales of transformations.

I now come to another kind of transformation. It was believed by the aged in Wales that witches could not only turn themselves into hares, but that by incantation they could change other people into animals. My friend, the

Rev. T. Lloyd Williams, Wrexham, lodged whilst he was at Ystrad Meurig School with a Mrs. Jones, Dolfawr, who was a firm believer in "Rhibo" or Rheibo, or witching, and this lady told my friend the following tales of *Betty'r Bont*, a celebrated witch in those parts.

A Man turned into a Hare.

One of the servant men at Dolfawr, some years before Mr. Williams lodged there, laughed at Betty'r Bont's supposed power. However, he lived to repent his folly. One night after he had gone to bed he found that he had been changed into a hare, and to his dismay and horror he saw a couple of greyhounds slipped upon him. He ran for bare life, and managed to elude his pursuers, and in a terrible plight and fright he ran to Dolfawr, and to his bed. This kind of transformation he ever afterwards was subjected to, until by spells he was released from the witch's power over him.

A Man changed into a Horse.

Mr. Williams writes of the same servant man who figures in the preceding tale:—"However, after that, she (Betty'r Bont) turned him into a grey mare, saddled him, and actually rode him herself; and when he woke in the morning, he was in a bath of perspiration, and positively declared that he had been galloping all night."

Singularly enough *Giraldus Cambrensis* mentions the same kind of transformation. His words are:—

"I myself, at the time I was in Italy, heard it said of some districts in those parts, that there the stable-women, who had learnt magical arts, were wont to give something to travellers in their cheese, which transformed them into beasts of burden, so that they carried all sorts of burdens, and after they had performed their tasks, resumed their own forms."—Bohn's Edition, p. 83.

From Brand's *Popular Antiquities*, p. 225, I find that a common name for *nightmare* was *witch-riding*, and the night-mare, he tells us, was "a spectre of the night, which seized men in their sleep and suddenly deprived them of speech and motion," and he quotes from Ray's Collection of Proverbs :—

> " Go in God's name, so *ride* no witches."

I will now leave this subject with the remark that people separated by distance are often brought together by their superstitions, and probably, these beliefs imply a common origin of the people amongst whom these myths prevail.

The following tales show how baneful the belief in witch-craft was ; but, nevertheless, there was some good even in such superstitions, for people were induced, through fear of being witched, to be charitable.

A Witch who turned a Blue Dye into a Red Dye.

An old hag went to a small farmhouse in Clocaenog parish, and found the farmer's wife occupied in dyeing wool blue. She begged for a little wool and blue dye. She was informed by Mrs. —— that she was really very sorry that she could not part with either, as she had only just barely enough for her own use. The hag departed, and the woman went on with her dyeing, but to her surprise, the wool came out of the pot dyed red instead of blue. She thought that possibly it was the dye that was to blame, and so she gave up for the night her employment, and the next day she went to Ruthin for a fresh supply of blue to finish her work, but again she failed to dye the wool blue, for red, and not blue, was the result of her dyeing. She, in surprise, told a neighbour of her unaccountable failure to dye her wool blue. This neighbour asked her if she had been visited by anyone, and she in answer told her that old so and so had been at her house begging. " Ah," was the response, "I see how it is you can never dye that wool blue, you have been witched, send the red wool and the part that you have not touched here to me, and I will finish the work for you." This was done, and the same colour was used by both women, but now it became blue, whilst with the other, it was red.

This tale was told me by a gentleman who does not wish his name to appear in print, as it would lead to the identification of the parties mentioned, and the descendants of the supposed witch, being respectable farmers, would rather that the tale of their canny grandmother were forgotten, but my informant vouches for the truth of the tale.

A Pig Witched.

A woman sold a pig at Beaumaris to a man called Dick y Green; she could not that day sell any more, but the following market day she went again to Beaumaris. Dick was there waiting her appearance, and he told her that the pig he bought was bewitched and she must come with him to undo the curse. Away the woman went with Dick, and when they came to the pig she said, "What am I to do now, Dick?" "Draw thy hand seven times down his back," said Dick, and say every time, "*Rhad Duw arnat ti*," i.e., "The blessing of God be on thee." The woman did so, and then Dick went for physic for the pig, which recovered.

Milk that would not churn, and the steps taken to counteract the malice of the Witch that had cursed the churn and its contents.

Before beginning this tale, it should be said that some witches were able to make void the curses of other witches. Bella of Denbigh, who lived in the early part of the present century, was one of these, and her renown extended over many counties.

I may further add that my informant is the Rev. R.
Jones, whom I have often mentioned, who is a native of
Llanfrothen, the scene of the occurrences I am about to
relate, and that he was at one time curate of Denbigh, so
that he would be conversant with the story by hearsay,
both as to its evil effects and its remedy.

About the year 1815 an old woman, supposed to be a
witch, lived at Ffridd Ucha, Llanfrothen, and she got her
living by begging. One day she called at Ty mawr, in the
same parish, requesting a charity of milk; but she was
refused. The next time they churned, the milk would not
turn to butter, they continued their labours for many hours,
but at last they were compelled to desist in consequence of the
unpleasant odour which proceeded from the churn. The milk
was thrown away, and the farmer, John Griffiths, divining
that the milk had been witched by the woman who had
been begging at their house, went to consult a conjuror,
who lived near Pwllheli. This man told him that he was to
put a red hot crowbar into the milk the next time they
churned. This was done, and the milk was successfully
churned. For several weeks the crowbar served as an
antidote, but at last it failed, and again the milk could not
be churned, and the unpleasant smell made it again impossible for anyone to stand near the churn. Griffiths, as
before, consulted the Pwllheli conjuror, who gave him a
charm to place underneath the churn, stating, when he
did so, that if it failed, he could render no further assistance. The charm did not act, and a gentleman whom he
next consulted advised him to go to Bell, or Bella, the
Denbigh witch. Griffiths did so, and to his great surprise
he found that Bell could describe the position of his house,
and she knew the names of his fields. Her instructions
were—Gather all the cattle to Gors Goch field, a meadow in

front of the house, and then she said that the farmer and a
friend were to go to a certain holly tree, and stand
out of sight underneath this tree, which to this day
stands in the hedge that surrounds the meadow mentioned
by Bell. This was to be done by night, and the farmer was
told that he should then see the person who had injured
him. The instructions were literally carried out. When
the cows came to the field they herded together in a
frightened manner, and commenced bellowing fearfully. In
a very short time, who should enter the field but the
suspected woman in evident bodily pain, and Griffiths and
his friend heard her uttering some words unintelligible to
them, and having done so, she disappeared, and the cattle
became quiet, and ever after they had no difficulty in
churning the milk of those cows.

The two following tales were told the writer by the Rev.
T. Lloyd Williams, Wrexham. The scene of the stories was
Cardiganshire, and Betty'r Bont was the witch.

A Witch who was refused a Goose, and her revenge.

A witch called at a farm when they were feathering geese
for sale, and she begged much for one. She was refused,
but it would have been better, according to the tale, had
her request been granted, for they could not afterwards rear
geese on that farm.

Another version of the preceding tale is, that the same
witch called at a farm when the family was seated at dinner
partaking of a goose; she requested a taste, but was refused,
when leaving the house door she was heard to mutter, "Let
there be no more geese at . . . . ." and her curse became
a fact.

A Witch refused Butter, and the consequence.

An old hag called at a farm and begged the wife to sell
her a pound of butter. This was refused, as they wanted to

pot the butter. The witch went away, therefore, empty handed. The next day when the maid went to the fields for the cows she found them sitting like cats before a fire, with their hind legs beneath them. I am indebted to my friend Mr. Lloyd Williams for this tale. A friend told me the following tale.

A Witch's Revenge, and her Discomfiture.

An old beggar woman was refused her requests by a farmer's wife, and it was noticed that she uttered words that might have been a threat, when going away from the door, and it was also observed that she picked up a few straws from the yard and carried them away with her. In the course of a few days, a healthy calf died, and the death of several calves followed in rapid succession. These misfortunes caused the wife to remember the old woman whom she had sent away from her door, and the farmer came to the conclusion that his cattle had been witched by this old woman, so he went to a conjuror, who told him to cut out the heart of the next calf that should die, and roast it before the fire, and then, after it had been properly roasted, he was to prick it all over with a fork, and if anyone should appear as a beggar, they were to give her what she asked. The instructions were carried out literally, and just as the heart was being pricked, the old woman whom the wife had driven away came up to the house in a dreadful state, and rushing into the house, said—"In the name of God, what are you doing here?" She was told that they were doing nothing particular, and while the conversation was being carried on, the pricking operation was discontinued and the old hag became less excited, and then she asked the farmer kindly to give her a few potatoes, which he gladly did, and the old woman departed; and no more calves died after that.

Tales of the kind related above are extremely common, and might be multiplied to almost any extent.. It would seem that the evil influence of witches was exerted not only at times when they were refused favours, but that, at will, they could accomplish mischief. Thus I have heard it said of an old woman, locally supposed to be a witch, that her very presence was ominous of evil, and disaster followed wherever she went; if she were inclined to work evil she was supposed to be able to do so, and that without any provocation.

I will give one tale which I heard in Garthbeibio of this old hag's doings.

A Horse Witched.

Pedws Ffoulk, a supposed witch, was going through a field where people were employed at work, and just as she came opposite the horse it fell down, as if it were dead. The workmen ran to the horse to ascertain what was the matter with it, but Pedws went along, not heeding what had occurred. This unfeeling conduct on her part roused the suspicion of the men, and they came to the conclusion that the old woman had witched the horse, and that she was the cause of its illness. They, therefore, determined to run after the woman and bring her back to undo her own evil work. Off they rushed after her, and forced her back to the field, where the horse was still lying on the ground. They there compelled the old creature to say, standing over the horse, these words—"*Duw arno fo*" (God be with him). This she did, and then she was allowed to go on her way· By and by the horse revived, and got upon his feet, and looked as well as ever, but this, it was thought, would not have been the case had not the witch undone her own curse.

In Anglesey, as I was informed by my brother, the late Rev. Elijah Owen, Vicar of Llangoed, it was believed that witches

made void their own curses of animals by saying over them
" *Rhad Duw ar y da* " (The Blessing of God be on the cattle)

Cows and Horses Witched.

The writer was told the name of the farm where the
following events were said to have taken place, but he is
not quite sure that his memory has not deceived him, so he
will only relate the facts without giving them a locality.

A farmer had a good mare that went mad, she foamed at
the mouth, rushed about the stall, and died in great agony.
But this was not all, his cows kept back their milk, and
what they could extract from them stank, nor could they
churn the milk, for it turned into froth.

A conjuror was consulted, and the farmer was told that
all this evil had been brought about by a witch who had
been refused milk at his door, and her mischief was counteracted by the conjuror thus consulted.

Occasionally we hear of injured persons retaliating upon
the witches who had brought about their losses. This,
however, was not often attempted, for people feared the
consequences of a failure, but it was, nevertheless, supposed
to be attainable.

I will relate a few instances of this punishment of witches
for their evil doings.

Witches Punished.

A neighbour, who does not wish to have his name recorded,
states that he can vouch for the incidents in the following
tale. A farmer who lost much stock by death, and suspected
it was the work of an old hag who lived in his neighbourhood, consulted a conjuror about the matter, and he
was told that his suspicions were correct, that his losses
were brought about by this old woman, and, added the
conjuror, if you wish it, I can wreak vengeance on the
wretch for what she has done to your cattle. The injured

farmer was not averse to punishing the woman, but he did
not wish her punishment to be over severe, and this he told
the conjuror, but said he, "I should like her to be deprived
of the power to injure anyone in future." This was accomplished, my informant told me, for the witch-woman took to
her bed, and became unable to move about from that very
day to the end of her life. My informant stated that he
had himself visited this old woman on her sick bed, and
that she did not look ill, but was disinclined to get up, and
the cause of it all was a matter of general gossip in the
neighbourhood, that she had been cursed for her evil doings.

Another tale I have heard is that a conjuror obliged a
witch to jump from a certain rock into the river that ran at
its foot, and thus put an end to her life.

Rough punishment was often inflicted upon these simple
old women by silly people.

The tales already given are sufficiently typical of the
faith of the credulous regarding witches, and their ability to
work out their evil desires on their victims. I will now
proceed briefly to relate other matters connected with witchcraft as believed in, in all parts of Wales.

How to break, or protect people from, a Witch's Spell.

There were various ways of counteracting the evils brought
upon people by witches.

1. The intervention of a priest or minister of religion
made curses of none effect.

The following tale was told me by my friend the Rector
of Rhydycroesau. When Mr. Jones was curate of Llanyblodwel a parishioner sent to ask the "parson" to come
to see her. He went, but he could not make out what he
had been sent for, as the woman was, to all appearance, in
her usual health. Perceiving a strong-looking woman before
him he said, "I presume I have missed the house, a sick

person wished to see me." The answer was, " You are quite
right, Sir, I sent for you, I am not well; I am troubled."
In the course of conversation Mr. Jones ascertained that
the woman had sent for him to counteract the evil machinations of her enemy. " I am witched," she said, " and a
parson can break the spell." The clergyman argued with
her, but all to no purpose. She affirmed that she was
witched, and that a clergyman could withdraw the curse.
Finding that the woman was obdurate he read a chapter
and offered up a prayer, and wishing the woman good day
with a hearty " God bless you," he departed. Upon a
subsequent visit he found the woman quite well, and he
was informed by her, to his astonishment, that he had
broken the spell.

2. Forcing the supposed witch to say over the cursed
animals, "*Rhad Duw ar y da*" ("God's blessing be on the
cattle "), or some such expressions, freed them from spells.

An instance of this kind is related on page 242, under
the heading, " A Horse Witched."

3. Reading the Bible over, or to, the bewitched freed them
from evil.

This was an antidote that could be exercised by anyone
who could procure a Bible. In an essay written in Welsh,
relating to the parishes of Garthbeibio, Llangadfan, and
Llanerfyl, in 1863, I find the following :—

"Gwr arall, ffarmwr mawr, a chanddo fuwch yn sal ar y
Sabbath, ar ol rhoddi *physic* iddi, tybiwyd ei bod yn marw,
rhedodd yntau i'r ty i nol y Bibl, *a darllenodd bennod iddi;*"
which rendered into English, is :—

Another man, a large farmer, having a cow sick on the
Sabbath day, after giving her physic, supposing she was
dying, ran into the house to fetch the Bible, and *read a
chapter to her.*

4. A Bible kept in a house was a protection from all evil.

This was a talisman, formerly only within the reach of the opulent. Quoting again from the essay above referred to, I find these words:—

"Byddai ambell Fibl mewn *ty mawr* yn cael ei gadw mewn cist neu goffr a chlo arno, tuag at gadw y ty rhag niwaid." That is:—

A Bible was occasionally kept in the bettermost farms in a chest which was locked, to protect the house from harm.

5. A ring made of the mountain ash acted as a talisman.

Rings made of this wood were generally placed under the doorposts to frustrate the evil designs of witches, and the inmates dwelt securely when thus protected. This tree was supposed to be a famous charm against witchcraft.

Mrs. Susan Williams, Garth, a farm on the confines of Efenechtyd parish, Denbighshire, told the writer that E. Edwards, Llwynybrain, Gwyddelwern, was famous for breaking spells, and consequently his aid was often required. Susan stated that they could not churn at Foel Fawn, Derwen. They sent for Edwards, who came, and offered up a kind of prayer, and then placed a ring made of the bark or of the wood of the mountain ash (she could not recollect which) underneath the churn, or the lid of the churn, and thus the spell was broken.

6. A horse-shoe found on a road or field, and nailed either on or above the door of a house or stable, was considered a protection from spells.

I have seen horse-shoes hanging by a string above a door, and likewise nailed with the open part upwards, on the door lintel, but quite as often I have observed that the open part is downwards; but however hung, on enquiry, the object is the same, viz., to secure luck and prevent evil.

7. Drawing blood from a witch or conjuror by anyone incapacitated these evil doers from working out their designs upon the person who spilt their blood.

I was told of a tailor's apprentice, who on the termination of his time, having heard, and believing, that his master was a conjuror, when saying good-bye doubled up his fingers and struck the old man on the nose, making his blood spurt in all directions. "There, master," said he, "there is no ill will between us, but you can now do me no harm, for I have drawn your blood, and you cannot witch me."

8. Drawing blood from a bewitched animal breaks the spell.

In the days of my youth, at Llanidloes, a couple of valuable horses were said to be bewitched, and they were bled to break the spell. If blood could not be got from horses and cattle, it was considered to be a positive proof that they were bewitched, and unless the spell could be broken, nothing, it was said, could save them from death.

9. It was generally thought that if a witch said the word "God" to a child or person, whom she had bewitched, it would "undo her work."

My friend Mr. Edward Hamer, in his "Parochial Account of Llanidloes," published in *The Montgomeryshire Collections*, vol. x., p. 242, records an instance of this belief. His words are:—

"About fifty years ago the narrator was walking up Long Bridge Street, when he saw a large crowd in one of the yards leading from the street to a factory. Upon making his way to the centre of this crowd, he saw an old woman in a 'fit,' real or feigned, he could not say, but he believed the latter, and over her stood an angry, middle-aged man, gesticulating violently, and threatening the old dame, that he would hang her from an adjacent beam if she would not pronounce the word 'God' to a child which was held in its mother's arms before her. It was in vain that the old woman protested her innocence; in vain that she said that by complying with his request she would stand before them a confessed witch; in vain that she fell into one fit after another, and prayed to be allowed to depart; not a sympathising face could she for some time see in the crowd, until the wife of a manufacturer, who lived close by, appeared on the scene, who also pleaded in vain on her behalf. Terrified beyond all measure, and scarcely knowing what she did, the old woman mumbled something to the child. It smiled. The angry parents were satisfied the spell was broken, the crowd dispersed, and the old woman was allowed to depart quietly."

10. The earth from a churchyard sprinkled over any place preserved it from spells.

Mr. Roberts, Plas Einion, Llanfair D. Clwyd, a very aged farmer, told me that when a certain main or cock fighting had been arranged, his father's servant man, suspecting unfair play, and believing that his master's birds had been bewitched, went to the churchyard and carried therefrom a quantity of consecrated earth, with which he slyly sprinkled the cock pit, and thus he averted the evil, and broke the spell, and all the birds fought, and won, according to their deserts.

11. Anything taken into a church belonging to a farm supposed to be cursed broke the spell or curse laid upon the place from which that thing was taken.

About twenty years ago, when the writer was curate of Llanwnog, Montgomeryshire, a Mrs. Hughes, a farmer's wife, who was a firm believer in omens, charms, and spells, told me that she knew nothing would come of the spell against so and so, and when asked to explain the matter, she said that she had seen straw taken from that farm to kindle the fire in the church, and thus, she said, the spell was broken.

12. A pin thrust into " Witch's Butter" would cause the witch to undo her work.

" Witch's Butter" is the name given to a kind of fungus that grows on decayed wood. The fungus resembles little lumps of butter, and hence its name. Should anyone think himself witched, all that he has got to do is to procure "witch's butter," and then thrust a pin into it. It was thought that this pin penetrated the wicked witch, and every pin thrust into the fungus went into her body, and thus she was forced to appear, and undo her mischief, and be herself relieved from bodily pain by relieving others.

13. A conjuror's charm could master a witch's spell.

It was thought that when a person was under a witch's spell he could get relief and punish the witch by procuring a charm from a conjuror. This charm was a bit of paper, often covered with illegible writing, but whatever was on it made no great difference, for the persons who procured the charms were usually illiterate. The process was as follows: —The party cursed took the charm, and thrust a pin through it, and having waited awhile to see whether the witch would appear or not, proceeded to thrust another pin through the paper, and if the witch were tardy in appearing, pin after pin was thrust into the paper, and every pin, it was thought, went into the body of the spiteful hag, and brought her ultimately to the house where her curse was being broken, in shocking pain, and when there it was believed she would say—

"Duw gatto bobpeth ag a feddwch chwi."

God preserve everything which you possess.

14. Certain plants were supposed to possess the power of destroying charms.

The Rev. D. James, Rector of Garthbeibio, was asked by Evan Williams, the Voel, a parishioner, whether he feared witches, and when answered in the negative, his interrogator appeared surprised; however, awhile afterwards, Williams went to the Rectory, and told the rector that he knew why he did not fear witches, and proceeded to tell him that he had seen a plant in the front of the rectory that protected the house from charms. This was what he called, *Meipen Fair*. In some parts of England the snapdragon is supposed to possess a like virtue, and also the elder tree.

Mr. Davies, schoolmaster, Llangedwyn, informed the writer that at one time hyssop was hung on the inside of the house door to protect the inmates from charms.

15. The seventh daughter could destroy charms. The seventh son was thought to possess supernatural power, and so also was the seventh daughter, but her influence seems to have been exerted against witchcraft.

16. The sign of the cross on the door made the inmates invulnerable, and when made with the finger on the breast it was a protection from evil.

The sign of the cross made on the person was once common in Wales, and the advice given by the aged when a person was in any difficulty was "*ymgroesa*," cross yourself. The custom of crossing the door on leaving the house lingered long in many places, and, I think, it is not altogether given up in our days.

17. Invoking the aid of the Holy Trinity. This was resorted to, as seen in the charm given on page 270, when animals were witched.

The way to find out whether a Hag is a Witch or not.

It was generally supposed that a witch could not pray, and one way of testing her guilty connection with the evil one was to ascertain whether she could repeat the Lord's

Prayer correctly. If she failed to do so, she was pronounced to be a witch. This test, as everyone knows, must have been a fallacious one, for there are good living illiterate people who are incapable of saying their *Pader*; but such was the test, and failure meant death.

Some fifty years ago, when the writer was a lad in school, he noticed a crowd in Short Bridge Street, Llanidloes, around an aged decrepit woman, apparently a stranger from the hill country, and on inquiring what was going on, he was told that the woman was a suspected witch, and that they were putting her to the test. I believe she was forced to go on her knees, and use the name of God, and say the Lord's Prayer. However, the poor frightened thing got successfully through the ordeal, and I saw her walk away from her judges.

Another manner for discovering a witch was to weigh her against the Church Bible; if the Bible went up, she was set at liberty, if, on the other hand, she were lighter than the Bible, she was a witch, and forfeited her life.

Swimming a witch was another method, and this was the one generally resorted to. The suspected person was taken to a river or pool of water, her feet and hands were tied, and she was thrown in; if she sank she was innocent, if she floated she was a witch, and never reached the bank alive.

Such as the preceding were some of the ridiculous trials to which poor, badly clad, aged, toothless, and wrinkled women were put by their superstitious neighbours to ascertain whether these miserable women were in league with the devil.

CONJURORS.

1. It was formerly believed that men could sell themselves to the devil, and thus become the possessors of supernatural power. These men were looked upon as malicious conjurors.

2. Another species of conjurors practised magical arts, having obtained their knowledge from the study of books. These were accounted able to thwart the designs of evil workers of every description.

3. There was another class of men supposed to have obtained strange power from their ancestors. They were looked upon as charmers and conjurors by descent.

1. Those who belonged to the first-mentioned class were not in communion with the Church, and the first step taken by them to obtain their object was to unbaptize themselves. The process was as follows:—The person who wished to sell himself to the devil went to a Holy Well, took water therefrom three times into his mouth, and spurted it out in a derisive manner, and thus having relieved himself, as it was thought, of his baptismal vow, he was ready and fit to make a contract with the evil one.

2. The second kind of conjurors obtained their knowledge of the occult science from the study of books. Generally learned men were by the ignorant supposed to possess uncanny power. When the writer lived in Carnarvonshire he was informed that Owen Williams, Waenfawr, had magical books kept in a box under lock and key, and that he never permitted anyone to see them. Poor Owen Williams, I wonder whether he knew of the popular rumour !

The following tale of Huw Llwyd's books I obtained from the Rev. R. Jones, rector of Llanycil.

Huw Llwyd and his Magical Books.

The story, as it has reached our days, is as follows :— It is said that Huw Llwyd had two daughters; one of an inquisitive turn of mind, like himself, while the other resembled her mother, and cared not for books. On his death bed he called his learned daughter to his side, and directed her to take his books on the dark science, and throw them into a pool, which he named, from the bridge that spanned the river. The girl went to Llyn Pont Rhyd-ddu with the books, and stood on the bridge, watching the whirlpool beneath, but she could not persuade herself to throw them over, and thus destroy her father's precious treasures. So she determined to tell him a falsehood, and say that she had cast them into the river. On her return home her father asked her whether she had thrown the books into the pool, and on receiving an answer in the affirmative, he, inquiring whether she had seen anything strange when the books reached the river, was informed that she had seen nothing. " Then," said he, " you have not complied with my request. I cannot die until the books are thrown into the pool." She took the books a second time to the river, and now, very reluctantly, she hurled them into the pool, and watched their descent. They had not reached the water before two hands appeared, stretched upward, out of the pool, and these hands caught the books before they touched the water and, clutching them carefully, both the books and the hands disappeared beneath the waters. She went home immediately, and again appeared before her father, and in answer to his question, she related what had occurred. " Now," said he, " I know you have thrown them in, and I can now die in peace," which he forthwith did.

3. Hereditary conjurors, or charmers, were thought to be beneficial to society. They were charmers rather than conjurors. In this category is to be reckoned:—

(a) The seventh son of a family of sons, born the one after the other.

(b) The seventh daughter in a family of daughters, born in succession, without a brother between. This person could undo spells and curses, but she could not herself curse others.

(c) The descendants of a person, who had eaten eagles'
flesh could, for nine generations, charm for the
shingles, or, as it is called in Welsh, *Swyno'r Ryri.*

Conjurors were formerly quite common in Wales; when
I say common, I mean that there was no difficulty in
obtaining their aid when required, and they were within
easy reach of those who wished to consult them. Some
became more celebrated than others, and consequently
their services were in greater requisition; but it may be said,
that each district had its wise man.

The office of the conjuror was to counteract the machina-
tions of witches, and to deliver people from their spells.
They were looked upon as the natural enemies of witches.
Instances have already been given of this antagonism.

But conjurors could act on their own account, and if they
did not show the same spiteful nature as witches, they,
nevertheless, were credited with possessing great and
dangerous power. They dealt freely in charms and spells,
and obtained large sums of money for their talismanic
papers. They could, it was believed, by their incantations
reveal the future, and oblige light-fingered people to restore
the things they had stolen.

Even a fishing rod made by a conjuror was sure to bring
luck to the fisherman. Lovers and haters alike resorted to
the wise man to attain through his aid their object.

There were but few, if any, matters beyond their compre-
hension, and hence the almost unbounded confidence placed
in these impostors by the superstitious and credulous.

Strange as it may seem, even in this century there are many
who still consult these deceivers, but more of this by and by.

I will now relate a few tales of the doings of these conjurors, and from them the reader can infer how baneful
their influence was upon the rustic population of Wales.

The Magician's Glass.

This glass, into which a person looked when he wished to solve the future, or to ascertain whom he or she was to marry, was used by Welsh, as well as other magicians. The glass gave back the features of the person sought after, and reflected the future career of the seeker after the hidden future. It was required that the spectator should concentrate all his attention on the glass, and, on the principle that they who gazed long should not gaze in vain, he obtained the desired glimpse. *Cwrt Cadno*, already referred to, professed to have such a glass.

But, the magician's glass is an instrument so often mentioned in connection with necromancy in all parts of the world, that more need not be said of it.

I will now give a few stories illustrative of the conjuror's power.

A Conjuror's Punishment of an Innkeeper for his exorbitant charges.

A famous conjuror, Dick Spot, was on his way to Llanrwst, and he turned into a public house at Henllan for refreshments. He called for a glass of beer and bread and cheese, and was charged tenpence for the same, fourpence for the beer, and sixpence for the bread and cheese. This charge he considered outrageous, but he paid the demand, and before departing he took a scrap of paper and wrote on it a spell, and hid it under the table, and then went on his way. That evening, soon after the landlord and landlady had retired for the night, leaving the servant girl to clear up, they were surprised to hear in the kitchen an unaccountable noise; shouting and jumping was the order of the day, or rather night, in that room. The good people heard the girl shout at the top of her voice—

"Six and four are ten,
Count it o'er again,"

and then she danced like mad round and round the
kitchen. They sternly requested the girl to cease yelling,
and to come to bed, but the only answer they received was—

"Six and four are ten,
Count it o'er again,"

and with accelerated speed she danced round and round
the kitchen.

The thought now struck the landlord that the girl had
gone out of her mind, and so he got up, and went to see
what was the matter with her, with the intention of trying to get her away from the kitchen. But the moment
he placed his foot in the kitchen, he gave a jump, and joined
the girl in her mad dance, and with her he shrieked out—

"Six and four are ten,
Count it o'er again."

So now the noise was doubled, and the good wife, finding
that her husband did not return to her, became very angry,
if not jealous. She shouted to them to cease their row, but
all to no purpose, for the dancing and the shouting continued.
Then she left her bed and went to the kitchen door, and
greatly disgusted she was to see her husband and maid
dancing together in that shameless manner. She stood at
the door a moment or two observing their frantic behaviour,
and then she determined forcibly to put a stop to the
proceedings, so into the room she bounded, but with a hop
and a jump she joined in the dance, and sang out in chorus
with the other two—

"Six and four are ten,
Count it o'er again."

The uproar now was great indeed, and roused the neighbours from their sleep. They from outside heard the mad
dance and the words, and guessed that Dick Spot had been
the cause of all this. One of those present hurried after
the conjuror, who, fortunately, was close at hand, and desired

him to return to the inn to release the people from his spell. "Oh," said Dick, " take the piece of paper that is under the table and burn it, and they will then stop their row." The man returned to the inn, pushed open the door, rushed to the table, and cast the paper into the fire, and then the trio became quiet. But they had nearly exhausted themselves by their severe exertions ere they were released from the power of the spell.

A Conjuror and Robbers.

A conjuror, or *Gwr Cyfarwydd*, was travelling over the Denbighshire hills to Carnarvonshire; being weary, he entered a house that he saw on his way, and he requested refreshments, which were given him by a young woman. "But," said she, "you must make haste and depart, for my brothers will soon be here, and they are desperate men, and they will kill you." But no, the stranger was in no hurry to move on, and though repeatedly besought to depart, he would not do so. To the great dread and fear of the young woman, her brothers came in, and, in anger at finding a stranger there, bade him prepare for death. He requested a few minutes' respite, and took out a book and commenced reading it. When he was thus engaged a horn began growing in the centre of the table, and on this the robbers were obliged to gaze, and they were unable even to move. The stranger went to bed, and found the robbers in the morning still gazing at the horn, as he knew they would be, and he departed leaving them thus engaged, and the tale goes, that they were arrested in that position, being unable to offer any resistance to their captors.

There are several versions of the Horn Tale afloat; instead of being made to grow out of a table, it was made to grow out of a person's head or forehead. There is a tradition

that Huw Llwyd was able to do this wonderful thing, and
that he actually did it.

The Conjuror and the Cattle.

R. H., a farmer in Llansilin parish, who lost several head
of cattle, sent or went to Shon Gyfarwydd, who lived in
Llanbrynmair, a well-known conjuror, for information concerning their death, and for a charm against further loss.
Both were obtained, and the charm worked so well that the
grateful farmer sent a letter to Shon acknowledging the
benefit he had derived from him.

This Shon was a great terror to thieves, for he was able
to spot them and mark them in such a way that they were
known to be culprits. I am indebted to Mr. Jones, Rector
of Bylchau, near Denbigh, for the three following stories, in
which the very dread of being marked by Shon was sufficient
to make the thieves restore the stolen property.

Stolen property discovered through fear of applying to the Llanbrynmair Conjuror.

Richard Thomas, Post Office, Llangadfan, lost a coat and
waistcoat, and he suspected a certain man of having stolen
them. One day this man came to the shop, and Thomas saw
him there, and, speaking to his wife from the kitchen in a
loud voice, so as to be heard by his customer in the shop,
he said that he wanted the loan of a horse to go to Llanbrynmair. Llanbrynmair was, as we know, the conjuror's
place of abode. Thomas, however, did not leave his house, nor
did he intend doing so, but that very night the stolen
property was returned, and it was found the next morning
on the door sill.

Reclaiming stolen property through fear of the Conjuror.

A mason engaged in the restoration of Garthbeibio Church
placed a trowel for safety underneath a stone, but by
morning it was gone. Casually in the evening he informed

his fellow workmen that he had lost his trowel, and that someone must have stolen it, but that he was determined to find out the thief by taking a journey to Llanbrynmair. He never went, but the ruse was successful, for the next morning he found, as he suspected would be the case, the trowel underneath the very stone where he had himself placed it.

Another similar Tale.

Thirty pounds were stolen from Glan-yr-afon, Garthbeibio. The owner made known to his household that he intended going to Shon the conjuror, to ascertain who had taken his money, but the next day the money was discovered, being restored, as was believed, by the thief the night before.

These stories show that the ignorant and superstitious were influenced through fear, to restore what they had wrongfully appropriated, and their faith in the conjuror's power thus resulted, in some degree, in good to the community. The *Dyn Hyspys* was feared where no one else was feared, and in this way the supposed conjuror was not altogether an unimportant nor unnecessary member of society. At a time, particularly when people are in a low state of civilization, or when they still cling to the pagan faith of their forefathers, transmitted to them from remote ages, then something can be procured for the good of a benighted people even through the medium of the *Gwr Cyfarwydd*.

Events occurred occasionally by a strange coincidence through which the fame of the *Dyn Hyspys* became greatly increased. An event of this kind is related by Mr. Edward Hamer. He states that:—

"Two respectable farmers, living in the upper Vale of the Severn (Cwm Glyn Hafren), and standing in relationship to each other of uncle and nephew, a few years ago purchased each a pig of the same litter, from another farmer. When bought, both animals were, to all appearance, in excellent health and condition, and for a short time after their removal to their new homes both continued to improve daily. It was not long, however, before both were taken ill very suddenly. As there appeared something very strange in the behaviour of his animal, the nephew firmly believed that he was 'witched,' and acting upon this belief, set out for the neighbouring conjuror. Having received certain injunctions from the 'wise man,' he returned home, carried them out, and had the satisfaction of witnessing the gradual recovery of his pig. The uncle paid no attention to the persuasions and even entreaties of his nephew; he would not believe that his pig was 'witched,' and refused to consult the conjuror. The pig died after an illness of three weeks, *and many thought the owner deserved little sympathy for manifesting so much obstinacy and scepticism.* These events occurred in the spring of the year 1870, and were much talked of at the time."—*Montgomeryshire Collections,* vol. x., p. 240.

Conjurors retained their repute by much knavery and collusion with others.

Tales are not wanted that expose their impostures. The Rev. Meredith Hamer, late of Berse, told me of the following exposure of a conjuror. I know not where the event occurred, but it is a typical case.

A Conjuror's Collusion exposed.

This man's house consisted of but few rooms. Between the kitchen and his study, or consulting room, was a slight partition. He had a servant girl, whom he admitted as a partner in his trade. This girl, when she saw a patient approach the house, which she was able to do, because there was only one approach to it, and only one entrance.

informed her master of the fact that someone was coming, and he immediately disappeared, and he placed himself in a position to hear the conversation of the girl with the person who had come to consult him. The servant by questioning the party adroitly obtained that information respecting the case which her master required, and when she had obtained the necessary information, he would appear, and forthwith tell the stranger that he knew hours before, or days ago, that he was to have the visit now paid him, and then he would relate all the particulars which he had himself heard through the partition, to the amazement of the stranger, who was ignorant of this means of communication.

At other times, if a person who wished to consult him came to the house when the conjuror was in the kitchen, he would disappear as before, stating that he was going to consult his books, and then his faithful helper would proceed to extort the necessary information from the visitor. On this, he would re-appear and exhibit his wonderful knowledge to the amazed dupe.

On one occasion, though, a knowing one came to the conjuror with his arm in a sling, and forthwith the wise man disappeared, leaving the maid to conduct the necessary preliminary examination, and her visitor minutely described how the accident had occurred, and how he had broken his arm in two places, &c.

All this the conjuror heard, and he came into the room and rehearsed all that he had heard; but the biter was bitten, for the stranger, taking his broken arm out of the sling, in no very polite language accused the conjuror of being an impostor, and pointed out the way in which the collusion had been carried out between him and his maid.

This was an exposure the conjuror had not foreseen!

The Conjuror's Dress.

Conjurors, when engaged in their uncanny work, usually wore a grotesque dress and stood within a circle of protection. I find so graphic a description of a doctor who dealt in divination in Mr. Hancock's "History of Llanrhaïadr-yn-Mochnant" that I will transcribe it:—"He" (the raiser of the devils) " was much resorted to by the friends of parties mentally deranged, many of whom he cured. Whenever he assumed to practise the 'black art,' he put on a most grotesque dress, a cap of sheepskin with a high crown, bearing a plume of pigeons' feathers, and a coat of unusual pattern, with broad hems, and covered with talismanic characters. In his hand he had a whip, the thong of which was made of the skin of an eel, and the handle of bone. With this he drew a circle around him, outside of which, at a proper distance, he kept those persons who came to him, whilst he went through his mystic sentences and performances."—*Montgomeryshire Collections*, vol. vi., pp. 329-30.

CHARMS.

The cure of diseases by charms is generally supposed to be a kind of superstition antagonistic to common sense, and yet there are undoubted cases of complete cures through the instrumentality of charms. Warts are, undoubtedly, removed by the faith of those persons who suffer from them in the power of the charmer and his charms. The writer has had innumerable instances of the efficacy of wart charms, but it is not his intention to endeavour to trace the effect of charms on highly sensitive people, but only to record those charms that he has seen or heard of as having been used.

Swyno'r 'Ryri (Charming the Shingles).

The shingles is a skin disease, which encircles the body like a girdle, and the belief was that if it did so the patient died. However, there was a charm for procuring its removal, which was generally resorted to with success; but the last person who could charm this disease in Montgomeryshire lies buried on the west side of the church at Penybontfawr, and consequently there is no one now in those parts able to charm the shingles. The inscription on his tombstone informs us that Robert Davies, Glanhafon Fawr, died March 13th, 1864, aged 29, so that faith in this charm has reached our days.

It was believed that the descendants of a person who had eaten eagle's flesh *to the ninth generation* could charm for shingles.

The manner of proceeding can be seen from the following quotation taken from "The History of Llanrhaiadr-yn-Mochnant," by Mr. T. W. Hancock, which appears in vol. vi., pp. 327-8 of the *Montgomeryshire Collections*.

A Charm for the Shingles.

"This custom (charming for the shingles) was more prevalent in this parish than in any other in Montgomeryshire. A certain amount of penance was to be done by the sufferer, who was to go to the charmer in the morning fasting, and he was also to be fasting. The mode of cure was simple—the charmer breathed gently on the inflamed part, and then followed a series of little spittings upon and around it. A few visits to the charmer, or sometimes a single one, was sufficient to effect a cure.

"The power of charming for the ''Ryri' is now lost, or in any event has not been practised in this parish, for several years past. The possession of this remarkable healing power by the charmer was said to have been derived from the circumstance *of either the charmer himself, or one of his ancestors within the ninth degree, having eaten of the flesh of the eagle*, the virtue being, it was alleged, transmitted from the person who had so partaken to his descendants for nine generations. The tradition is that the disorder was introduced into the country by a malevolent eagle.

"Some charmers before the operation of spitting, muttered to themselves the following incantation:—

> Yr Eryr Eryres
> Mi a'th ddanfonais
> Dros naw môr a thros naw mynydd,
> A thros naw erw o dir anghelfydd ;
> Lle na chyfartho ci, ac na frefo fuwch,
> Ac na ddelo yr eryr byth yn uwch."

> Male eagle, female eagle,
> I send you (by the operation of blowing, we presume)
> Over nine seas, and over nine mountains,
> And over nine acres of unprofitable land,
> Where no dog shall bark, and no cow shall low,
> And where no eagle shall higher rise."

The charmer spat first on the rash and rubbed it with his finger over the affected parts, and then breathed nine times on it.

Jane Davies, an aged woman, a native of Llanrhaiadr-yn-Mochnant, with whom I had many long conversations on several occasions, told the narrator that she had cut a cat's ear to get blood, wherewith to rub the patient's breast who was suffering from the shingles, to stop its progress, until the sufferer could be visited by the charmer, and she said that the cat's blood always stopped it spreading.

There were several charms for many of the ailments to which man is subject, which were thought to possess equal curative virtues.

Toothache charms.

By repeating the following doggerel lines the worst case of toothache could be cured—

> Peter sat on a marble stone,
> Jesus came to him all alone.
> What's up, Peter? The toothache, my lord ;
> Rise up Peter, and be cured of this pain,
> And all those *who carry these few lines* for my sake.

This charm appeared in the *Wrexham Advertiser* as one that was used in *Coedpoeth* and *Bulch Gwyn.* But the words appear in "*Y Gwyliedydd*" for May, 1826, page 151. The Welsh heading to the charm informs us that it was obtained from an Irish priest in county Cork, Ireland. The words are :—

Fel yr oedd Pedr yn eistedd ar faen Mynor,
Crist a ddaeth atto, ac efe yn unig.
Pedr, beth a ddarfu i ti ? Y Ddanodd, fy Arglwydd Dduw.
Cyfod, Pedr, a rhydd fyddi ;
A bydd pob dyn a dynes iach oddiwrth y ddanodd
Y rhai a gredant i'r geiriau hyn,
Yr wyf fi yn gwneuthur yn enw Duw.

The first two lines of the English and Welsh are the same but the third and succeeding lines in Welsh are as follows :—

Peter, what is the matter ? The toothache, my Lord God.
Rise Peter, and thou shalt be cured ;
And every man and woman who believes these words
Shall be cured of the toothache,
Which I perform in the name of God.

Another version of this charm was given me by Mrs. Reynolds, Pembroke House, Oswestry—

As Jesus walked through the gates of Jerusalem,
He saw Peter weeping. Jesus said unto him, why weepest thou ?
I have got the toothache. Jesus touched his tooth,
And Jesus said, have faith and believe,
Thy tooth shall ache no more.
I return you humble and hearty thanks
For the blessing which you have bestowed on me.

A young man told me that his brother once suffered greatly from toothache, and a woman gave him a charm like the above, written on paper. He rubbed the charm along the tooth, and he kept it in his pocket until it crumbled away, and as long as he preserved it he never was trouble with the toothache.

Rosemary Charm for Toothache.

" Llosg ei bren (Rhosmari) hyd oni bo yn lo du, ac yna dyro ef mewn cadach lliain cry, ac ira dy ddanedd ag ef; ac fo ladd y pryfed, ac a'u ceidw rhag pob clefyd."—*Y Brython*, p. 339.

" Burn a Rosemary bough until it becomes black, and then place it in a strong linen cloth, and anoint thy teeth with it, and it will kill the worm, and preserve thee from every kind of fever."

It was thought at one time that toothache was caused by a worm in the tooth, as intimated above.

Whooping Cough Charm.

Children suffering from whooping cough were taken to a seventh son, or lacking a seventh son of sons only, to a fifth son of sons only, who made a cake, and gave it to the sufferers to be eaten by them, and they would recover. The visit was to be thrice repeated. Bread and butter were sometimes substituted for the cake.

The writer has been told of instances of the success of this charm.

Another charm was—buy a penny roll, wrap it in calico, bury it in the garden, take it up next day. The sufferer from whooping-cough is then to eat the roll until it is consumed.

Charm for Fits.

A ring made out of the offertory money was a cure for fits. About the year 1882 the wife of a respectable farmer in the parish of Efenechtyd called at the rectory and asked the rector's wife if she would procure a shilling for her from the offering made at Holy Communion, out of which she was going to have a ring made to cure her fits. This coin was to be given unsolicited and received without thanks.

The Rev. J. D. Edwards, late vicar of Rhosymedre, informed the writer that his parishioners often obtained silver

coins from the offertory for the purpose now named. So as
to comply with the conditions, the sufferers went to Mrs.
Edwards some time during the week before " Sacrament
Sunday," and asked her to request Mr. Edwards to give him
or her a shilling out of the offertory, and on the following
Monday the afflicted person would be at the Vicarage, and
the Vicar, having already been instructed by Mrs. Edwards,
gave the shilling without uttering a word, and it was
received in the same manner.

Another charm for fits was to procure a human being's
skull, grind it into powder, and take it as medicine.

Charm for Cocks about to fight.

The charm consisted of a verse taken from the Bible,
written on a slip of paper, wrapped round the bird's leg, as
the steel spurs were being placed on him. The verse so
employed was, Eph. vi., 16 :—" Taking the shield of faith,
wherewith ye shall be able to quench all the fiery darts of
the wicked.

William Jones, Pentre Llyffrith, Llanfyllin, was a celebrated cock charmer. There was also a well-known charmer
who lived at Llandegla, Denbighshire, who refused a charm
to a certain man. When asked why he had not complied
with his request, he said—" He will not need charms for his
birds, for he will be a dead man before the main comes off."
This became true, for the man died, as foretold.

Charm for Asthma.

Place the Bible for three successive nights under the
bolster of the sufferer, and it will cure him.

Charms for Warts.

1. Drop a pin into a holy well and your warts will disappear, but should anyone take the pin out of the well, the
warts you have lost will grow on his fingers.

2. Rub the warts with the inside of a bean pod, and then throw the pod away.

3. Take wheat on the stalk, rub the warts with the wheat's beard or bristles at the end of the ear, take these to four crosses or roads that cross each other, bury the straw, and the warts will decay with the decay of the straw.

4. Rub the warts with elderberry leaves plucked by night, and then burn them, and the warts will disappear.

5. Rub the warts with a bit of flesh meat, wrap the flesh up in paper, throw it behind your back, and do not look behind you to see what becomes of it, and whoever picks it up gets your warts.

6. Take a snail and pierce it through with a thorn, and leave it to die on the bush; as it disappears so will your warts.

Charm for removing a Stye from the eye.

Take an ordinary knitting needle, and pass it back and fore over the stye, but without touching it, and at the same time counting its age, thus—One stye, two styes, three styes, up to nine, and then reversing the order, as nine styes, eight styes, down to one stye, and *no* stye. This counting was to be done in one breath. If the charmer drew his breath the charm was broken, but three attempts were allowed. The stye, it was alleged, would die from that hour, and disappear in twenty-four hours.

Charms for Quinsy.

Apply to the throat hair cut at midnight from the black shoulder stripe of the colt of an ass.

Charming the Wild Wart.

Take a branch of elder tree, strip off the bark, split off a piece, hold this skewer near the wart, and rub the wart three or nine times with the skewer, muttering the while an incantation of your own composing, then pierce the wart with a thorn. Bury the skewer transfixed with the thorn in a dunghill. The wart will rot away just as the buried things decay.

Charm for Rheumatism.

Carry a potato in your pocket, and when one is finished, supply its place with another.

Charm for removing the Ringworm.

1. Spit on the ground the first thing in the morning, mix the spittle with the mould, and then anoint the ringworm with this mixture.

2. Hold an axe over the fire until it perspires, and then anoint the ringworm with the sweat.

Cattle Charms.

Mr. Hamer in his "Parochial Account of Llanidloes" published in *The Montgomeryshire Collections*, Vol. x., p.249, states that he has in his possession two charms that were actually used for the protection of live stock of two small farms. One of them opens thus :—

"In the name of the Father, and of the Son, and of the Holy Ghost. Amen . . . . and in the name of Lord Jesus Christ my redeemer, that I will give relief to——creatures his cows, and his calves, and his horses, and his sheep, and his pigs, and all creatures that alive be in his possession, from all witchcraft and from all other assaults of Satan. Amen."

Mr. Hamer further states that :—

"At the bottom of the sheet, on the left, is the magical word, *Abracadabra*, written in the usual triangular form ; in the centre. a number of planetary symbols, and on the right, a circular figure filled in with lines and symbols, and beneath them the words, ' By Jah, Joh, Jab.' It was the custom to rub these charms over the cattle, &c. a number of times, while some incantation was being mumbled. The

paper was then carefully folded up, and put in some safe
place where the animals were housed, as a guard against
future visitations."

In other cases the charm was worn by the cattle, as is
shown by the following tale:—

Charm against Foot and Mouth Disease.

The cattle on a certain farm in Llansilin parish suffered
from the above complaint, and old Mr. H——— consulted
a conjuror, who gave him a written charm which he was
directed to place on the horns of the cattle, and he was told
this would act both as a preventive and a cure. This
farmer's cattle might be seen with the bit of paper, thus
procured, tied to their horns. My informant does not wish to
be named, nor does she desire the farmer's name to be
given, but she vouches for the accuracy of her information,
and for my own use, she gave me all particulars respecting
the above. This took place only a few years ago, when the
Foot and Mouth Disease first visited Wales.

I obtained, through the kindness of the Rev. John Davies,
vicar of Bryneglwys, the following charm procured from
Mr. R. Jones, Tynywern, Bryneglwys, Denbighshire, who
had it from his uncle, by whom it was used at one time.

Yn enw y Tad, a'r Mab, a'r Ysbryd.

Bod I grist Iesu y gysegredig a oddefe ar y groes,
Pan godaist Sant Lasarys o'i fedd wedi farw,
Pan faddeuaist Bechodau I fair fagdalen, a thrygra
wrthyf fel bo gadwedig bob peth a henwyf fi ag a
croeswyf fi ⚕ trwy nerth a rhinwedd dy eiriau
Bendigedig di fy Arglwydd Iesu Crist. Amen.
Iesu Crist ain harglwydd ni gwared ni rhag pop
rhiwogaeth o Brofedigaeth ar ysbrydol o uwch deiar
nag o Is deiar, rhag y gythraelig o ddun nei ddynes
a chalon ddrwg a reibia dda ei berchenog ei
ddrwg rhinwedd ei ddrwg galon ysgymynedig

a wahanwyd or ffydd gatholig ⁙ trwy nerth a rhinwedd
dy eiriau Bendigedig di fy Arglwydd Iesu Crist. Amen.

Iesu Crist ain harglwydd ni Gwared ni rhag y glwy
ar bar, ar Llid, ar genfigain ar adwyth . . . . . .
ar Pleined Wibrenou ar gwenwyn
deiarol, trwy nerth a rhinwedd dy eiriau
Bedigedig di Fy Arglwydd Iesu Crist. Amen.

It was somewhat difficult to decipher the charm, and four
words towards the end are quite illegible, and consequently
they are omitted. The following translation will show the
nature of the charm :—

In the Name of the Father, the Son, and the Spirit.

May Christ Jesus the sanctified one, who suffered death on
the cross,
When thou didst raise Lazarus from his tomb after his death,
When Thou forgavest sins to Mary Magdalen, have mercy
on me, so that everything named by me and
crossed by me ⁙ may be saved by the power and virtue
of thy blessed words my Lord Jesus Christ. Amen.

Jesus Christ our Lord save us from every
kind of temptation whether spiritual above the earth
or under the earth, from the devilish man or woman
with evil heart who bewitcheth the goods of their owner ;
his evil virtue, his evil excommunicated heart
cut off from the Catholic Faith ⁙ by the power and virtue
of thy blessed words my Lord Jesus Christ. Amen.

Jesus Christ our Lord save us from the disease and the
affliction, and the wrath, and the envy, and the mischief, and
the . . . . . and the planet of the sky and the earthly
poison, by the power and virtue
of Thy blessed words, my Lord Jesus Christ.

Amen.

The mark ⁙ indicates that crosses were here made by
the person who used the charm, and probably the words
of the charm were audibly uttered.

Another Cattle Charm Spell.

Mr. Hughes, Plasnewydd, Llansilin, lost several head of cattle. He was told to bleed one of the herd, boil the blood, and take it to the cowhouse at midnight. He did so, and lost no more after applying this charm.

A Charm for Calves.

If calves were scoured over much, and in danger of dying, a hazel twig the length of the calf was twisted round the neck like a collar, and it was supposed to cure them.

A Charm for Stopping Bleeding.

Mrs. Reynolds, whom I have already mentioned in connection with a charm for toothache, gave me the following charm. It bears date April 5, 1842:—

> Our Blessed Saviour Jesus Christ was born at Bethlehem,
> By the Virgin Mary,
> Baptized in the River Jordan,
> By St. John the Baptist.
> He commanded the water to stop, and it obeyed Him.
> And I desire in the name of Jesus Christ,
> That the blood of this vein (or veins) might stop,
> As the water did when Jesus Christ was baptized.
>
> Amen.

Charm to make a Servant reliable.

" Y neb a fyno gael ei weinidog yn gywir, doded beth o'r lludw hwn yn nillad ei weinidog ac efe a fydd cywir tra parhao'r lludw."—*Y Brython*, vol. iii., p. 137.

Which is :—Whosoever wishes to make his servant faithful let him place the ashes (of a snake) in the clothes of his servant, and as long as they remain there he will be faithful.

There are many other wonderful things to be accomplished with the skin of an adder, or snake, besides the preceding. The following are recorded in *Y Brython*, vol. iii., p. 137.

Charms performed with Snake's Skin.

1. Burn the skin and preserve the ashes. A little salve made out of the ashes will heal a wound.

2. A little of the ashes placed between the shoulders will make a man invulnerable.

3. Whoso places a little of the ashes in the water with which he washes himself, should his enemies meet him, they will flee because of the beauty of his face.

4. Cast a little of the ashes into thy neighbour's house, and he will leave it.

5. Place the ashes under the sole of thy foot, and everybody will agree with thee.

6. Should a man wrestle, let him place some of the ashes under his tongue, and no one can conquer him.

7. Should a man wish to know what is about to occur to him, let him place a pinch of the ashes on his head, and then go to sleep, and his dreams will reveal the future.

8. Should a person wish to ascertain the mind of another, let him throw a little of the ashes on that person's clothes, and then let him ask what he likes, the answer will be true.

9. Has already been given above. (See page 272).

10. If a person is afraid of being poisoned in his food, let him place the ashes on the table with his food, and poison cannot stay there with the ashes.

11. If a person wishes to succeed in love, let him wash his hands and keep some of the ashes in them, and then everybody will love him.

12. The skin of the adder is a remedy against fevers.

The Charms performed with Rosemary.

Rosemary dried in the sun and made into powder, tied in a cloth around the right arm, will make the sick well.

The smoke of rosemary bark, sniffed, will, even if you are in gaol, release you.

HH

The leaves made into salve, placed on a wound, where the flesh is dead, will cure the wound.

A spoon made out of its wood will make whatever you eat therewith nutritious.

Place it under the door post, and no snake nor adder can ever enter thy house.

The leaves placed in beer or wine will keep these liquids from becoming sour, and give them such a flavour that you will dispose of them quickly.

Place a branch of rosemary on the barrel, and it will keep thee from fever, even though thou drink of it for a whole day.

Such were some of the wonderful virtues of this plant, as given in the *Brython*, vol. iii., 339.

Charm for Clefyd y Galon, or Heart Disease.

The Rev. J. Felix, vicar of Cilcen, near Mold, when a young man lodged in Eglwysfach, near Glandovey. His landlady, noticing that he looked pale and thin, suggested that he was suffering from *Clefyd y galon*, which may be translated as above, or love sickness, a complaint common enough among young people, and she suggested that he should call in David Jenkins, a respectable farmer and a local preacher with the Wesleyans, to cure him. Jenkins came, and asked the supposed sufferer whether he believed in charms, and was answered in the negative. However, he proceeded with his patient as if he had answered in the affirmative. Mr Felix was told to take his coat off, he did so, and then he was bidden to tuck up his shirt above his elbow. Mr. Jenkins then took a yarn thread and placing one end on the elbow measured to the tip of Felix's middle finger, then he told his patient to take hold of the yarn at one end, the other end resting the while on the elbow, and he was to take fast hold of it, and stretch it. This he did, and the yarn lengthened, and this was a sign that he was actually sick of heart disease. Then the charmer tied this yarn around the patient's left arm above the elbow, and there it was left, and on the next visit measured again, and he was pronounced cured.

The above information I received from Mr. Felix, who is still alive and well.

There were various ways of proceeding in this charm. Yarn was always used and the measurement as above made, and sometimes the person was named and his age, and the Trinity was invoked, then the thread was put around the neck of the sick person, and left there for three nights, and afterwards buried in the name of the Trinity under ashes. If the thread shortened above the second joint of the middle finger there was little hope of recovery ; should it lengthen that was a sign of recovery.

Clefyd yr Ede Wlan or Yarn Sickness.

About twenty years ago, when the writer was curate of Llanwnog, Montgomeryshire, a young Welsh married woman came to reside in the parish suffering from what appeared to be that fell disease, consumption. He visited her in her illness, and one day she appeared much elated as she had been told that she was improving in health. She told the narrator that she was suffering from *Clwyf yr ede wlan* or the woollen thread sickness, and she said that the yarn had *lengthened*, which was a sign that she was recovering. The charm was the same as that mentioned above, supplemented with a drink made of a quart of old beer, into which a piece of heated steel had been dipped, with an ounce of meadow saffron tied up in muslin soaked in it, taken in doses daily of a certain prescribed quantity, and the thread was measured daily, thrice I believe, to see if she was being cured or the reverse. Should the yarn shorten it was a sign of death, if it lengthened it indicated a recovery. However, although the yarn in this case lengthened, the young woman died. The charm failed.

Sufficient has been said about charms to show how prevalent faith in their efficiency was. Ailments of all descriptions had their accompanying antidotes; but it is singularly strange that people professing the Christian religion should cling so tenaciously to paganism and its forms, so that even in our own days, such absurdities as charms find a resting-place in the minds of our rustic population, and often, even the better-educated classes resort to charms for obtaining cures for themselves and their animals.

But from ancient times, omens, charms, and auguries have held considerable sway over the destinies of men. That charming book, *Plutarch's Lives*, abounds with instances of this kind. Indeed, an excellent collection of ancient Folk-lore could easily be compiled from extant classical authors. Most things die hard, and ideas that have once made a lodgment in the mind of man, particularly when they are connected in any way with his faith, die the very hardest of all. Thus it is that such beliefs as are treated of in this chapter still exist, and they have reached our days from distant periods, filtered somewhat in their transit, but still retaining their primitive qualities.

We have not as yet gathered together the fragments of the ancient religion of the Celts, and formed of them a consistent whole, but evidently we are to look for them in the sayings and doings of the people quite as much as in the writings of the ancients. If we could only ascertain what views were held respecting any particular matter in ancient times, we might undoubtedly find traces of them even in modern days. Let us take for instance only one subject, and see whether traces of it still exist. Cæsar in his

Commentaries states of the Druids that, "One of their
principal maxims is that the soul never dies, but that after
death it passes into the body of another being. This maxim
they consider to be of the greatest utility to encourage
virtue and to make them regardless of life."

Now, is there anything that can be associated with such
teaching still to be found? The various tales previously
given of hags turning themselves and others into various
kinds of animals prove that people believed that such transi-
tions were in life possible, and they had only to go a step
further and apply the same faith to the soul, and we arrive
at the transmigration of souls.

It is not my intention to make too much of the following
tale, for it may be only a shred, but still as such it is worthy
of record. A few years ago I was staying at the Rectory,
Erbistock, near Ruabon, and the rector, the Rev. P. W.
Sparling, in course of conversation, said that a parishioner,
one Betsy Roberts, told him that she knew before anyone
told her, that a certain person died at such and such a time.
The rector asked her how she came to know of the
death if no one had informed her, and if she had not been
to the house to ascertain the fact. Her answer was, "I knew
because I saw a hare come from towards his house and cross
over the road before me." This was about all that the
rector could elicit, but evidently the woman connected the
appearance of the hare with the death of the man. The
association of the live hare with the dead man was here a
fact, and possibly in the birthplace of that woman such a
connection of ideas was common. Furthermore, it has
often been told me by people who have professed to have
heard what they related, that being present in the death
chamber of a friend they have heard a bird singing beautifully outside in the darkness, and that it stopped immediately

on the death of their friend. Here again we have a strange connection between two forms of life, and can this be a lingering Druidic or other ancient faith ?

In the *Dictionary of the Welsh Language* by the Rev. Canon Silvan Evans, part i., p. 8, under the word *Abred*, we have an exhaustive statement on the subject of transmigration, which I will take the liberty to transcribe, for it certainly throws light on the matter now treated of.

"*Abred* .... 1. The state or condition through which, by a regular upward gradation, all animated beings pass from the lowest point of existence in which they originate, towards humanity and the highest state of happiness and perfection. All the states of animation below that of humanity are necessarily evil; in the state of humanity, good and evil are equally balanced; and in all the states above humanity, good preponderates and evil becomes impossible. If man, as a free agent, attaches himself to evil, he falls in death into such an animal state of existence as corresponds with the turpitude of his soul, which may be so great as to cast him down into the lowest point of existence, from which he shall again return through such a succession of animal existences as is most proper to divest him of his evil propensities. After traversing such a course, he will again rise to the probationary state of humanity, where according to contingencies he may rise or fall; yet, should he fall, he shall rise again, and should this happen for millions of ages, the path of happiness is still open to him, and will so remain to all eternity, for sooner or later he will infallibly arrive at his destined station or happiness, from which he can never fall. This doctrine of metamorphosis or evolution, attributed to the Druids and the Welsh bards, is succinctly but fully stated by its hierophant, Iolo Morganwg, in his ' Poems' (1794), ii., 195-256, and elucidated by documents which had not previously been made public, but of which none are of an early date."

Thus writes the Welsh lexicographer on this matter. The word *abred* is archaic, as is the idea for which it stands; but as already said, very little has been lost of ideas which were once the property of kindred races; so here we have no exception to the general rule, though the word *abred* and the theory it represented come down to modern times strengthless, resembling the lifeless mummy of an Egyptian king that once represented a living people and principle. Still, the word and the idea it stands for have descended, in form, to our days, and tell us something about the faith of our forefathers regarding the immortality of the soul.

RHAMANTA, OR OMEN SEEKING.

Rhamanta was a kind of divination that could be resorted to without the intervention of any outside party, by anyone wishful to ascertain the future with reference to herself or himself. It differed, therefore, from the preceding tales of conjurors or witches, insomuch that the services of neither of these parties were required by the anxious seekers of coming events. They could themselves uplift the veil, using, however, for this purpose certain means, which were credited with possessing the power of opening to their view events which were about to happen.

As there was something uncanny in this seeking for hidden information, young women generally in companies of three sought for the information their inquisitiveness required. This was usually done in the dead of night, and twelve o'clock was the hour when they resorted to their incantations. Some of the expedients adopted were harmless, though silly; others were cruel. To the effective carrying out of the matter it was generally necessary that at least one of the party should have slept within the year on an oat-straw bed, or a bed made of the leaves of mountain ash, mixed with the seeds of a spring fern, and a pillow of Maiden Hair.

The nights generally resorted to for the purpose mentioned above were All Hallow Eve, S. John's Eve, and Mayday Eve, but there were other times also when the lovesick could get a glimpse of their life partners.

I have said that some of the means employed were innocent and others cruel. Before proceeding I will record instances of both kinds. It was thought that if a young woman placed a snail under a basin on *Nos Wyl Ifan*, S. John's Eve, it would by its movements trace the name of her coming husband underneath, or at least his initials. One can very well imagine a young woman not over particular as to form, being able to decipher the snail's wanderings, and making them represent her lover's name. Should the snail have remained immovable during the night, this indicated her own or her lover's death; or at the least, no offer of marriage in the coming year.

It was usual for young women to hunt for *Llysiau Ifan* (S. John's Wort) on *Nos Wyl Ifan*, at midnight, and it was thought that the silvery light of a glowworm would assist them in discovering the plant. The first thing, therefore, was to search for their living lanthorn. This found, they carried the glowworm in the palm of the hand, and proceeding in their search they sought underneath or among the fern for St. John's Wort. When found, a bunch was carried away, and hung in the young woman's bedroom. If in the morning the leaves appeared fresh, it was a sign that she should be married within the year; if, however, the leaves were found hanging down or dead, this indicated her death, or that she was not to get a husband within that year. We can well understand that a sharp young person would resort to means to keep the plant alive, and thus avert what she most feared.

The following instance of *Rhamanta* I received from a young woman who witnessed the work done. She gave me the name of the party, but for special reasons I do not supply names.

A young woman was madly in love with a young man, and she gave the servant man a jug of beer for procuring a frog for her. This he did; and she took the poor creature to the garden, and thrust several pins into its back. The tortured creature writhed under the pain, but the cruel girl did not cease until the required number had been inserted. Then she placed the frog under a vessel to prevent its escape, and turning to my informant, she said, "There, he will now come to our house this evening." The man certainly came, and when he entered she smiled at my informant, and then both went together to the lacerated frog, and the pins were extracted one by one from its back, and the wounded animal was set at liberty. My informant said that the hard-hearted girl mumbled something both when inserting and extracting the pins.

It was believed that the spirit of a person could be invoked and that it would appear, after the performance of certain ceremonies, to the person who was engaged in the weird undertaking. Thus a young woman who had gone round the church seven times on All Hallow Eve came home to her mistress, who was in the secret that she was going to *rhamanta*, and said, "Why did you send master to frighten me?" But the master had not left the house. His wife perceived that it was the spirit of her husband that had appeared to the girl, and she requested the girl to be kind to her children, "for," said she, "you will soon be mistress here." In a short time

II

afterwards the wife died, and the girl became her successor.

I obtained the preceding tale from the Rev. P. Edwards, son of the Rector of Llanwyddelan, Montgomeryshire, and the lady who related the tale of herself to Mr. Edwards said the occurrence took place when she was servant girl.

There are several versions of the above tale to be met with in many places in Wales.

I will give one, omitting names, from my work on " *Old Stone Crosses,*" p. 203 :—"An aged woman in Gyffylliog parish, who is still alive (1886), saw her husband by *rhamanta,* and so did her fellow-servant. I am indebted to Mr. Jones, Woodland Farm, to whom the woman related it, for the story I am about to give. When young women, she and her fellow-servant, in accordance with the practice of the country, determined to obtain a sight of the men whom they were to marry. The mistress was let into the secret that that night one of the two was going to raise the veil of the future, and the other the following night. As the clock began striking twelve the fellow-servant began striking the floor with a strap, repeating the doggerel lines

" Am gyd-fydio i gyd-ffatio,"

and almost immediately she saw her master come down stairs. The girl innocently the next day asked her mistress why she had sent her master down stairs to frighten her. The answer of her mistress was, ' Take care of my children.' This girl ultimatly married her master. The next night it was the other girl's turn, and she saw a dark man, whom she had never seen before; but in the course of a week or so, a stranger came into the farmyard, and she at once perceived that it was the person whom she had seen when divining. Upon inquiry, she ascertained that he was a married man, but in time his wife died, and the girl became his wife."

There were several ways of proceeding by young girls who

were anxious to ascertain whom they were to marry. One
of these was by means of yarn. This divination was
usually performed by two young girls after the family had
retired for the night. It has been called *Coel ede wlan*, or
the yarn test, and under this name I will describe the process

Coel Ede Wlan, or the Yarn Test.

Two young women took a ball of yarn and doubled the
threads, and then tied tiny pieces of wood along these threads
so as to form a miniature ladder. Then they went upstairs
together, and opening the window threw this artificial ladder
to the ground, and then the one who was performing the
incantation commenced winding the yarn back, saying
the while :—

> " Y fi sy'n dirwyn
> Pwy sy'n dal ? "
> I am winding,
> Who is holding ?

This was done three times, and if no lover made his
appearance, then for that year her chances of marriage were
gone. The next evening the other girl in the same manner
tried her fortune, and possibly better luck would attend her
trial. It was believed that the spirit of the coming husband
would mount this ladder and present himself to his future
wife.

The Rev. R. Jones, rector of Llanycil, told me the following tale. Two young men from Festiniog went to court two
young girls in the parish of Maentwrog, servants at a farm
called Gellidywyll. As they were going towards the farm
one of them said, " Let me rest awhile." He at once seated
himself on the ground, and apparently he fell asleep immediately. This surprised his friend, but he was thoroughly
frightened when he saw *a blue light emanate* from his
mouth, and he attempted to awaken the man, but he failed
to arouse him, he seemed as if dead. However, after awhile,

the blue light was seen returning, and it entered the mouth of the sleeper, and he instantly awoke, and they proceeded together towards Gellidywyll. At the very time that the man felt an irresistible inclination to sleep, his love had used the yarn incantation, and the unconscious man during his short sleep dreamt that he had seen his sweetheart in the window, and the girl said that he had appeared to her at the window. In a few months after this proof of true love they were married.

Another form of incantation was to walk around the church seven or nine times on certain nights. This I will call the *Twca Test* or *Knife Test.* This was a very common form of incantation.

Divination with the Twca or Knife.

The proceeding was as follows :—The party who wished to know whom he, or she, was to marry, went to the church secretly and walked around it seven times, repeating the while these words :—

> " Dyma'r Twca,
> Lle mae'r wain ? "
> Here's the knife,
> Where's the sheath ?

And it was thought that the spirit of his or her life partner would appear to the person who held the knife, with the sheath in his or her hand, and that it would be found that the one fitted the other exactly. I have been told by a person who resorted to this test that if the person was to become a wife, her lover would certainly appear to her; if she was to die an old maid then a coffin would meet her. The superstition is mentioned in *Bardd Cwsg*—

" Fe glywai rai yn son am fyned i droi o gwmpas yr Eglwys i weled eu cariadau, a pheth a wnaeth y catffwl ond ymddangos i'r ynfydion yn ei lun ei hun." That is in English :—

"He heard some persons talking of going round the church to see their sweethearts, but what did the stupid one (the devil) do, but appear to the foolish things in his own person."

The Washing Test.

Another well-known and often practised form of divination was for a young woman to take an article to wash, such as a stocking, to the water-spout or *pistyll*, and with her she carried two pieces of wood wherewith to strike the article which was being washed. She went on her knees and commenced striking the stocking, saying the while:—

"Am gyd-fydio i gyd-ffatio."
We'll live together to strike together.

It was thought that her future husband would then appear, take hold of the other piece of wood, and join her in her work; should the wraith appear, a marriage within six months followed.

Troi Crysau or Clothes Drying Test.

You g maidens washed linen after the household had retired, and placed the articles by the fire to dry, and then watched to see who should come at midnight to turn the clothes. In this case, again, the evil one is said to have entered the kitchen to perform this work for the young woman, and also it is affirmed that a coffin has, ere this, moved along through the room, a sure prognostication that she was doomed to die single. *Bardd Cwsg* mentions this practice.

He writes in the third part of his book, where a devil is accused in the Parliament of Hell, thus:—"Aeth nos *Ystuyll* ddiweddaf i ymweled a dwy ferch ieuanc yng Nghymru *oedd yn troi crysau*, ac yn lle denu'r genethod i faswedd, yn rhith llanc glandeg, myned ag elor i sobreiddio un; a myned a thrwst rhyfel at y llall mewn corwynt uffernol."

" He went on the night of *Epiphany* to visit two young
girls in Wales, *who were turning shirts*, and, instead of en-
ticing them to folly, in the form of a handsome young man,
he took to the one a coffin to sober her, and to the other he
appeared in a hellish whirlwind, with a horrible noise."

Happy, however, is the young woman should the man she
loves appear, for he is to be her husband.

Hemp Seed Sowing.

A young married woman, a native of Denbighshire, told
me that if a young woman sowed hemp seed, the figure
of her lover would appear and follow her. This was to be
done by night on Hallow Eve. I find from *English Folk-
Lore*, p. 15, that this divination is practised in Devonshire
on St. Valentine's Eve, and that the young woman runs
round the church repeating, without stopping, the following
lines :—

> " I sow hempseed, hempseed I sow,
> He that loves me best
> Come, and after me now."

Sage Gathering.

A young person who went of a night to the garden, and
stripped the leaves of the sage tree, would, as the clock
struck twelve, be joined by her lover. This was to be done
on All Hallow Eve.

Pullet's Egg Divination.

Mr. J. Roberts, Plas Einion, Llanfair Dyffryn Clwyd, told me
the following :—When he was a young man, he, his sister, and
the servant man, formed a company to find out by divination their future life partners. They procured a pullet's egg,
it was emptied into a cup, to this was added flour and salt,
in equal proportions, these ingredients were mixed together,
made into three small cakes, and baked. They all ate one
half of their cake, and the other half was placed in their
respective stockings, to be placed under their bolsters.

They went upstairs backward, and thus to bed, preserving the while, absolute silence. It was believed, he said, that they should that night, in their dreams, if everything were carried out properly, see their partners, who would come to their bedsides to offer them a drink of water.

The Candle and Pin Divination.

The process is as follows:—A couple of young women meet, and stick pins in a candle, and if the divination acts properly the last pin drops out of the candle at 12 o'clock at night, and then the future husband of the girl to whom that pin belongs appears.

I must not name the lady whom I am indebted to for the following information, but she told me that when she was a young woman, she, and her friend, took part in this prying into the future, and exactly at 12 o'clock her companion's pin fell out of the candle, and at that very instant there was a knocking at the door, and in great fright both ran upstairs, but the knocking continued, and her friend put her head out of the window to enquire who was there, and my inform- ant told me that the man at the door became her friend's husband, though at the time they were consulting the future she was desperately in love with another man.

There were other ways in which people could *Rhamant*. Enough has been said on this subject, but there are other practices resorted to, having much the same object in view, which I will now relate.

To ascertain the condition of the Person whom you are to Marry.

Water in Basin Divination.

Should young persons wish to know whether their hus- bands were to be bachelors, or their wives spinsters, the following test was to be resorted to :—

Three persons were necessary to carry out the test. These

three young ladies were to join in the undertaking and they were to proceed as follows:—On *Nos Calan Gauaf,* All Hallow Eve, at night, three basins were to be placed on a table, *one filled with clear spring water, one with muddy water, and the other empty.* The young ladies in turn were led blindfolded into the room, and to the table, and they were told to place their hands on the basins. She who placed her hand on the clear spring water was to marry a bachelor, whilst the one who touched the basin with muddy water was to wed a widower, and should the empty basin be touched it foretold that for that person a life of single blessedness was in store.

Hairs of a Lover found under a Holly Tree.

This test is to be carried out on All Hallow Eve. The young person walks backwards to a holly tree, takes a handful of grass from underneath it, and then carries the leaves to the light, and she then sees among the grass several hairs of her true lover.

The Bible and Key Divination.

A key is taken, and placed on the 16th verse of the 1st chapter of Ruth:—"And Ruth said, intreat me not to leave thee, or to return from following after thee; for whither thou goest, I will go; and where thou lodgest I will lodge; thy people shall be my people, and thy God my God."

The Bible is then closed with that part of the key that enters the lock on this verse. The person who wishes to look into the future takes the garter off his left leg, and then ties the Bible round with his garter, which also passes through the loop of the key. He has with him a friend who joins in carrying out the test. Both men place one of their big or central fingers on the key underneath the loop, and press the key, so as to keep the Bible steady and the key from falling. Then the man, who does not consult the future, reads the verse above written, and should the Bible turn towards the other man, it is an affirmative answer that the young lady he loves will accept him.

The writer received this account from a man who had himself consulted the future by the Bible and Key.

Testing a Lover's Love by Cracking of Nuts.

This divination is common to many countries, but the writer knows that it is resorted to on *All Hallows Eve* in Denbighshire by young ladies, partly, it may be in fun, and partly in earnest. The plan of proceeding is as follows :— Nuts are placed on the bars of the fire grate, equal in number to the young lady's lovers, and the nut that cracks first, and jumps off the bar, represents her true love. She has, of course fixed in her mind the lover each nut stands for. So common is this test that in the North of England *All Hallows Eve* is called " *Nutcrack night.*"

Gay describes the ceremony:—

Two hazel nuts I throw into the flame
And to each nut I give a sweetheart's name ;
This with the loudest bounce me sore amazed,
That in a flame of brightest-colour blazed ;
As blazed the nut, so may thy passions grow,
For 'twas thy nut that did so brightly glow.

Burns, in his poem of *Hallowe'en* also mentions the nut divination.

The auld guidwife's weel-hoordet nits
Are round an' round divided,
An' monie lads' and lasses' fates
Are there that night decided ;
Some kindle, couthie, side by side,
An' burn thegither trimly ;
Some start awa' wi' saucy pride,
And jump out-owre the chimlie
Fu' high that night.

Jean slips in twa' wi' tentie e'e ;
　Wha 'twas, she wadna tell ;
But this is Jock, an' this is me,
　She says in to hersel' :
He bleez'd owre her, and she owre him,
　As they wad never mair part ;
'Till, fuff ! he started up the lum,
　An' Jean had e'en a sair heart
　　To see't that night.

The Apple Pip Trial of Lovers.

The fair lady takes as many pips as she has lovers, and these she places on the point of a knife, which she inserts between the bars of the fire grate. Each pip represents a lover, and the pip that swells out and jumps into the fire indicates that he is the best lover for whom the pip stands.

SPIRITUALISM.

The next subject I shall treat of is curious, and partakes of the nature of spiritualism. I hardly know by what other word to describe it, therefore I will give particulars, so as to make the matter intelligible to the reader, and call it " Spiritualism."

It was believed that it was possible for the spirit to leave the body, and then, after an absence of some time, to return again and re-enter it. The form the spirit assumed when it quitted the body was a bluish light like that of a candle, but somewhat longer. This light left the body through the mouth, and re-entered the same way.

The writer was informed by a certain female friend at Llandegla that she had seen a bluish light leave the mouth of a person who was sick, light which she thought was the life, or spirit of that person, but the person did not immediately die.

For another tale of this kind I am indebted to Mr. R.
Roberts, who lives in the village of Clocaenog, near Ruthin.
He was not himself a witness of the occurrence, but
vouches for the accuracy of the report. It is as follows:—

A Spirit leaving and re-entering the body.

A man was in love with two young girls, and they were
both in love with him, and they knew that he flirted with
them both. It is but natural to suppose that these young
ladies did not, being rivals, love each other. It can well
be believed that they heartily disliked each other. One
evening, according to custom, this young man spent the
night with one of his sweethearts, and to all appearance
she fell asleep, or was in a trance, for she looked very pale.
He noticed her face, and was frightened by its death-like
pallor, but he was greatly surprised to see *a bluish
flame proceed out of her mouth*, and go towards the door.
He followed this light, and saw it take the direction of the
house in which his other love lived, and he observed that
from that house, too, a like light was travelling, as if to
meet the light that he was following. Ere long these lights
met each other, and they apparently fought, for they
dashed into each other, and flitted up and down, as if
engaged in mortal combat. The strife continued for some
time, and then the lights separated and departed in the
direction of the respective houses where the two young
women lived. The man returned to the house of the young
woman with whom he was spending the night, following
close on the light, which he saw going before him, and
which re-entered her body through her mouth; and then
she immediately awoke.

Here, presumedly, these two troubled young ladies met
in a disembodied form to contend for the possession of this
young man.

A tale much like the preceding occurs on page 283.

There is something akin to this spectral appearance believed in in Scotland, where the apparition is called *Wraith*, which word is defined in *Jameson's Etymological Dictionary*, published by Gardner, 1882, thus :—

" *Wraith, &c.* : Properly an apparition in the exact likeness of a person, supposed by the vulgar to be seen before, or soon after, death."

This definition does not correspond exactly to what has been said of the Welsh spirit appearance, but it teaches the possibility, or shows the people's faith in the possibility, of the soul's existence apart from the body. It would seem that in Scotland this spectre is seen before, or after, death ; but the writer has read of a case in which the *wraith* of a person appeared to himself and was the means of saving his life, and that he long survived after his other self had rescued him from extreme danger.

Lately a legend of Lake Ogwen went the round of the papers, but the writer, who lived many years in the neighbourhood of that lake, never heard of it until he saw it in the papers in 1887. As it bears on the subject under consideration, I will in part transcribe the story :—

" On one of these occasions a friend who had known something of the Welsh gipsies repeated to Rossetti an anecdote which had been told him as a ' quite true fack ' by a Romani girl—an anecdote touching another Romani girl *whose wraith had been spirited away in the night from the* ' *camping place* ' by the incantations of a wicked lover, had been seen rushing towards Ogwen Lake in the moonlight, ' While all the while that 'ere same chavi wur asleep an' a-sobbin' in her daddy's livin' waggin.' "—*Bye-Gones*, Ap. 13, 1887.

This tale resembles in many respects the one given on page 291, for there is in both a lover and a sleeping girl, and the girl does not die, but there are minor differences in the tales, as might be expected.

In Germany like tales are current. Baring-Gould, in his *Myths of the Middle Ages*, pp. 423-4, says :—

"The soul in German mythology is supposed to bear some analogy to a mouse. In Thuringia, at Saalfeld, a servant girl fell asleep whilst her companions were shelling nuts. They observed *a little red mouse creep out of her mouth* and run out of the window. One of the fellows present shook the sleeper but could not wake her, so he moved her to another place. Presently the mouse ran back to the former place and dashed about seeking the girl; not finding her, it vanished; at the same moment the girl died."

One other tale on this subject I will give, which appeared in the *North Wales Chronicle* for April 22, 1883, where it is headed—

A Spiritualistic Story from Wales.

" In an article relating to spiritualism in the February number of the *Fortnightly Review*, a story was told which is here shortened. The anecdote is given on the authority of a Welsh gentleman named Roberts, who resided at Cheetham, near Manchester, and the scene of the adventure is Beaumaris, the date 184—. The narrator was then an apprentice in a draper's shop. His master was strict, and allowed his apprentice but half an hour for dinner, which he had to take at his lodgings, some distance away from the shop. At whatever time he left the shop he had to be back there punctually at half past twelve. One day he was late, and while hastily swallowing his meal, his aunt being at the table, he looked up and saw that the clock pointed to *half past* twelve! He was thunderstruck, and, with the fear of his master before him, all but lost consciousness, and was indeed in a dazed state for a few minutes, as was noticed by those at the table. Shaking this off by an effort, he again looked at the clock, and, to his relief and astonishment, saw that the hands only pointed to a *quarter past* twelve. Then he quickly finished his dinner and returned to the shop at the appointed time. There he was told that at a *quarter past* twelve he had returned to the shop, put up his hat, moved about in an absent manner, had been scolded, and had thereupon put on his hat again and walked out. Several persons on the one hand corroborated this story, whilst on the other his aunt was positive that, although at that moment he had fallen into a strange fit of abstraction, he had never left the table. This is the narrative, attested by a gentleman now living. The year 184— is not so far back ; perhaps there are still those residing on the upper side of the turf at Beaumaris who remember the circumstance."

This tale in its nature is not unlike the others herein given. It belongs to the supernatural side of life.

However improbable these stories may appear, they point to the notion that spirits can exist independently of the body. The Irish *fetch*, the Scotch *wraith*, and the Welsh *Canwyll Corph* are alike in their teaching, but of this latter I shall speak more particularly when treating of death portents.

A Doctor called from his bed by a Voice.

Mr. Hugh Lloyd, Llanfihangel-Glyn-Myfyr, who received the story from Dr. Davies, the gentleman who figures in the tale, informed me of the following curious incidents :—

Doctor Davies, of Cerrig-y-drudion, had gone to bed and slept, but in the night he heard someone under his bedroom window shout that he was wanted in a farmhouse

called Craigeirchan, which was three miles from the
doctor's abode, and the way thereto was at all times beset
with difficulties, such as opening and shutting the many
gates ; but of a night the journey to this mountain farm
was one that few would think of taking, unless called to do
so by urgent business. The doctor did not pay much
attention to the first request, but he lay quietly on the bed
listening, and almost immediately he heard the same voice
requesting him to go at once to Craigeirchan, as he was
wanted there. He now got up to the window, but could
not see anyone; he therefore re-entered his bed, but for
the third time he heard the voice telling him to go to
the farm named, and now he opened the window and said
that he would follow the messenger forthwith. The doctor
got up, went to the stable, saddled the horse, and off he
started for a long dismal ride over a wild tract of mountain
country; such a journey he had often taken. He was not
surprised that he could not see, nor hear, anyone in advance,
for he knew that Welsh lads are nimble of foot, and could,
by cutting across fields, &c., outstrip a rider. At last he
neared the house where he was wanted, and in the distance
he saw a light, and by this sign he was convinced that there
was sickness in the house. He drove up to the door and
entered the abode, to the surprise but great joy of the
inmates. To his inquiry after the person who had been
sent for him, he was told that no one had left the house, nor
had anyone been requested by the family to go to the doctor.
But he was told his services were greatly wanted, for the
wife was about to become a mother, and the doctor was in-
strumental in saving both the life of the child and mother.

What makes this tale all the more curious is the fact, that
the doctor was an unbeliever in such things as ghosts, &c.,
and he had often enjoyed a quiet laugh over the tales he

heard of a supernatural kind. Mr. Lloyd asked the doctor whether he had heard of the woman's condition, but he affirmed he was ignorant of everything connected with the place and family.

Another Tale of a Doctor.

I received the following tale from the Rev. Philip Edwards, formerly curate at Selattyn, near Oswestry :—

There was, or perhaps is—for my informant says he believes the lady is still alive—in a place called Swydd-ffynnon, Cardiganshire, a Mrs. Evans, who had a strange vision. Mr. Edwards's father called one evening upon Mrs. Evans, and found her sitting by the fire in company with a few female friends, greatly depressed. On enquiring as to the cause of her distress, she stated that she had had a strange sight that very evening. She saw, she said, in the unoccupied chamber at the further end of the house, a light, and, whilst she was wondering what light it was, she observed a tall, dark, stranger gentleman, who had a long, full beard, enter the house and go straight to the room where the light was, but before going in he took off his hat and placed it on the table ; then he took off his gloves and threw them into the hat, and then he placed his riding whip across the hat, and without uttering a single word he entered the lit-up room. Shortly afterwards she saw the stranger emerge from the room and leave the house, and on looking again towards the room she saw that the light had disappeared. It was, she said, this apparition that had disconcerted her. Some time after this vision Mrs. Evans was in a critical state, and as she lived far away from a doctor my informant's father was requested to ride to Aberystwyth for one. He found, however, that the two doctors who then resided in that town were from home. But he was informed at the inn that there was a London doctor staying at Hafod. He determined, whether he could or could not, induce this gentleman to accompany him to Swyddffynnon, to go there. The gentleman, on hearing the urgency of the case, consented to visit the sick woman. Mr. Edwards and the doctor rode rapidly to their destination, and Mr. Edwards was surprised to find that the doctor did everything exactly as had been stated by Mrs. Evans. There was also a light in the chamber, for there the neighbours had placed the still-born child, and it was the providential help of the London doctor that saved Mrs. Evans's life. I may add that the personal appearance of this gentleman corresponded with the description given of him by Mrs. Evans.

DEATH PORTENTS.

These are common, in one form or other, to all nations. I will give a list of those which were formerly in high repute in Wales.

The Corpse Bird, or Deryn Corph.

This was a bird that came flapping its wings against the window of the room in which lay a sick person, and this visit was considered a certain omen of that person's death. The bird not only fluttered about the lighted window, but also made a screeching noise whilst there, and also as it flew away. The bird, singled out for the dismal honour of being a death prognosticator, was the tawny, or screech owl. Many are the instances, which have been told me by persons who heard the bird's noise, of its having been the precursor of death. This superstition is common to all parts of Wales.

A Crowing Hen.

This bird, too, is supposed to indicate the death of an inmate of the house which is its home; or, if not the death, some sore disaster to one or other of the members of that family. The poor hen, though, as soon as it is heard crowing, certainly foretells its own death, for no one will keep such an uncanny bird on the premises, and consequently the crowing hen loses its life.

It is a common saying that—

> A whistling woman, and a *crowing hen*,
> Are neither good for God nor men.

Should a hen lay a small egg it was to be thrown over the head, and over the roof of the house, or a death would follow.

A Cock Crowing in the Night.

This, too, was thought to foretell a death, but whose death, depended on the direction of the bird's head whilst crowing. As soon as the crowing was heard someone went to ascertain the position of the cock's head, and when it was seen that his head was turned from their own house towards someone else's abode, the dwellers in that house slept in peace, believing that a neighbour, and not one of themselves, was about to die. It was supposed, that to make the prognostication sure, the cock would have to crow three times in succession before or about midnight, and in the same direction.

The Corpse Candle—Canwyll Corph.

The corpse candle, or *canwyll corph*, was a light like that of a candle, which was said to issue from the house where a death was about to occur, and take the course of the funeral procession to the burial place. This was the usual way of proceeding, but this mysterious light was also thought to wend its way to the abode of a person about to die. Instances could be given of both kinds of appearances.

I have met with persons in various parts of Wales who told me that they had seen a corpse candle. They described it as a pale bluish light moving slowly along a short distance above the ground. Strange tales are told of the course the light has taken. Once it was seen to go over hedges and to make straight for the churchyard wall. This was not then understood, but when the funeral actually took place the ground was covered with snow, and the drift caused the procession to proceed along the fields and over the hedges and churchyard wall, as indicated by the corpse candle.

It was ill jesting with the corpse candle. The Rev. J. Jenkins, Vicar of Hirnant, told me that a drunken sailor at Borth said he went up to a corpse candle and attempted to light his pipe at it, but he was whisked away, and when he came to himself he discovered that he was far off the road in the bog.

The Rev. Edmund Jones, in his book entitled *A Relation of Ghosts and Apparitions, &c.*, states :—

" Some have seen the resemblance of a skull carrying the candle ; others the shape of the person that is to die carrying the candle between his fore-fingers, holding the light before his face. Some have said that they saw the shape of those who were to be at the burying."

Those who have followed the light state that it proceeded to the church, lit up the building, emerged therefrom, and then hovered awhile over a certain spot in the churchyard, and then sank into the earth at the place where the deceased was to be buried.

There is a tradition that St. David, by prayer, obtained the corpse candle as a sign to the living of the reality of another world, and that originally it was confined to his diocese. This tradition finds no place in the Life of the Saint, as given in the *Cambro-British Saints*, and there are there many wonderful things recorded of that saint.

It was thought possible for a man to meet his own Candle There is a tale of a person who met a Candle and struck it with his walking-stick, when it became sparks, which, however, re-united. The man was greatly frightened, became sick, and died. At the spot where he had struck the candle the bier broke and the coffin fell to the ground, thus corroborating the man's tale.

I will now record one tale not of the usual kind, which was told me by a person who is alive.

Tale of a Corpse Candle.

My informant told me that one John Roberts, Felin-y-Wig, was in the habit of sitting up a short time after his family had retired to rest to smoke a quiet pipe, and the last thing he usually did before retiring for the night was to take a peep into the night. One evening, whilst peering around, he saw in the distance a light, where he knew there was no house, and on further notice he observed that it was slowly going along the road from Bettws-Gwerfil-Goch towards Felin-y-Wig. Where the road dipped the light disappeared, only, however, to appear again in such parts of the road as were visible from John Roberts's house. At first Roberts thought that the light proceeded from a lantern, but this was so unusual an occurrence in those parts that he gave up this idea, and intently followed the motions of the light. It approached Roberts's house, and evidently this was its destination. He endeavoured to ascertain whether the light was carried by a man or woman, but he could see nothing save the light. When, therefore, it turned into the lane approaching Roberts's house, in considerable fear he entered the house and closed the door, awaiting, with fear, the approach of the light. To his horror, he perceived the light passing through the shut door, and it played in a quivering way underneath the roof, and then vanished. That very night the servant man died, and his bed was right above the spot where the light had disappeared.

Spectral Funerals, or Drychiolaeth.

This was a kind of shadowy funeral which foretold the real one. In South Wales it goes by the name *toilu, toili,* or *y teulu* (the family) *anghladd,* unburied ; in Montgomeryshire it is called *Drychiolaeth,* spectre.

I cannot do better than quote from Mr. Hamer's *Parochial Account of Llanidloes (Montgomeryshire Collections,* vol. x., p. 256), a description of one of these phantom funerals. All were much alike. He writes :—

" It is only a few years ago that some excitement was caused amongst the superstitious portion of the inhabitants by the statement of a certain miner, who at the time was working at the Brynpostig mine. On his way to the mine one dark night, he said that he was thoroughly frightened in China Street on seeing a spectral funeral leaving the house of one Hoskiss, who was then very ill in bed. In his fright the miner turned his back on the house, with the intention of going home, but almost fainting he could scarcely move out of the way of the advancing procession, which gradually approached, at last surrounded him, and then passed on down Longbridge Street, in the direction of the church. The frightened man managed with difficulty to drag himself home, but he was so ill that he was unable to go to work for several days."

The following weird tale I received from the Rev. Philip Edwards, whom I have already mentioned (p. 282). I may state that I have heard variants of the story from other sources.

While the Manchester and Milford Railway was in course of construction there was a large influx of navvies into

Wales, and many a frugal farmer added to his incomings by
lodging and boarding workmen engaged on the line.
Several of these men were lodged at a farm called Pender-
lwyngoch, occupied by a man named Hughes.

One evening when the men were seated round the fire,
which burned brightly, they heard the farm dogs bark, as
they always did at the approach of strangers. This aroused
the attention of the men, and they perceived from the
furious barking of the dogs that someone was coming
towards the house. By-and-by they heard the tramp of
feet, mingled with the howling of the frightened dogs, and
then the dogs ceased barking, just as if they had slunk
away in terror. Before many minutes had elapsed the
inmates heard the back door opened, and a number of
people entered the house, carrying a heavy load resembling
a dead man, which they deposited in the parlour, and all
at once the noise ceased. The men in great dread struck a
light, and proceeded to the parlour to ascertain what had
taken place. But they could discover nothing there,
neither were there any marks of feet in the room, nor could
they find any footprints outside the house, but they saw the
cowering dogs in the yard looking the picture of fright.
After this fruitless investigation of the cause of this dread
sound, the Welsh people present only too well knew the
cause of this visit. On the very next day one of the men
who sat by the fire was killed, and his body was carried by
his fellow-workmen to the farm house, in fact everything
occurred as rehearsed the previous night. Most of the
people who witnessed the vision are, my informant says,
still alive.

Cyhyraeth—Death Sound.

This was thought to be a sound made by a crying spirit.
It was plaintive, yet loud and terrible. It made the hair

stand on end and the blood become cold; and a whole neighbourhood became depressed whenever the awful sound was heard. It was unlike all other voices, and it could not be mistaken. It took in its course the way the funeral procession was to go, starting from the house of the dead, and ending in the churchyard where the deceased was to be buried. It was supposed to announce a death the morning before it occurred, or, at most, a few days before. It was at one time thought to belong to persons born in the Diocese of Llandaff, but it must have travelled further north, for it is said to have been heard on the Kerry Hills in Montgomeryshire. The function of the *Cyhyraeth* was much the same as that of the Corpse Candle, but it appealed to the sense of sound instead of to the sense of sight. Dogs, when they heard the distressing sound of the *Cyhyraeth*, showed signs of fear and ran away to hide.

Lledrith—Spectre of a Person.

This apparition of a friend has in the Scotch wraith, or Irish fetch its counterpart. It has been said that people have seen friends walking to meet them, and that, when about to shake hands with the approaching person, it has vanished into air. This optical illusion was considered to be a sign of the death of the person thus seen.

Tolaeth—Death Rapping or Knocking.

The death rappings are said to be heard in carpenters' workshops, and that they resembled the noise made by a carpenter when engaged in coffin-making. A respectable miner's wife told me that a female friend told her, she had often heard this noise in a carpenter's shop close by her abode, and that one Sunday evening this friend came and told her that the *Tolaeth* was at work then, and if she would come with her she should hear it. She complied, and there she heard this peculiar sound, and was thoroughly frightened,

There was no one in the shop at the time, the carpenter and his wife being in chapel. Sometimes this noise was heard by the person who was to die, but generally by his neighbours. The sounds were heard in houses even, and when this was the case the noise resembled the noise made as the shroud is being nailed to the coffin.

A Raven's Croaking.

A raven croaking hoarsely as it flew through the air became the angel of death to some person over whose house it flew. It was a bird of ill omen.

The Owl.

This bird's dismal and persistent screeching near an abode also foretold the death of an inmate of that house.

A Solitary Crow.

The cawing of a solitary crow on a tree near a house indicates a death in that house.

The Dog's Howl.

A dog howling on the doorsteps or at the entrance of a house also foretold death. The noise was that peculiar howling noise which dogs sometimes make. It was in Welsh called *yn udo*, or crying.

Missing a Butt.

Should a farmer in sowing wheat, or other kind of corn, or potatoes, or turnips, miss a row or butt, it was a token of death.

Stopping of a Clock.

The unaccountable stopping of the kitchen clock generally created a consternation in a family, for it was supposed to foretell the death of one of the family.

A Goose Flying over a House.

This unusual occurrence prognosticated a death in that house,

Goose or Hen Laying a Small Egg.

This event also was thought to be a very bad omen, if not a sign of death.

Hen laying Two Eggs in the same day.

Should a hen lay two eggs in the same day, it was considered a sign of death. I have been told that a hen belonging to a person who lived in Henllan, near Denbigh, laid an egg early in the morning, and another about seven o'clock p.m. in the same day, and the master died.

Thirteen at a Table.

Should thirteen sit at a table it was believed that the first to leave would be buried within the year.

Heather.

Should any person bring heather into a house, he brought death to one or other of the family by so doing.

Death Watch.

This is a sound, like the ticking of a watch, made by a small insect. It is considered a sign of death, and hence its name, *Death Watch.*

A working man's wife, whose uncle was ill in bed, told the writer, that she had no hopes of his recovery, because death ticks were heard night and day in his room. The man, who was upwards of eighty years old, died.

Music and Bird Singing heard before Death.

The writer, both in Denbighshire and Carnarvonshire, was told that the dying have stated that they heard sweet voices singing in the air, and they called the attention of the watchers to the angelic sounds, and requested perfect stillness, so as not to lose a single note of the heavenly music.

A young lad, whom the writer knew—an intelligent and promising boy—whilst lying on his death-bed, told his mother that he heard a bird warbling beautifully outside the house, and in rapture he listened to the bird's notes.

His mother told me of this, and she stated further, that she had herself on three different occasions previously to her eldest daughter's death, in the middle of the night, distinctly heard singing of the most lovely kind, coming, as she thought, from the other side of the river. She went to the window and opened it, but the singing immediately ceased, and she failed to see anyone on the spot where she had imagined the singing came from. My informant also told me that she was not the only person who heard lovely singing before the death of a friend. She gave me the name of a nurse, who before the death of a person, whose name was also given me, heard three times the most beautiful singing just outside the sick house. She looked out into the night, but failed to see anyone. Singing of this kind is expected before the death of every good person, and it is a happy omen that the dying is going to heaven.

In the *Life of Tegid*, which is given in his *Gwaith Barddonawl*, p. 20, it is stated :—

" Yn ei absenoldeb o'r Eglwys, pan ar wely angeu, ar fore dydd yr Arglwydd, tra yr oedd offeiriad cymmydogaethol yn darllen yn ei le yn Llan Nanhyfer, boddwyd llais y darllenydd gan fwyalchen a darawai drwy yr Eglwys accen uchel a pherseiniol yn ddisymwth iawn. . . . Ar ol dyfod o'r Eglwys cafwyd allan mai ar yr amser hwnw yn gywir yr ehedodd enaid mawr Tegid o'i gorph i fyd yr ysprydoedd."

Which translated is as follows :—

In his absence from Church, when lying on his death-bed, in the morning of the Lord's Day, whilst a neighbouring clergyman was taking the service for him in Nanhyfer Church, the voice of the reader was suddenly drowned by the beautiful song of a thrush, that filled the whole Church. . . . It was ascertained on leaving the church that at that very moment the soul of Tegid left his body for the world of spirits.

In the *Myths of the Middle Ages*, p. 426, an account is given of "The Piper of Hamelin," and there we have a description of this spirit song :—

> Sweet angels are calling to me from yon shore,
> Come over, come over, and wander no more.

Miners believe that some of their friends have the gift of seeing fatal accidents before they occur, A miner in the East of Denbighshire told me of instances of this belief and he gave circumstantial proof of the truth of his assertion. Akin to this faith is the belief that people have seen coffins or spectral beings enter houses, both of which augur a coming death.

In *The Lives of the Cambro-British Saints*, p. 444, it is stated that previously to the death of St. David "the whole city was filled with the music of angels."

The preceding death omens do not, perhaps, exhaust the number, but they are quite enough to show how prevalent they were, and how prone the people were to believe in such portents. Some of them can be accounted for on natural grounds, but the majority are the creation of the imagination, strengthened possibly in certain instances by remarkable coincidences which were remembered, whilst if no death occurred after any of the omens, the failure was forgotten.

BIRDS AND BEASTS.

Folk-lore respecting animals is common in Wales. It has been supposed that mountainous countries are the cradles of superstitions. But this is, at least, open to a doubt; for most places perpetuate these strange fancies, and many of them have reached our days from times of old, and the exact country whence they came is uncertain. Still, it cannot be denied that rugged, rocky, sparsely inhabited uplands, moorlands, and fens, are congenial abodes for wild fancies, that have their foundation in ignorance, and are perpetuated by the credulity of an imaginative people that lead isolated and solitary lives.

The bleating of the sheep, as they wander over a large expanse of barren mountain land, is dismal indeed, and well might become ominous of storms and disasters. The big fat sheep, which are penned in the lowlands of England, with a tinkling bell strapped to the neck of the king of the flock, convey a notion of peace and plenty to the mind of the spectator, that the shy active mountain sheep, with their angry grunt and stamping of their feet never convey. Still, these latter are endowed with an instinct which the English mutton-producer does not exercise. Welsh sheep become infallible prognosticators of a change of weather; for, by a never failing instinct, they leave the high and bare mountain ridges for sheltered nooks, and crowd together when they detect the approach of a storm. Man does not observe atmospheric changes as quickly as sheep do, and as sheep evidently possess one instinct which is strongly developed and exercised, it is not unreasonable to suppose that man in a low state of civilisation might credit animals with possessing powers which, if observed, indicate or foretell other events beside storms.

Thus the lowly piping of the solitary curlew, the saucy burr of the grouse, the screech of the owl, the croaking of the raven, the flight of the magpie, the slowly flying heron, the noisy cock, the hungry seagull, the shrill note of the woodpecker, the sportive duck, all become omens.

Bird omens have descended to us from remote antiquity. Rome is credited with having received its pseudo-science of omens from Etruria, but whence came it there? This semi-religious faith, like a river that has its source in a far distant, unexplored mountain region, and meanders through many countries, and does not exclusively belong to any one of the lands through which it wanders; so neither does it seem that these credulities belong to any one people or age; and it is difficult, if not impossible, to trace to their origin, omens, divination, magic, witchcraft, and other such cognate matters, which seem to belong to man's nature.

Readers of Livy remember how Romulus and Remus had recourse to bird omens to determine which of the brothers should build Rome. Remus saw six vultures, and Romulus twelve; therefore, as his number was the greater, to him fell the honour of building the famous city.

But this was not the only bird test known to the Romans. Before a battle those people consulted their game fowl to ascertain whether or not victory was about to attend their arms. If the birds picked up briskly the food thrown to them victory was theirs, if they did so sluggishly the omen was unpropitious, and consequently the battle was delayed.

Plutarch, in his "Life of Alexander," gives us many proofs of that great general's credulity. The historian says:—
"Upon his (Alexander's) approach to the walls (of Babylon) he saw a great number of crows fighting, some of which fell down dead at his feet." This was a bad sign. But I will not pursue the subject. Enough has been said

to prove how common omens were. I will now confine my remarks to Wales.

Birds singing before February.

Should the feathered songsters sing before February it is a sign of hard, ungenial weather. This applies particularly to the blackbird and throstle. The following lines embody this faith:—

Os cân yr adar cyn Chwefror, hwy griant cyn Mai.

If birds sing before February, they will cry before May.

Thus their early · singing prognosticates a prolonged winter.—*Bye-Gones*, vol. i., p. 88.

Birds flocking in early Autumn.

When birds gather themselves together and form flocks in the early days of autumn, it is thought to foretell an early and severe winter.

On the other hand, should they separate in early spring, and again congregate in flocks, this shews that hard weather is to be expected, and that winter will rest on the lap of May.

Birds' Feathers.

Feather beds should be made of domestic birds' feathers, such as geese, ducks, and fowls. Wild fowl feathers should not be mixed with these feathers; for, otherwise, the sick will die hard, and thus the agony of their last moments will be prolonged.

The Cock.

Cæsar, Bk. v., c. 12, tells us that the Celtic nation did not regard it lawful to eat the cock.

It was thought that the devil assumed occasionally the form of a cock. It is said that at Llanfor, near Bala, the evil spirit was driven out of the church in the form of a cock, and laid in the river Dee.

Formerly the cock was offered to the water god. And at certain Holy Wells in Wales, such as that in the parish of Llandegla, it was customary to offer to St. Tecla a cock for a male patient, and a hen for a female. A like custom prevailed at St. Deifer's Well, Bodfari. Classical readers may remember that Socrates, before his death, desired his friend Crito to offer a cock to Æsculapius. "Crito," said he, and these were his last words, "we owe a cock to Æsculapius, discharge that debt for me, and pray do not forget it;" soon after which he breathed his last.

In our days, the above-mentioned superstitions do not prevail, but the cock has not been resigned entirely to the cook. By some means or other, it still retains the power of announcing the visit of a friend; at least, so says the mountain farmer's wife.

The good-wife in North Wales, when the cock comes to the door-sill and there crows many times in succession, tells her children that "Some one is coming to visit us, I wonder who it is." Before nightfall a friend drops in, and he is informed that he was expected, that the cock had crowed time after time by the door, and that it was no good sending him away, for he would come back and crow and crow, "and now," adds she, "you have come." "Is it not strange," says the good woman, "that he never makes a mistake," and then follows a word of praise for chanticleer, which the stranger endorses.

However much the hospitable liked to hear their cock crow in the day time, he was not to crow at night. But it was formerly believed that at the crowing of the cock, fairies, spirits, ghosts, and goblins rushed to their dread abodes. Puck was to meet the Fairy King, "ere the first cock crow."

Cock-fighting.

Cock-fighting was once common in Wales, and it was said that the most successful cock-fighters fought the bird that resembled the colour of the day when the conflict took place; thus, the blue game-cock was brought out on cloudy days, black when the atmosphere was inky in colour, black-red on sunny days, and so on.

Charms for cocks have already been mentioned (p. 267). These differed in different places. In Llansantffraid, Mont-gomeryshire, a crumb from the communion table, taken therefrom at midnight following the administration of the Holy Communion, was an infallible charm. This was placed in the socket of the steel spur, which was then adjusted to the natural spur.—*Bye-Gones*, vol. i., p. 88.

The Goose.

Should a goose lay a soft egg, a small egg, or two eggs in a day, it is a sign of misfortune to the owner of that goose.

An old woman in Llandrinio parish, Montgomeryshire, who lived in a cottage by the side of the Severn, and who possessed a breed of geese that laid eggs and hatched twice a year, when I asked her the time that geese should begin to lay, said :—

Before St. Valentine's Day
Every good goose will lay.

and she added :—

By St. Chad,
Every good goose, and bad.

St. Chad's Day is March the 2nd.

Mr. Samuel Williams, Fron, Selattyn, gave me the following version of the above ditty :—

On Candlemas Day,
Every good goose begins to lay.

Another rendering is:—

> Every good goose ought to lay
> On Candlemas Day.

Candlemas Day is February 2nd.

Geese should sit so as to hatch their young when the moon waxes and not when it wanes, for, otherwise, the goslings would not thrive. The lucky one in the family should place the eggs for hatching under the goose or hen.

For the following paragraph I am indebted to "Ffraid," a writer in *Bye-Gones*, vol. i., p. 88 :—

"The goose is thought to be a silly bird, and hence the expression, 'You silly goose,' or 'You stupid goose,' as applied to a person. The falling snow is believed to be the effect of celestial goose-feathering, and the patron of geese—St. Michael—is supposed to be then feathering his protegés. The first goose brought to table is called a Michaelmas goose; a large annual fair at Llanrhaiadr-yn-Mochnant is called 'Ffair y cwarter Gwydd,' the quarter goose fair. Seven geese on grass land are supposed to eat as much grass as will keep a cow. Permanent grass land is called 'Tir Gwydd,' goose land. A bed of goose feathers is required to complete a well-furnished house. The fat of geese, called 'goose-oil,' is a recipe for many ailments. A small bone in the head of a goose, called the 'goose's tooth,' is carried in the pocket for luck, and is a sure preventative against toothache."

Much of the above paragraph is common to most parts of Wales, but the writer used to be told, when he was a lad, that the snow was caused by "the old woman feathering her geese," and a Michaelmas goose was called a green goose, as well as a "Michaelmas goose."

NN

The Crow.

The crow figures much in Welsh folk-lore. In many ways he is made to resemble the magpie; thus, when one crow or one magpie was seen, it was thought to foretell misfortune, as implied by the saying :—

> Un frân ddu,
> Lwc ddrwg i mi.

But should the spectator shout out in a defiant way :—

> Hen frân ddu,
> Gras Duw i mi,

no harm would follow. The former lines in English would be:—

> One crow I see,
> Bad luck to me.

But this foretold evil, brought about by the old black crow, could be counteracted by repeating the following words, (a translation of the second couplet), with a pause between each line, and thus the last line would assume the form of a prayer :—

> Old Black Crow !
> God, grace bestow ;

or the evil could be hurled back upon the Old Black Crow by the repetition of these words :—

> Hen frân ddu,
> Gras Duw i mi,
> Lwc ddrwg i ti.

Freely translated, these lines would be :—

> Old Black Crow !
> God's grace to me,
> Bad luck to thee.

In the English-speaking parts of Wales, such as along the borders of Montgomeryshire, adjoining Shropshire, I have heard the following doggerel lines substituted for the Welsh:--

> Crow, crow, get out of my sight,
> Before I kill thee to-morrow night.

The bad luck implied by the appearance of one crow

could also be overcome, as in the case of the magpie, by making a cross on the ground, with finger or stick.

Although one crow implied bad luck, two crows meant good luck; thus we have these lines :—

> Dwy frân ddu,
> Lwc dda i mi.
>
> Two black crows,
> Good luck to me.

Many prognostications were drawn from the appearance of crows. A crow seen on the highest branch of a tree implied that the person seeing it should shortly see his or her sweetheart. The manner in which they flew foretold a wedding or a burying. When they fly in a long line there is to be a wedding, if crowded together a funeral.

There is a common expression in Montgomeryshire— "Dwy frân dyddyn"—" The two crows of the farm "—just as if each farm had its two crows, either as guardians of the farm—for two crows implied good luck—or as if they were located by couples in various places, which places became their feeding ground and homes. This, however, is not true of rooks, which feed in flocks and roost in flocks.

Crows' Feathers.

In Montgomeryshire it was, at one time, supposed that if a person picked up a crow's feather he was sure to meet a mad dog before the day was over.

But in other parts it was considered lucky to find a crow's feather, if, when found, it were stuck on end into the ground. This superstition lingered long in Llanfihangel Glyn Myfyr, a remote, hilly parish in Denbighshire.

Some years ago, crows' wing or tail feathers could be seen stuck upright in the ground in many parts of Wales, but at present such a thing cannot be seen. The practice and the superstition have come to an end.

A Rookery deserted was a sign of bad luck, but when they nested near a house it was a sign of good luck.

The writer visited, in the year 1887, a gentleman's park, where for generations the rooks had made a lodgment, and by several persons his attention was called to the ominous fact that the rooks had left the ancestral trees which ornamented the spacious and well-wooded park, and had even carried their nests away with them. He was informed that the desertion boded no good to the highly respected family that occupied that ancient seat.

The writer also visited a friend, who lives in an ancient abode, a mile or two from the rook-rejected park, and, with a smile, he was informed by the lady of the house that a colony of rooks had taken possession of the trees that surrounded her house. He gladly wished her luck, to which she responded—" It has been a long time coming."

Both these places are in East Denbighshire.

The writer remembers a case in which a rookery was deserted just before misfortune fell upon the gentleman who occupied the house around which grew the trees occupied by the rooks. This gentleman one morning noticed the rooks carrying away their nests to a new home. He called his servant man to him, and desired him to go after the rooks and destroy their nests in their new abode, in the fond hope that they would thus be induced to return to their old home. This was done more than once, but the rooks would not take the hint; they persisted in gathering up the scattered sticks that strewed the ground, but these they replaced in the trees above, which now had become their new home. When it was found that they would not return, the man desisted, and his master, as he had feared, met with dire misfortune shortly afterwards (see p. 304).

The Cuckoo. *Y Gôg.*

The cuckoo is a sacred bird. It is safe from the game-keeper's gun. Its advent is welcomed with pleasure. "Have you heard the cuckoo?" is a question put by the fortunate person who first hears its notes to every person he meets. When it is ascertained that the cuckoo has arrived, parents give their children pence for luck, and they themselves take care not to leave their houses with empty pockets, for should they do so, those pockets, if the cuckoo is heard, will be empty all the year. Those who hear the cuckoo for the first time thrust immediately their hand in their pockets, and turn their money, or toss a piece into the air, and all this is for luck for the coming year ushered in by the cheering sound of the cuckoo's notes.

It is believed that the cuckoo is in our country for several days before its welcome two notes are heard, and that the cause of its huskiness is, that it is tired, and has not cleared its voice by sucking birds' eggs.

Generally the cuckoo is heard for the first time yearly about the same place, and the hill tops not far from the abodes of man are its favourite resort. Thus we have the ditty :—

> Cynta' lle y cân y cogydd,
> Yw y fawnog ar y mynydd.
> The place where first the cuckoo sings,
> Is by the peat pits on the hills.

The cuckoo is supposed to be accompanied by the wry-neck, hence its name, "Gwas-y-gog," the cuckoo's servant. The wryneck was thought to build the nest, and hatch and feed the young of the cuckoo.

Many superstitions cluster round the cuckoo; thus, should a person be in doubt as to the way to take, when going from home, to secure success in life, he, or she, waits

for the cuckoo's return, and then should the bird be heard
for the first time, singing towards the east, as it flies, that
is the direction to take, or any other direction as the case
may be; and it is, or was, even thought that the flight of
the cuckoo, singing as it flies before a person, for the
first time in the year, indicated a change of abode for that
person, and the new home lay in the direction in which the
cuckoo flew.

Should the cuckoo make its appearance before the leaves
appear on the hawthorn bush, it is a sign of a dry, barren
year.

> Os cân y gôg ar ddrain-llwyn llwm,
> Gwerth dy geffyl a phryn dy bwn.

> If the cuckoo sings on a hawthorn bare,
> Sell thy horse, and thy pack prepare.

The Welsh words I heard at Llanuwchllyn, a good many
years ago, just as the cuckoo's voice was heard for the first
time in those parts, and there were then no leaves out on
the hedgerows. I do not recollect whether the prophecy
became true, but it was an aged Welshman that made use
of the words. Another version of the same is heard in
Llanwddyn parish :—

> Os cân y gôg ar bincyn llwm,
> Gwerth dy geffyl a phryn dy bwn.

> If the cuckoo sings on a sprig that's bare,
> Sell thy horse, and thy pack prepare.

The latter ditty suits a hilly country, and the former
applies to the lowlands where there are hedgerows.

The early singing of the cuckoo implies a plentiful crop
of hay, and this belief is embodied in the following ditty :—

> Mis cyn Clamme cân y côge,
> Mis cyn Awst y cana' inne.

That is :—

> If the cuckoo sings a month before May-day,
> I will sing a month before August.

Calan Mai, May-day, abbreviated to *Clamme*, according to the Old Style, corresponds with our 12th of May, and the above saying means, that there would be such an abundant hay harvest if the cuckoo sang a month before May-day, that the farmer would himself sing for joy on the 12th of July. It was the custom in the uplands of Wales to begin the hay harvest on the 1st of July.

The above I heard in Montgomeryshire, and also the following :—

> Mis cyn Clamme cân y côge,
> Mis cyn hynny tyf mriallu.

That is :—

> If the cuckoo sings a month before May-day,
> Primroses will grow a month before that time.

I do not know what this means, unless it implies that early primroses foretell an early summer.

But, speaking of the song of the cuckoo, we have the following lines :—

> Amser i ganu ydi Ebrill a Mai,
> A hanner Mehefin, chwi wyddoch bob rhai.

This corresponds somewhat with the English :—

> The cuckoo sings in April,
> The cuckoo sings in May,
> The cuckoo sings to the middle of June,
> And then she flies away.

In Mochdre parish, Montgomeryshire, I was told the following :—

> In May she sings all day,
> In June she's out of tune.

The following Welsh lines show that the cuckoo will not
sing when the hay harvest begins :—

> Pan welith hi gocyn,
> Ni chanith hi gwcw.
> When she sees a heap,
> Silence she will keep.

In certain parts of Wales, such as Montgomeryshire,
bordering on Shropshire, it is thought that the cuckoo
never sings after Midsummer-day.   This faith finds corroborative support in the following lines :—

> The cuckoo sings in April,
> The cuckoo sings in May,
> The cuckoo sings in Midsummer,
> But never on that day.

In Flintshire, in Hawarden parish, it is believed that she
mates in June, as shown by these words:—

> The cuckoo comes in April,
> The cuckoo sings in May,
> The cuckoo mates in June,
> And in July she flies away.

In Montgomeryshire I have often heard these lines :—

> The cuckoo is a fine bird,
> She sings as she flies,
> She brings us good tidings,
> And never tells us lies ;
> She sucks young birds' eggs,
> To make her voice clear,
> And the more she sings " Cuckoo,"
> The summer is quite near.

The last two lines are varied thus :—

> And then she sings, " Cuckoo "
> Three months in every year.

Or :—

> And when she sings " Cuckoo "
> The summer is near.

The cuckoo was credited with sucking birds' eggs, to make room for her own, as well as to acquire a clear voice. Perhaps the rustic belief is at fault here. The writer has seen a cuckoo rise from the ground with an egg in her mouth, but he has seen it stated that the cuckoo always lays her eggs on the ground, and carries them in her mouth until she discovers a nest wherein to deposit them, and when she has done this her mother's care is over.

A White Cock.

A white cock was looked upon as an unlucky bird, thus:—

> Na chadw byth yn nghylch dy dŷ,
> Na cheiliog gwyn, na chath ddu.
> Never keep about thy house,
> A white cock, nor black cat.

Crane.

The crane is often mistaken for the heron. When the crane flies against the stream, she asks for rain, when with the stream she asks for fair weather.

This bird is said to be thin when the moon wanes, and fat at the waxing of the moon.

Ducks.

When ducks sportively chase each other through the water, and flap their wings and dive about, in evident enjoyment of their pastime, it is a sign that rain is not far off.

Eagle.

Persons who had eaten eagle's flesh had power to cure erysipelas, and this virtue was said by some to be transmitted to their descendants for ever, whilst others affirmed it only lasted for nine generations. See page 263, where this subject is fully treated.

The Goat Sucker.

A curious notion prevailed respecting this bird, arrived at, presumably, in consequence of its peculiar name—the *goat sucker*—viz., that it lives on the milk of the goat, which it obtains by sucking the teats of that animal.

Putting Hens to Sit.

Placing the eggs in the nest for hens, geese, and ducks to sit on was considered an important undertaking. This was always done by the lucky member of the family. It was usual to put fowl to sit so as to get the chick out of the egg at the waxing, and not at the waning, of the moon. It was thought that the young birds were strong or weak according to the age of the moon when they were hatched.

March chickens were always considered the best. A game bird hatched in March was thought to be stronger and more plucky than those that broke their shells in any other month, and, further, to obtain all extraneous advantages, that bird which was hatched at full moon began life with very good prospects.

A singular custom prevailed at Llansantffraid, Montgomeryshire, when putting hens, and other fowl, to sit. I obtained the information from the late Vicar, the Rev. R. H. M. Hughes, M.A., an observant gentleman, who took a lively interest in all matters connected with his parish. I was staying with him, and he made the remark that in his parish it was considered lucky to place the hen, when she first began to sit, with her head towards the church. This the cottagers in the village could easily do, for the parish church was in their midst. I do not know whether this kind of proceeding prevailed in other places.

The number of eggs placed under a hen varied with her size, but one general rule was followed, viz., an odd number of

eggs was always placed under her; eleven or thirteen was
the usual number, but never ten or twelve,

The Heron.

The heron as it flies slowly towards the source of a river is
said to be going up the river to bring the water down, in
other words, this flight is a sign of coming rain.   The same
thing is said of the crane.

Fable of why the Heron frequents the banks of rivers and lakes.

It is from thirty to forty years ago that I heard the fable I
am about to relate, and the circumstances under which I
heard it are briefly as follows.   I was walking towards
Bangor from Llanllechid, when I saw a farmer at work
hedging.   I stopped to chat with him, and a bramble which
had fastened itself on his trousers gave him a little trouble
to get it away, and the man in a pet said, " Have I not paid
thee thy tithe?"   " Why do you say those words, Enoch?"
said I, and he said, " Have you not heard the story?"   I
confessed my ignorance, and after many preliminary
remarks, the farmer related the following fable :—

The heron, the cat, and the bramble bought the tithe of
a certain parish.   The heron bought the hay, mowed it,
harvested it, and cocked it, and intended carrying it the
following day, but in the night a storm came on, and carried
the hay away, and ever since then the heron frequents the
banks of the rivers and lakes, looking for her hay that was
carried away, and saying " Pay me my tithe."

The cat bought the oats, cut them, and even threshed
them, and left them in the barn, intending the following
day to take them to the market for sale.   But when she
went into the barn, early the next morning, she found the
floor covered with rats and mice, which had devoured the
oats, and the cat flew at them and fought with them, and

drove them from the barn, and this is why she is at enmity with rats and mice even to our day.

The bramble bought the wheat, and was more fortunate than the heron and cat, for the wheat was bagged, and taken to the market and sold, but sold on trust, and the bramble never got the money, and this is why it takes hold of everyone and says " Pay me my tithe," for it forgot to whom the wheat had been sold.

The Jackdaw.

This bird is considered sacred, because it frequents church steeples and builds its nest there, and it is said to be an innocent bird, though given to carrying off things and hiding them in out-of-the-way places. When ignorance of a fault is pleaded, it is a common saying—"l have no more knowledge of the fact than the Devil has of the jackdaw" (see *Bye-Gones*, Vol. I., 86). The Devil evidently will have nothing to do with this bird, because it makes its home in the church steeple, and he hates the church and everything belonging to it.

The Magpie.

The magpie was considered a bird of ill-omen. No one liked to see a magpie when starting on a journey, but in certain parts of Montgomeryshire, such as the parish of Llanwnog, *if the magpie flew from left to right it foretold good luck ;* in other parts, such as Llansantffraid, if seen at all, it was considered a sign of bad luck.

However, fortunately, a person could make void this bad luck, for he had only to spit on the ground, and make a cross with his finger, or stick, through the spittle, and boldly say—

"Satan, I defy thee,"

and the curse, or bad luck, indicated by the appearance of the magpie, could not then come.

The number of magpies seen implied different events. It
was a common saying:—

> One's grief, two's mirth,
> Three's a marriage, four's a birth ;

and another rendering of the above heard in Montgomeryshire was:—

> One for bad luck,
> Two for good luck,
> Three for a wedding,
> Four for a burying.

Another ditty is as follows :—

> One's joy, two's greet (crying),
> Three's a wedding, four's a sheet (death).

As stated above, one is grief, or bad luck, if it flies from
right to left, but if from left to right it implied success or
joy. So these various readings can only be reconciled by a
little verbal explanation, but " four's a birth " cannot be
made to be an equivalent to " four's a sheet," a winding
sheet, or a burying, by any amount of ingenuity.

Should a magpie be seen stationary on a tree, it was
believed that the direction in which it took its flight foretold either success or disaster to the person who observed
it. If it flew to the left, bad luck was to follow ; if to the
right, good luck ; if straight, the journey could be under-
taken, provided the bird did not turn to the left whilst
in sight, but disappeared in that direction.

I heard the following tale in Denbighshire:—In days of
old, a company of men were stealthily making their way
across the country to come upon the enemy unawares. All
at once they espied a magpie on a tree, and by common
consent they halted to see which way it would take its
flight, and thus foretell the fortune which would attend
their journey. One of the party, evidently an unbeliever
in his comrades' superstition, noiselessly approached the

bird, and shot it dead, to the great horror of his companions. The leader of the party, in great anger, addressed the luckless archer—"You have shot the bird of fate, and you shall be shot." The dauntless man said, "I shot the magpie, it is true, but if it could foretell our fate, why could it not foresee its own?" The archer's reasoning was good, but I do not know whether people were convinced by logic in those distant times, any more than they are in ours.

I will relate one other tale of the magpie, which I heard upwards of twenty years ago in the parish of Llanwnog, Montgomeryshire.

I was speaking to a farmer's wife—whose name it is not necessary to give, as it has nothing to do with the tale— when a magpie flew across our view. "Ah!" she ejaculated, "you naughty old thing, what do you want here?" "I see," said I, "you think she brings bad luck with her.' "Oh, yes," was the response, "I know she does." "What makes you so positive," said I, "that she brings bad luck with her?" My question elicited the following story. My friend commenced:—"You know the brook at the bottom of the hill. Well, my mother met with very bad luck there, a good many years ago, and it was in this way—she was going to Newtown fair, on our old horse, and she had a basket of eggs with her. But, just as she was going to leave the 'fould,' a magpie flew before her. We begged of her not to go that day—that bad luck would attend her. She would not listen to us, but started off. However, she never got further than the brook, at the bottom of the hill, for, when she got there, the old mare made straight for the brook, and jerked the bridle out of mother's hand, and down went the mare's head to drink, and off went the basket, and poor mother too. All the eggs were broken, but I'm glad to say mother was not much the worse for her fall. But ever since then I know it is unlucky to see a magpie. But sir," she added, "there is no bad luck for us to-day, for *the magpie flew from left to right.*"

The magpie was thought to be a great thief, and it was popularly supposed that if its tongue were split into two with silver it could talk like a man.

The cry of the magpie is a sign of rain. To man its dreaded notes indicated disaster, thus :—

> Clyw grechwen nerth pen, iaith pi—yn addaw
> Newyddion drwg i mi.

> List ! the magpie's hoarse and bitter cry
> Shews that misfortune's sigh is nigh.

If this bird builds her nest at the top of a tree the summer will be dry; if on the lower branches, the summer will be wet.

The Owl.

The hooting of an owl about a house was considered a sign of ill luck, if not of death. This superstition has found a place in rhyme, thus :—

> Os y ddylluan ddaw i'r fro,
>   Lle byddo rhywun afiach
> Dod yno i ddweyd y mae'n ddinâd,
>   Na chaiff adferiad mwyach.

> If an owl comes to those parts,
>   Where some one sick is lying,
> She comes to say without a doubt,
>   That that sick one is dying.

Peacock.

The peacock's shrill note is a sign of rain. Its call is supposed to resemble the word *gwlaw,* the Welsh for rain.

Pigeon.

If the sick asks for a pigeon pie, or the flesh of a pigeon, it is a sign that his death is near.

If the feathers of a pigeon be in a bed, the sick cannot die on it.

The Raven.

The raven has ever enjoyed a notoriously bad name as a bird of ill-omen.

He was one of those birds which the Jews were to have in abomination (Lev., xi., 5—13).

But other nations besides the Jews dreaded the raven.

> The raven himself is hoarse
> That croaks the fatal entrance of
> Duncan under thy battlements.
>
> *Macbeth*, Act i., s. 5.

Thus wrote Shakespeare, giving utterance to a superstition then common. From these words it would seem that the raven was considered a sign of evil augury to a person whose house was about to be entered by a visitor, for his croaking forebode treachery. But the raven's croaking was thought to foretell misfortune to a person about to enter another's house. If he heard the croaking he had better turn back, for an evil fate awaited him.

In Denmark the appearance of a raven in a village is considered an indication that the parish priest is to die, or that the church is to be burnt down that year. (*Notes and Queries*, vol. ii., second series, p. 325.) The Danes of old prognosticated from the appearance of the raven on their banners the result of a battle. If the banner flapped, and exhibited the raven as alive, it augured success; if, however, it moved not, defeat awaited them.

In Welsh there is a pretty saying :—

> Duw a ddarpar i'r frân.
> God provides for the raven.

But this, after all, is only another rendering of the lovely words :—

> Your heavenly Father feedeth them.

Such words imply that the raven is a favoured bird. (See p. 304).

Robin Redbreast.

Ill luck is thought to follow the killer of dear Robin Redbreast, the children's winter friend. No one ever shoots Robin, nor do children rob its nest, nor throw stones at it. Bad luck to anyone who does so. The little bird with its wee body endeavoured to staunch the blood flowing from the Saviour's side, and it has ever since retained on its breast the stain of His sacred blood, and it consequently enjoys a sacred life. It is safe from harm wherever English is spoken.

There is another legend, which is said to be extant in Carmarthenshire, accounting for the Robin's *red breast.* It is given in *Bye-Gones,* vol. i., p. 173, from Mr. Hardwick's *Traditions, Superstitions, Folk-lore, &c.* :—" Far, far away, is a land of woe, darkness, spirits of evil, and fire. Day by day does the little bird bear in its bill a drop of water to quench the flame. So near to the burning stream does he fly that his dear little feathers are scorched ; and hence is he named Bronchuddyn (qu. Bronrhuddyn), i.e., breast-burned, or breast-scorched. To serve little children, the robin dares approach the infernal pit. No good child will hurt the devoted benefactor of man. The robin returns from the land of fire, and therefore he feels the cold of winter far more than the other birds. He shivers in brumal blasts, and hungry he chirps before your door. Oh, my child, then, in pity throw a few crumbs to poor red-breast."

The Sea Gull.

It is believed that when sea gulls leave the sea for the mountains it is a sign of stormy weather.

A few years ago I was walking from Corwen to Gwyddelwern, and I overtook an aged man, and we entered into conversation. Noticing the sea gulls hovering about, I said, there is going to be a storm. The answer of my old companion was, yes, for the sea gull says before starting from the sea shore :—

> Drychin, drychin,
> Awn i'r eithin ;

and then when the storm is over, they say one to the other, before they take their flight back again to the sea :—

> Hindda, hindda,
> Awn i'r morfa.

which first couplet may be translated :—

> Foul weather, foul weather,
> Let's go to the heather ;

and then the two last lines may be rendered :—

> The storm is no more,
> Let's go to the shore.

This was the only occasion when I heard the above stanza, and I have spoken to many aged Welshmen, and they had not heard the words, but every one to whom I spoke believed that the sea gulls seen at a distance from the sea was a sign of foul weather.

The Swallow.

The joy with which the first swallow is welcomed is almost if not quite equal to the welcome given to the cuckoo. "One swallow does not make a summer" is an old saw.

There is a superstition connected with the swallow that is common in Wales, which is, that if it forsakes its old nest on a house, it is a sign of ill luck to that house. But swallows rarely forsake their old nests, and shortly after their arrival they are busily engaged in repairing the breaches, which the storms of winter or mischievous children have made in their abodes; and their pleasant twitterings are a pleasure to the occupants of the house along which they build their nests, for the visit is a sign of luck.

The flight of the swallow is a good weather sign. When the swallow flies high in the air, it is a sign of fair weather; when, on the other hand, it skims the earth, it is a sign of rain.

It was a great misfortune to break a swallow's nest, for—

Y neb a doro nyth y wenol,
Ni wel fwyniant yn dragwyddol.
Whoever breaks a swallow's nest,
Shall forfeit everlasting rest.

The Swan.

The eggs of the swan are hatched by thunder and lightning. This bird sings its own death song.

The Swift.

This bird's motions are looked upon as weather signs. Its feeding regions are high up in the air when the weather is settled for fair, and low down when rain is approaching.

Its screaming is supposed to indicate a change of weather from fair to rain.

Tit Major, or Sawyer.

The Rev. E. V. Owen, Vicar of Llwydiarth, Montgomeryshire, told me that the Tit's notes are a sign of rain, at least, that it is so considered in his parish. The people call the bird "Sawyer," and they say its notes resemble in sound the filing of a saw. A man once said to my friend:—"I dunna like to hear that old sawyer whetting his saw." "Why not," said Mr. Owen. "'Cause it'll rain afore morning" was the answer. This bird, if heard in February, when the snow or frost is on the ground, indicates a breaking up of the weather. Its sharp notes rapidly repeated several times in succession are welcome sounds in hard weather, for they show that spring is coming.

The Wren.

The Wren's life is sacred, excepting at one time of the year, for should anyone take this wee birdie's life away, upon him some mishap will fall. The wren is classed with the Robin:—

> The robin and the wren
> Are God's cock and hen.

The cruel sport of hunting the wren on St. Stephen's Day, which the writer has a dim recollection of having in his boyhood joined in, was the one time in the year when the wren's life was in jeopardy.

The Rev. Silvan Evans, in a letter to the *Academy*, which has been reproduced in *Bye-Gones*, vol. vii., p. 206, alludes to this sport in these words:—

"Something similar to the 'hunting of the wren' was not unknown to the Principality as late as about a century ago, or later. In the Christmas holidays it was the custom of a certain number of young men, not necessarily boys, to visit the abodes of such couples as had been married within the year. The order of the night—for it was strictly a nightly performance—was to this effect. Having caught a wren, they placed it on a miniature bier made for the occasion, and carried it in procession towards the house which they intended to visit. Having arrived they serenaded the master and mistress of the house under their bedroom window with the following doggerel:—

> Dyma'r dryw,
> Os yw e'n fyw,
> Neu dderyn tô
> I gael ei rostio.

That is:—

> Here is the wren,
> If he is alive,
> Or a sparrow
> To be roasted.

If they could not catch a wren for the occasion, it was lawful to substitute a sparrow (aderyn tô). The husband, if agreeable, would then open the door, admit the party, and regale them with plenty of Christmas ale, the obtaining of which being the principal object of the whole performance."

The second line in the verse, "*Os yw e'n fyw*," intimates that possibly the wren is dead—"If he is alive." This would generally be the case, as it was next to impossible to secure the little thing until it had been thoroughly exhausted, and then the act of pouncing upon it would itself put an end to its existence.

Perhaps the English doggerel was intended to put an end to this cruel sport, by intimating that the wee bird belonged to God, was one of His creatures, and that therefore it should not be abused.

There is a Welsh couplet still in use :—

> Pwy bynnag doro nyth y dryw,
> Ni chaiff ef weled wyneb Duw.
>
> Whoever breaks a wren's nest,
> Shall never see God's face.

This saying protects the snug little home of the wren. Much the same thing is said of the Robin's nest, but I think this was put, " Whoever robs a robin's nest shall go to hell."

Another Welsh couplet was :—

> Y neb a doro nyth y dryw,
> Ni chaiff iechyd yn ei fyw.
>
> Whoever breaks the wren's nest,
> Shall never enjoy good health.

Although the robin and the wren were favourites of heaven, still it was supposed that they were under some kind of curse, for it was believed that the robin could not fly through a hedge, it must always fly over, whilst on the other hand, the wren could not fly over a hedge, but it was obliged to make its way through it. (See Robin, p. 329).

The Wood Pigeon.

The thrice repeated notes of five sounds, with an abrupt note at the end, of which the cooing of the wood pigeon

consists, have been construed into words, and these words
differ in different places, according to the state of the
country, and the prevailing sentiments of the people. Of
course, the language of the wood pigeon is always the
language of the people amongst whom he lives. He always
speaks Welsh in Wales, and English in England, but in
these days this bird is so far Anglicised that it blurts out
English all along the borders of Wales.

In the cold spring days, when food is scarce and the wood
pigeon cold, it forms good resolutions, and says :—

> Yn yr haf
> Tŷ a wnaf;
> Gwnaf.

> In the summer
> I'll make a house; .
> I will.

However, when the summer has come with flower, and
warmth, the wood pigeon ridicules its former resolution and
changes its song, for in June it forgets January, and now
it asks :—

> Yn yr ha'
> Tŷ pwy wna' ?
> Pwy?

> In the summer
> Who'll make a house?
> Who?

For then a house is quite unnecessary, and the trouble to
erect one great. The above ditty was told me by the Rev.
John Williams, Rector of Newtown, a native of Flintshire.

In the English counties bordering upon Wales, such as
Herefordshire, the wood pigeon encouraged Welshmen to
drive off Englishmen's cattle to their homes, by saying:—

> Take two cows, Taffy,
> Take two cows, Taffy,
> Take two.

and ever since those days the same song is used; but another version is :—

> Take two cows Davy,
> Take two cows Davy,
> Two.

The late Rev. R. Williams, Rector of Llanfyllin, supplied me with the above, and he stated that he obtained it from Herefordshire.

In the uplands of Denbighshire the poor wood pigeon has a hard time of it in the winter, and, to make provision for the cold winter days, he, when he sees the farmer sowing spring seeds, says :—

> Dyn du, dyn da,
> Hau pys, hau ffa,
> Hau ffachys i ni
> Fwyta.

which rendered into English is :—

> Black man, good man,
> Sow peas, sow beans,
> Sow vetches for us
> To eat.

Mr. Hugh Jones, Pentre Llyn Cymmer, a farmer in Llanfihangel Glyn Myfyr, a descendant of the bard Robert Davies, Nantglyn, supplied me with the preceding ditty.

The Magpie teaching a Wood Pigeon how to make a nest.

The wood pigeon makes an untidy nest, consisting of a few bits of twigs placed one on the other without much care. There is a fable in the Iolo MSS., p. 159, in Welsh, and the translation appears on page 567 in English, as follows :—

The magpie, observing the slight knowledge of nest building possessed by the wood pigeon, kindly undertook the work of giving his friend a lesson in the art, and as the lesson proceeded, the wood pigeon, bowing, cooed out :—

> *Mi wn ! Mi wn ! Mi wn !*
> I know ! I know ! I know !

The instructor was at first pleased with his apt pupil, and proceeded with his lesson, but before another word could be uttered, the bird swelling with pride at its own importance and knowledge, said again :—

I know! I know! I know!

The magpie was annoyed at this ignorant assurance, and with bitter sarcasm said: "Since you know, do it then," and this is why the wood pigeon's nest is so untidy in our days. In its own mind it knew all about nest building, and was above receiving instruction, and hence its present clumsy way of building its nest. This fable gave rise to a proverb, "As the wood pigeon said to the magpie : 'I know.'"

It is believed that when wood pigeons are seen in large flocks it is a sign of foul weather.

Woodpecker.

The woodpecker's screech was a sign of rain. This bird is called by two names in Welsh which imply that it foretold storms ; as, *Ysgrech y coed*, the wood screech, and *Caseg y drycin*, the storm mare.

These names have found a place in Welsh couplets :—

" Ysgrech y coed!
Mae'r gwlaw yn dod."
The Woodpecker's cry!
The rain is nigh.

Bardd Nantglyn, Robert Davies, Nantglyn, has an englyn to the woodpecker :—

"*I Gaseg y Drycin.*"

" Och! rhag Caseg, grêg rwygiant,—y drycin,
Draw accw yn y ceunant,
Ar fol pren, uwch pen pant,
Cyn 'storm yn canu 'sturmant."

Barddoniaeth R. Davies, p. 61.

My friend Mr. Richard Williams, Celynog, Newtown, translates this stanza as follows:—

Ah! 'tis the hoarse note of the Woodpecker,
　　In yonder ravine,
On the round trunk of a tree, above the hollow,
Sounding his horn before the coming storm.

Yellow Hammer. (Penmelyn yr Eithin).

There is a strange belief in Wales that this bird sacrifices her young to feed snakes.

Ass.

The stripe over the shoulders of the ass is said to have been made by our Lord when He rode into Jerusalem on an ass, and ever since the mark remains.

It was thought that the milk of an ass could cure the "decay," or consumption. This faith was common fifty years ago in Llanidloes, Montgomeryshire. I do not know whether it is so now. People then believed that ass's milk was more nutricious than other kind of food for persons whose constitutions were weak.

The Bee.

The little busy bee has been from times of old an object of admiration and superstition. It is thought that they are sufficiently sensitive to feel a slight, and sufficiently vindictive to resent one, and as they are too valuable to be carelessly provoked to anger, they are variously propitiated by the cottager when their wrath is supposed to have been roused. It is even thought that they take an interest in human affairs; and it is, therefore, considered expedient to give them formal notice of certain occurrences.

Buying a Hive of Bees.

In the central parts of Denbighshire people suppose that a hive of bees, if bought, will not thrive, but that a present of a hive leads to its well-doing.

A cottager in Efenechtyd informed the writer that a friend gave her the hive she had, and that consequently she had had luck with it; but, she added, "had I bought it, I could not have expected anything from it, for bought hives do badly." This was in the centre of Denbighshire.

Time of Bee Swarming.

The month in which bees swarm is considered of the greatest importance, and undoubtedly it is so, for the sooner they swarm, the longer their summer, and therefore the greater the quantity of honey which they will accumulate. A late swarm cannot gather honey from every opening flower, because the flower season will have partly passed away before they leave their old home.

This faith has found expression in the following lines:—

> A swarm of bees in May
> Is worth a load of hay;
>
> A swarm of bees in June
> Is worth a silver spoon;
>
> A swarm of bees in July
> Is not worth a fly.

These words are often uttered by cottagers when a swarm takes place in the respective months named in the lines. It is really very seldom that a swarm takes place in our days in May, and many a swarm takes place in July which is of more value than a fly. But however, be this as it may, the rhyme expresses the belief of many people.

The Day of Swarming.

Sunday is the favourite day for bee swarming. Country people say, when looking at their bees clustering outside the hive, and dangling like a rope from it, " Oh, they won't swarm until next Sunday," and it is true that they are often right in their calculations, for bees seem to prefer the peaceful Day of Rest to all other days for their flight. The kettle and pan beating are often heard of a Sunday in those parts of the country where bees are reared. It is possible that the quietness of the day, and the cessation of every-day noise, is appreciated by the little creatures, and that this prevailing stillness entices them to take then their flight from their old home to seek a new one.

Luck comes with a Strange Swarm.

It is considered very lucky indeed to find that a strange swarm of bees has arrived in the garden, or tree, belonging to a cottager. The advent of the bees is joyfully welcomed, and the conversation of the neighbours on such an occasion intimates that they think that good fortune has come with them to the person whom they have condescended to honour with their presence.

Occasionally, if bees settle down on property of doubtful ownership, a good deal of wrangling and bad feeling arises between the rival claimants for their possession.

It is considered unlucky for Bees to fly away from their owner.

As the coming of a strange swarm of bees is indicative of good luck to the person to whom they come, so the decamping of a swarm shows that misfortune is about to visit the person whom they leave.

Bees in a Roof.

It was thought lucky when bees made their home in the roof, or indeed in any part of a house, and this they could easily do when houses were thatched with straw. Many a swarm of bees found shelter in the roofs of ancient churches, but in our days bees are seldom found in either houses or churches.

Informing Bees of a Death in a Family.

Formerly it was the custom to tell the bees of a death in the family. The head of the house whispered the news to the bees in the hive. If this were neglected, it was thought that another death would soon follow the previous one. Instead of speaking to the bees, it was the custom, in some parts of Wales, to turn the bee-hive round before starting the funeral. This was always done by the representative of the family, and it also was thought to be a protection against death.

Mrs. Jones, Rhydycroesau Rectory, informed me that an old man, David Roberts of Llanyblodwel, once came to her in deep grief, after the funeral of his grandchild, because he had forgotten to turn the bee-hive before the funeral started for the church. He said that he was in such distress at the loss of the child, that he had neglected to tell the bees of the death, and, said he, some other member of the family is now sure to go. He informed Mrs. Jones that he had turned the hive at the death of his old woman, and that consequently no death had followed hers in his family.

Putting Bees in Mourning.

This is done after a death in a family, and the bees are put into mourning by tying a piece of black ribbon on a bit of wood, and inserting it into the hole at the top of the hive.

Stolen Bees.

It was believed that stolen bees would not make honey, and that the hive which had been stolen would die.

A Swarm entering a House.

Should a swarm enter a house, it was considered unlucky, and usually it was a sign of death to someone living in that house.

The culture of bees was once more common than it is, and therefore they were much observed, and consequently they figure in the folk-lore of most nations.

Cat.

The cat was thought to be a capital weather glass. If she stood or lay with her face towards the fire, it was a sign of

frost or snow; if she became frisky, bad weather was near.
If the cat washed her face, strangers might be expected; and
if she washed her face and ears, then rain was sure to come.
A *black* cat was supposed to bring luck to a house, thus :—

> Cath ddu, mi glywais dd'wedyd,
> A fedr swyno hefyd,
> A chadw'r teulu lle mae'n byw
> O afael pob rhyw glefyd.

> A black cat, I've heard it said,
> Can charm all ill away,
> And keep the house wherein she dwells
> From fever's deadly sway.

Cats born in May, or May cats, were no favourites. They
were supposed to bring snakes or adders into the house.
This supposition has found utterance :—

> Cathod mis Mai
> Ddaw a nadrodd i'r tai.

> Cats born in May
> Bring snakes to the house.

In some parts the black cat was otherwise thought of than
is stated above, for this injunction is heard :—

> Na chadw byth yn nghylch dy dŷ
> Na cheiliog gwyn na chath ddu.

> Never keep about thy house
> A white cock or *black* puss.

Cats are so tenacious of life that they are said to have
nine lives. We have already spoken of witches transforming themselves into cats.

A singular superstition connected with cats is the supposition that they indicate the place to which the dead have
gone by ascending or descending trees immediately after
the death of a person.

The Rev. P. W. Sparling, Rector of Erbistock, informed
me that one day a parishioner met him, and told him that
his brother, who had lately died, was in hell, and that he

wished the Rector to get him out. Mr. Sparling asked him how he knew where his brother was, and in answer the man said that he knew, because he had seen his brother in the form of a white cat descend a tree immediately after his death. On further inquiry, the man stated that since the cat came *down the tree*, it was a sign that his brother had gone down to hell; but had the cat *gone up the tree*, it would have shown that he had gone up to heaven.

I have heard it stated, but by whom I have forgotten, that if a *black* cat leaves a house where a person dies, immediately after that person's death, it shows he has gone to the bad place; but if a white cat, that he has gone to heaven.

COWS.

Cows Kneeling on Christmas Morn.

In the upland parishes of Wales, particularly those in Montgomeryshire, it was said, and that not so long ago, that cows knelt at midnight on Christmas eve, to adore the infant Saviour. This has been affirmed by those who have witnessed the strange occurrence.

Cows bringing forth two calves are believed to bring luck to a farmer; but in some parts of Wales a contrary view is taken of this matter.

If the new born calf is seen by the mistress of the house with its head towards her, as she enters the cowhouse to view her new charge and property, it is a lucky omen, but should any other part of the calf present itself to the mistress's view, it is a sign of bad luck.

Witches were thought to have great power over cows, and it was not unusual for farmers to think that their cows, if they did not thrive, had been bewitched.

Crickets.

It is lucky to have crickets in a house, and to kill one is sure to bring bad luck after it. If they are very numerous

in a house, it is a sign that peace and plenty reign there.
The bakehouse in which their merry chirp is heard is the
place to bake your bread, for it is a certain sign that the
bread baked there will turn out well.

An aged female Welsh friend in Porthywaen told me that
it is a sign of death for crickets to leave a house, and she
proved her case by an apt illustration. She named all the
parties concerned in the following tale :—"There were hundreds of crickets in . . . . house ; they were ' sniving,'
swarming, all about the house, and were often to be seen outside the house, or at least heard, and some of them perched on
the wicket to the garden ; but all at once they left the place,
and very soon afterwards the son died. The crickets, she
said, knew that a death was about to take place, and they
all left that house, going no one knew where."

It was not thought right to look at the cricket, much less
to hurt it. The warm fireplace, with its misplaced or dis-
placed stones, was not to be repaired, lest the crickets
should be disturbed, and forsake the place, and take with
them good luck. They had, therefore, many snug, warm
holes in and about the chimneys. Crickets are not so
plentiful in Wales as they once were.

Hare.

Cæsar, bk. v., ch. xii., states that the Celts "do not regard
it lawful to eat the *hare*, the cock, and the goose; they,
however, breed them for amusement and pleasure." This
gives a respectable age to the superstitions respecting these
animals.

Mention has already been made of witches turning themselves into hares. This superstition was common in all parts
of North Wales. The Rev. Lewis Williams, rector of Prion,
near Denbigh, told me the following tales of this belief:—
A witch that troubled a farmer in the shape of a hare, was

shot by him. She then transformed herself into her natural form, but ever afterwards retained the marks of the shot in her nose.

Another tale which the same gentleman told me was the following:—A farmer was troubled by a hare that greatly annoyed him, and seemed to make sport of him. He suspected it was no hare, but a witch, so he determined to rid himself of her repeated visits. One day, spying his opportunity, he fired at her. She made a terrible noise, and jumped about in a frightful manner, and then lay as if dead. The man went up to her, but instead of a dead hare, he saw something on the ground as big as a donkey. He dug a hole, and buried the thing, and was never afterwards troubled by hare or witch.

In Llanerfyl parish there is a story of a cottager who had only one cow, but she took to Llanfair market more butter than the biggest farmer in the parish. She was suspected of being a witch, and was watched. At last the watcher saw a hare with a tin-milk-can hanging from its neck, and it was moving among the cows, milking them into her tin-can. The man shot it, and it made for the abode of the suspected witch. When he entered, he found her on the bed bleeding.

It was supposed that there was something uncanny about hares. Rowland Williams, Parish Clerk, Efenechtyd, an aged man, related to me the following tale, and he gave the name of the party concerned, but I took no note of the name, and I have forgotten it:—A man on his way one Sunday to Efenechtyd Church saw a hare on its form. He turned back for his gun, and fired at the hare. The following Sunday he saw again a hare on the very same spot, and it lifted its head and actually stared at him. The man was frightened and went to church; the third Sunday he again saw a hare

on the very same form, and this hare also boldly looked at
him. This third appearance thoroughly convinced the man
that there was something wrong somewhere, and he afterwards avoided that particular place.

The pretty legend of Melangell, called Monacella, the
patroness of hares, is well known. One day the Prince of
Powis chased a hare, which took refuge under the robe of
the virgin Melangell, who was engaged in deep devotion.
The hare boldly faced the hounds, and the dogs retired to a
distance howling, and they could not be induced to seize
their prey. The Prince gave to God and Melangell a piece
of land to be henceforth a sanctuary. The legend of the
hare and the saint is represented in carved wood on
the gallery in the church of Pennant. Formerly it
belonged to the screen. Hares were once called in the
parish of Pennant Melangell *Wyn Melangell*, or St. Monacella's lambs. Until the last century no one in the parish
would kill a hare, and it was believed that if anyone cried
out when a hare was being pursued, " God and St. Monacella
be with thee," it would escape.

Haddock.

The haddock has a dark spot on each side its gills, and
superstition ascribes these marks to the impression of
S. Peter's thumb and finger, when he took the tribute
money out of the mouth of a fish of the same species in the
sea of Galilee.

Hedgehog.

It was believed that hedgehogs sucked cows, and so firmly
were the people convinced of this fact, that this useful little
animal was doomed to death, and I have seen in many
Churchwardens' accounts entries to the effect that they had
paid sums of money for its destruction. The amount given
in most parishes was two pence. I will give a few entries,

from many that I have by me, to show that parishes paid this sum for dead hedgehogs.

In Cilcen Churchwardens' Accounts for the year 1710 I find the following entry:—

> To Edward Lloyd for killing a hedgehog   00 . 00 . 02.

One hundred years afterwards I find in Llanasa Churchwardens' Accounts for 1810-1811 this entry:—

> 9 hedgogs   ...   .   1 . 6.

It was thought, should the cow's teats be swollen of a morning, that she had been sucked the previous night by a hedgehog.

Formerly dead hedgehogs could be seen in company with foxes, polecats, and other vermin suspended from the boughs of the churchyard yew trees, to prove that the Churchwardens paid for work actually done.

Horse.

A white horse figures in the superstition of school children. When the writer was a lad in school at Llanidloes, it was believed that if a white horse were met in the morning it was considered lucky, and should the boy who first saw the horse spit on the ground, and stealthily make the sign of a cross with his toe across the spittle, he was certain to find a coin on the road, or have a piece of money given to him before the day was over; but he was not to divulge to anyone what he had done, and for the working of the charm it was required that he should make sure that the horse was perfectly white, without any black hairs in any part of the body.

In Welshpool a like superstition prevails. Mr. Copnall, the master of the Boys' National School in that town, has kindly supplied me with the following account of this matter:—

" It is lucky to meet a white horse on the road, if, when you meet it, you spit three times over your little finger; if you

neglect this charm you will be unlucky. I asked the
children if it signified whether it was the little finger on the
right or left hand; some boys said the left, but the majority
said it made no difference which hand."

It was said that horses could see spirits, and that they
could never be induced to proceed as long as the spirit stood
before them. They·perspired and trembled whilst the spirit
blocked the way, but when it had disappeared, then the
horses would go on.

Lady-bird.

This pretty spotted little beetle was used formerly in the
neighbourhood of Llanidloes as a prognosticator of the
weather. First of all the lady-bird was placed in the palm
of the left hand, or right; I do not think it made any
difference which hand was used, and the person who held
it addressed it as follows :—

> Iâr fach gooh, gwtta,
> Pa un ai gwlaw, neu hindda?

and then having said these words, the insect was thrown
skywards, the person repeating the while—

> Os mai gwlaw, cwympa lawr,
> Os mai têg, hedfana;

which in English would be—

> Lady-bird, lady-bird, tell to me
> What the weather is going to be;
> If fair, then fly in the air,
> If foul, then fall to the ground.

The first two lines were said with the beetle in the hand,
and the last two whilst it was thrown upwards; if it came
to the ground without attempting to fly, it indicated rain;
if, however, when thrown into the air it flew away, then fair
weather was to be expected. The writer has often resorted
to this test, but whether he found it true or false he cannot
now say.

Mice.

A mouse nibbling clothes was a sign of disaster, if not death, to the owner. It was thought that the evil one occasionally took the form of a mouse. Years ago, when Craig Wen Farm, Llawr-y-glyn, near Llanidloes, Montgomeryshire, was haunted—the rumour of which event I well remember—the servant girl told her mistress, the tenant of the farm, that one day she was going through the corn field, and that a mouse ran before her, and she ran after it to catch it, but that when she was opposite the barn, *the mouse stopped and laughed at her*, and ran into a hole. The mouse, therefore, was the evil spirit, and the cause of all the mischief that followed.

Moles.

Moles are said to have no eyes. If mole hills move there will be a thaw. By the moving of mole hills is meant bits of earth tumbling off the mound. A labourer in Llanmerewig parish, Montgomeryshire, called my attention to this fact. It was a frosty day, and apparently no change was near, but it will thaw, said he, and certain I am, that by the next morning a thaw had set in.

Pigs.

Pigs used to be credited with the power of seeing the wind. Devils were fond of assuming the form of, or entering into, pigs. Pigs littered in February could not be reared. This I was told by a native of Llansantffraid, Montgomeryshire.

The Snake, Serpent.

The snake was supposed to be able to understand what men said. A tale was told me by an aged man at Penrhos, Montgomeryshire, of an event which took place in the last century. His father, he said, saw a number of snakes, or *nethers*, as he called them, basking in the sun, and he said when passing them, " I will make you jump to-morrow." The next day he, provided with a rod, passed the spot, but no adder could be seen. The next day he passed again the same spot without his rod, and the man was now obliged to run for his life, so furiously did the snakes attack him.

Traditions of Flying Snakes were once common in all parts of Wales.

Flying Serpents.

The traditional origin of these imaginary creatures was that they were snakes, which by having drunk the milk of a woman, and by having eaten of bread consecrated for the Holy Communion, became transformed into winged serpents or dragons.

These dangerous creatures had their lurking places in many districts, and they attacked everyone that crossed their paths. There was said to have been one such den on Moel Bentyrch. Old Mrs. Davies, Plas, Dolanog, who died 1890, aged 92, told the Rev. D. R. Evans, B.A., son of the Vicar of Dolanog, that once, when she was a young woman, she went to Llanfair market, and on the way she sat on a stile, and she saw smoke and fire issuing from a hole on Moel Bentyrch, where the *Gwiber*, or Flying Serpent, had its abode. She ran, and never stopped until she had placed a good distance between her and the hill. She believed that both the smoke and fire were caused by the serpent. There is also a tradition still current in Dolanog that this flying serpent was destroyed by wrapping some red material round a post into which sharp nails were driven. The serpent, attacking this post with furious onslaughts, was lacerated by the sharp spikes, and died. A like tradition is current in Llanrhaiadr-yn-Mochnant in connection with the *Post Coch*, or *Post-y-Wiber*, or Maen Hir y Maes-Mochnant.

Mr. Hancock in his "History of Llanrhaiadr-yn-Mochnant," writes as follows :—

"The legend connected with this stone pillar is, that it was raised in order to prevent the devastation which a

winged serpent or dragon (a *Wiber*) was committing in the
surrounding country. The stone was draped with scarlet
cloth, to allure and excite the creature to a furor, scarlet
being a colour most intolerably hateful and provoking to it.
It was studded with iron spikes, that the reptile might
wound or kill itself by beating itself against it. Its destruction, it is alleged, was effected by this artifice. It is said to
have had two lurking places in the neighbourhood, which
are still called *Nant-y-Wiber*, one at Penygarnedd, the
other near Bwlch Sychtyn, in the parish of Llansilin, and
this post was in the direct line of its flight. Similar legends
referring to winged serpents exist in various parts of Wales.
In the adjoining parish of Llanarmon-Dyffryn-Ceiriog there
is a place called *Sarffle* (the serpent's hole)."—*Montgomeryshire Collections*, vol. ix., 237.

Snake Rings, or Glain Nadroedd.

Mention is made in *Camden* of snake rings. Omitting
certain remarks not connected with the matter directly, he
writes:—" In some parts of Wales we find it a common
opinion of the vulgar that about Midsummer Eve (though
in the time they do not all agree) 'tis usual for snakes to
meet in companies, and that by joyning heads together and
hissing, a kind of Bubble is form'd like a ring about the
head of one of them, which the rest by continual hissing,
blow on till it comes off at the tail, and then it immediately
hardens, and resembles a glass ring; which whoever finds
(as some old women and children are persuaded) shall
prosper in all his undertakings." The above quotation is in
Gibson's additions to Camden, and it correctly states the
popular opinion. Many of these rings formerly existed,
and they seemed to be simply glass rings. They were
thought to possess many healing virtues, as, for instance, it
could cure wens and whooping cough, and I believe I have
heard it said that it could cure the bite of a mad dog.

Sheep.

It was thought that the devil could assume any animal's form excepting that of the sheep. This saying, however, is somewhat different from what a farmer friend told me of *black sheep*. He said his father, and other farmers as well, were in the habit of killing all their black lambs, because they were of the same colour as the devil, and the owners were afraid that Satan had entered, or would enter into them, and that therefore these sheep were destroyed. He stated that his father went on his knees on the ground and prayed, either before or after he had killed the black lambs. It is a common saying that the black sheep is the ringleader of all mischief in a flock of sheep. The expression, "He is a black sheep," as applied to a person, conveys the idea that he is a worthless being, inclined to everything that is bad.

It is even now in country places thought to be a lucky omen if anyone sees the head of the first spring lamb towards him. This foretells a lucky and prosperous year to the person whose eyes are thus greeted.

Spider.

The long-legged spider, or, as it is generally called in Wales, the Tailor, is an object of cruel sport to children. They catch it, and then handle it roughly, saying the while:—

> Old Harry long-leg
> Cannot say his prayers,
> Catch him by the right leg,
> Catch him by the left leg.
> And throw him down stairs ;

and then one leg after the other is plucked off, and the poor creature is left to die miserably. This was done in Llanidloes.

The Squirrel.

Hunting this sprightly little animal became at Christmas the sport of our rustic population. A number of lads gathered together, and proceeded to the woods to hunt the squirrel. They followed it with stones and sticks from tree to tree, shouting and screaming, to frighten it on and on, until it was quite unable to make further progress, and then they caught it. The writer, when a lad, has often joined in this cruel hunt, but whether the squirrel was killed when caught he is unable to recall to mind. Generally it escaped.

The Blind Worm, or Slow Worm.

This reptile is a snake, varying from twelve to eighteen inches long. Its head is small, and its movements very rapid. At the slightest noise, it darts away in a moment, and hides among rocks, stones, or rank grass. It is said to have no eyes, but this is a popular mistake--hence, however, its name, *Blind Worm*. This beautiful timid creature is often wantonly cut into pieces by its cruel and mistaken captors, for they credit it with the possession of evil propensities. It is said that, could it see, it would be a formidable enemy to man and beast. This supposition has found strength and sanction in doggerel verse. The Blind Worm is said to address the adder as follows :—

> If I could see,
> As well as thee,
> Man nor beast
> Should ne'er pass me.

Another version of these lines, heard in Shropshire, on the borders of Wales, is :—

> If I had one eye,
> As thou hast two,
> No man should live,
> Nor beast should loo (low).

These doggerel lines indicate clearly the dread in which this innocent snake is held.

LIST OF SUBSCRIBERS.

A

Acton, T. A., Regent Street, Wrexham
Adcane, Miss, Plas Llanfawr, Holyhead
Andrews, Mr Wm., *The Hull Press*, 1, Dock Street, Hull
Arnold, Prof. E. P., M.A, 10, Bryn Têg, Bangor

B

Ballinger, John, Mr., Cardiff Free Library, Cardiff
Barnes, J. R., Esq., The Quinta, Chirk
Bennett, Edgar, Esq., 2, Court Ash, Yeovil
Bennett, N., Esq., Glanyrafon, Llanidloes
Bangor, The Lord Bishop of, The Palace, Bangor, N.W.
Bowen, Alfred E., Esq., Town Hall, Pontypool
Bryan, B., Esq., Pen-lan, Ruthin
Bryan, R F., Esq.,
Bury, Mrs., Ellesmere, Shropshire

C

Chapman, Henry, Mr., Dolfor School, Near Newtown
Cunliffe, R., Esq., Llaurhaiadr Hall, Denbigh

D

Daniels, Rev. J., Curate, Carmarthen
Davies-Cooke, Philip B., Esq., Gwysanny, Mold
Davies, Rev. L. W., Manafon Rectory, Welshpool
Davies, Rev. D. W., M.A., The Vicarage, St. Asaph
Davies, Rev. Joseph, B.A., Curate, Holywell
Davies, Rev. C. H., M.A., Tregarth, Bangor
Davies, Rev. E. T., B.A., The Vicarage, Pwllheli
Davies, Rev. J., B.A., Bryneglwys Vicarage, Corwen
Davies, Rev. J. J., Machynlleth
Davies, W. Cadwaladr, Esq., Penybryn, Bangor, N. Wales
Davies, Rev. T. R., Curate, The Hut, Farnham Royal, Windsor
Davies, Thos. Mr., Draper, 121, High Holborn, London
Davies, Rev. T. A., B.A.,
D'Erisleigh, R. S., Esq., Salisbury College, Stoneycroft, Liverpool

Drinkwater, Rev. C. H., St. George's Vicarage, Shrewsbury
Duckworth, Thos., Esq., Librarian, Worcester Public Library
    Worcester

E

Edwards, Rev. D., M.A., Vicarage, Rhyl
Edwards, Mr. R., Litherland, Near Liverpool
Edwards, T. C., D.D., Principal, College, Bala
Edwards, Rev R., Rectory, Bettws, Gwerfil Goch, Near Corwen
Edwards, Rev. E J., B.A., Vicar, Tremeirchion, St. Asaph
Elias, Miss Elizabeth, 2, Chapel Street, Conway
Ellis, Rev. Robert, The Rectory, Llansannan, Abergele
Evans, Mr E., School House, Gwernaffield, Mold
Evans, Rev. E., The Vicarage, Llanarmon, Mold
Evans, Rev. J. T., Bettws Vicarage, Abergele
Evans, Rev. J., B.A., Tallarn Green, Malpas
Evans, Rev. D. W., M.A., St. George's Vicarage, Abergele
Evans, Rev. T. H., Minera Vicarage, Wrexham
Evans, Rev. W., B.A., 5, King Street, Aberystwyth
Evans, Rev. J. O., M.A., Peterston Rectory, Cardiff
Evans, Rev. J. Silas, B.A., Vicarage, St. Asaph
Evans, J. G. Esq., 7, Clarendon Villa, Oxford
Evans, J. E., Esq., 12, Albion Road, South Hampstead
    London, N.W.
Evans, Mr Arthur,

F

Felix, Rev. John, Cilcen Vicarage, Mold·
Fisher, Rev. J., B.A., Ruthin
Fletcher, Miss Fanny Lloyd, Nerquis Hall, Mold
Fletcher, Rev. W. H., M.A., The Vicarage, Wrexham

G

Gardner, H., Esq., C. 18, Exchange, Liverpool.
George, Rev. T., B.A., Nerquis Vicarage, Mold
Gilbert, T. H., Esq., 12½, Cheapside, London, E.C.
Green, Rev. G. K. M., Exhall Rectory, Alcester, Redditch
Griffith, Rev. D., B.A., Clocaenog Rectory, Ruthin
Griffith, H. J. Lloyd, M.A, Frondeg, Holyhead

H

Haines, W., Esq., Y Bryn, Near Abergavenny
Harland, E. Sydney, Esq., Barnwood Court, Gloucester
Harper, W. J., Mr., Wern Shop, Rhosesmor, Holywell
Hope, John H., Mr., National School, Holywell

Hughes, Rev. H. T., M.A., Bistre Vicarage, Chester
Hughes, Rev. T., M.A., Buttington Vicarage, Near Welshpool
Hughes, H., Mr., Glyn National School, Llangollen
Hughes, T. G., Esq., 47, Everton Road, Liverpool
Hughes, Rev. Jonathan,
Hughes, Rev. Morgan, Derwen Rectory, Corwen
Humphreys, Mr. W. R., School House, Penycae, Ruabon

J

James, Rev. E. R., R.D., The Rectory, Marchwiel, Wrexham
James, Rev. D. Pennant, Rectory, Oswestry
Jenkins, Rev. W., Chaplain of H.M. Prison, Ruthin
Jenkins, Rev. J., B.A., Bodawen, Penmaenmawr
Jenkins, Rev. L. D, B.A., Penycae Vicarage, Ruabon
Johnson, Mr. R., National Provincial Bank, Mold
Jones, Rev. D., Llanberis Rectory, Carnarvon
Jones, Rev. D., Llanrhaiadr-yn-Mochnant Vicarage, Oswestry
Jones, Sir Pryce Pryce, Dolerw, Newtown
Jones, Pryce Edward, Esq., M.P., Newtown Hall, Newtown
Jones, Rev. J. Thompson, B.A., Towyn Vicarage, Abergele
Jones, Rev. W., M.A., Trofarth Vicarage, Abergele
Jones, Prof. J. Morris, M.A., University College, Bangor
Jones, Rev. Rees, Carrog Rectory, Corwen
Jones, Rev. Hy., M.A., Llanychan Rectory, Ruthin
Jones, Dr. A. Emrys, 10, Saint John Street, Manchester
Jones, Miss M., Bryn Siriol, Mold
Jones, Rev. Evan,
Jones, Rev. Jno., Curate, Llanbedr, Ruthin
Jones, Rev. G. J., Curate of Ysceifiog, Holywell
Jones, Mr. H. W., Tanyberllan, Penmaenmawr
Jones, Rev. Stephen, Curate, Mold
Jones, Rev. W., Curate of Northop, Flintshire
Jones, Mr. Powell, School House, Llanelidan, Ruthin
Jones, Rev. Pierce, Aber Rectory, Bangor
Jones, Rev. Griffith Arthur, M.A., St. Mary's, Cardiff
Jones, Rev. Griffith, The Vicarage, Mostyn, Holywell
Jones, Lewis, Esq., *Journal* Office, Rhyl
Jones, J. R., Delbury School, Craven Arms, Salop
Jones, Mr. T., The Schools, Ffynnongroyw, Holywell, N.W.
Jones, Mr. J. E., National School, Llawr y Bettws, Corwen
Jones, Mr. L. P., National Schools, Rhosesmor, Holywell
Jones, Rev. Enoch, M.A.
Jones, Rev. W., Llanasa Vicarage, Holywell
Jones, F., Esq., Pyrocanth House, Ruthin
Jones, R. Prys, Esq., B.A., Board School, Denbigh
kones, Rev. Wynne, M.A., Rhosddu, Wrexham

K

Kenrick, Mr. Robert, 24, Marine Terrace, Aberystwyth

L

Lewis, Rev. D., Rectory, Merthyr Tydfil
Lewis, Rev. H. Elvet, Llanelly, Carmarthenshire
Lewis, Dr., Llansantffraid, Oswestry
Lewis, Rev. J. P., The Vicarage, Conway
Lindsay, W. M., Esq., Librarian, Jesus College, Oxford
Lloyd, Rev. T. H., M.A., Vicarage, Llansantffraid-yn-Mechain, Oswestry
Lloyd, Rev. John, The Rectory, Dolgelley
Lloyd, E. O. V., Esq., M.A., Rhaggatt, Corwen
Lloyd, Rev. L. D., B.A., Curate, Rhosddu, Wrexham
Lloyd, Rev. T., B.A., The Rectory, Bala
Lloyd, John Edward, Professor, M.A., University College, Bangor
Luxmore, E. B., Esq., Bryn Asaph, St. Asaph

M

Mainwaring, Col., Galltfaenan, Trefnant, R.S.O., N. Wales
Marsh, Miss Ellen, late of Tybrith, Carno, Mont.
M'Gonigle, Rev. T. G., Weston, Shrewsbury
M'Gormick, Rev. T. H. J., Holy Trinity, Ilkestone, Derbyshire
Minshall, P. H., Esq., Solicitor, Oswestry
Morgan, Rev. John, M.A., Rectory, Llandudno
Morris, Edward, Esq., M.A., Copthorne House, Ruthin Road Wrexham
Morris, Rev. John., M.A., The Rectory, Llanelidan, Ruthin
Muspratt, Miss, Trelawney, Flint

N

Nayler-Leyland, Mrs., Nantclwyd Hall, Ruthin
Nicholas, Rev. W. Ll., M.A, Flint Rectory, Flint
Nixon and Jarvis, Bank Place, Bangor
Nutt, David, 270, Strand, London, W.C.

O

Oldfield, J. E., Esq., B.A., Fferm, Bettws, Abergele
Owen, Rev. R. M., M.A., The Vicarage, Bagillt
Owen, Mr, School House, Burton, Gresford
Owen, E. H., Esq., F.S.A., Ty Coch, Nr Carnarvon
Owen, Rev. E. J., Penmaen Villa, Llanfairfechan, Carnarvonshire

Owen, Rev. T., B.A., Curate, Rhosllanerchrugog, Ruabon
Owen, Hon. Mrs. Bulkeley, Tedsmore
Owen, Isambard, M.D., 5, Hertford Street, Mayfair, London, W.
Owen, Rev. W. P., B.A., Curate, Holy Trinity, Oswestry
Owen, T. Morgan, Esq., H.M.I. of Schools, Bronwylfa, Rhyl, 4 copies
Owen, Rev. T. W., M.A., Empingham Rectory, Rutlandshire
Owen, A. C. Humphreys, Esq., Glansevern, Garthmyl, Mont.
Owen, Morris, Esq., Market street, Carnarvon
Owen, Rev. J., Dyserth Vicarage, Rhyl
Owen, Rev. W. D., B.A., Gwernaffield Vicarage, Mold.

P

Palmer, Alfred Neobard, 19, King Street, Wrexham
Parkins, Trevor, Esq , M.A., Gresford
Parkins, W. T., Esq., M.A., Glasfryn, Gresford, Wrexham
Parry, H., Glyn Mare, Conway
Pennant, Hon. Gertrude Douglas, Hans Place, London, S.W.
Pennant, P. P., Esq., Nantlys, St. Asaph
Phillips, Rev. John
Pierce, W., Board School, Holywell
Pierce, Mr Ellis, Bookseller, Dolyddelen
Pierce, W. M., National School, Denbigh
Price, Mr., School House, Bryneglwys, Corwen
Prichard, Thos., Esq., Llwydiarth Esgob, Llanerchymedd, R.S.O.,
    Anglesey
Probert, Mr John, Castle Estate Office, Ruthin
Pryce, The Ven. Archdeacon, Trefdraeth Rectory, Anglesey

R

Rees, Miss M., Clifton House, Denbigh
Rees, Mr, School House, Nerquis, Mold
Reece, Rev. T. F., B.A., Llanfwrog Rectory, Ruthin
Reichel, H. R., Esq., Pen'rallt, Bangor
Reynolds, Llywarch, Old Church Place, Merthyr Tydfil
Richardson, The Rev. Chancellor William, M.A., The Rectory,
    Corwen
Roberts, Rev. J., Fron, Garthmyl, Mont
Roberts, Mr W. S., School House, Cwmddu, Crickhowel, S. Wales
Roberts, Rev. E. S., B.A., Curate of Penarth, Cardiff
Roberts, G. W., Esq., M.D., Denbigh
Roberts, Rev. J. R., B.A., Curate of St. James's, Bangor
Roberts, Rev. R., Curate, Blaenau Festiniog
Roberts, Mr. W. Ll., Penyceunant, Penybont Fawr, Llanrhaiadr,
    Oswestry

Roderick, Rev. E. M , M.A., The Vicarage, Mold
Rowden, Mr B., Rose Cottage, Maesydre, Mold
Rowlands, Rev. D., M A., Normal College, Bangor

S

Selby, Mr. Jas. P., School House, Trevor, Ruabon
Shelby, Mr. T. F., 11, Cross Street, Rhosddu, Wrexham
St. Davids, The Lord Bishop, Abergwili Palace, Carmarthen
St. Asaph, Right Rev. Lord Bishop of, The Palace, St. Asaph.
Swansea, The Rt. Rev. the Lord Bishop, The Vicarage, Carmarthen

T

Taylor, Henry, Esq., F.S.A., Angar Park, Chester
Thomas, Rev. D. J., M.A., Vice Principal, The College, Winchester
Thomas, D. Lleufer, Esq., Cefn Hendre, Llandilo
Thomas, Ven. Archdeacon, Meifod Vicarage, Welshpool
Thomas, Rev. J. W., M.A., Rhosymedre Vicarage, Ruabon
Thomas, Rev. J. W., M.A., Bwlchycibau, Oswestry
Thomas, Miss, Park Mostyn, Denbigh
Thomas, Rev. H. E., Assistant Curate, Llangollen
Thomas, Rev. J. Howell, B.A., Curate of Brymbo, Wrexham
Turnour, Dr. A. E., Denbigh

V

Vaughan, Rev. T. H., B.A., Curate, Rhyl
Venables, R. G., Esq., Ludlow

W

Walmsley, James, Esq., Plas-y-nant, Ruthin
West Neville, Esq., Glanyrafon, Llanyblodwel, Oswestry
West, W. Cornwallis, M.P., Ruthin Castle, Ruthin
Whittington, Rev. W. P., The Grammar School, Ruthin
Williams, Rev. R. A., Waenfawr Vicarage, near Carnarvon
Williams, Rev. Lewis, Vicar of Prion, Denbigh
Williams, Rev. R. O., M.A., The Vicarage, Holywell
Williams, Rev. David, Llandyrnog Rectory, Denbigh
Williams, Rev. E. O., Melidan Vicarage, Rhyl
Williams, Rev. T. T., B.A, Penloin, Llanrwst
Williams, Mr T., Islawrdref Board School, Near Dolgelley
Williams, W. Llewellyn, Esq., Brown Hill, Llangadock, S. Wales
Williams, Rev. Lloyd, B.A., Organizing Sec., S.P.C.K., Wrexham
Williams, Rev. T. Ll., M.A., The Vicarage. St. Asaph
Williams, Rev. G., M.A., Trefonen

Williams, W. P., Esq., Caer Onen, Bangor
Williams, Mr T. Ll., 64, Love Lane, Denbigh
Williams, Mr R, 106, Clarence Street, Lower Broughton, Manchester
Wilson, Capt. Hy., Hope, Mold
Wilson, Alfred, Bookseller, 18, Gracechurch Street, London, S.C.
Wood, R. H., Esq F.S.A., Pantglas, Trawsfynydd
Wykes, Mr C. H., Board School, Rhosddu, Wrexham
Wynne, Miss F. E., 62, Park Street, Grosvenor Square, London